Public Libraries, Public Policies, and Political Processes

Public Libraries, Public Policies, and Political Processes

Serving and Transforming Communities in Times of Economic and Political Constraint

Paul T. Jaeger, Ursula Gorham,
John Carlo Bertot, and Lindsay C. Sarin

ROWMAN & LITTLEFIELD
Lanham • Boulder • New York • Toronto • Plymouth, UK

Published by Rowman & Littlefield
4501 Forbes Boulevard, Suite 200, Lanham, Maryland 20706
www.rowman.com

10 Thornbury Road, Plymouth PL6 7PP, United Kingdom

British Library Cataloguing in Publication Information Available

Library of Congress Cataloging-in-Publication Data

Jaeger, Paul T., 1974–
Public libraries, public policies, and political processes : serving and transforming communities in times of economic and political constraint / Paul T. Jaeger, Ursula Gorham, John Carlo Bertot, and Lindsay C. Sarin.
pages cm
Includes bibliographical references and index.
ISBN 978-1-4422-3346-1 (pbk. : alk. paper) — ISBN 978-1-4422-3347-8 (electronic)
1. Public libraries—Political aspects—United States. 2. Public libraries—Government policy—United States. 3. Public libraries—United States—Finance. 4. Libraries and society—United States.
I. Gorham, Ursula, 1975– II. Bertot, John Carlo. III. Sarin, Lindsay C. IV. Title.
Z731.J34 2014
027.473—dc23
2014001961

Printed in the United States of America

Contents

List of Figures

List of Tables

Preface

In 2005, Glen Holt penned an editorial in *Public Library Quarterly* that strongly encouraged readers to reflect on the reasons that the quality and capacities of public libraries are not viewed as critical infrastructure at the local level or as a matter of national interest at the federal level. The editorial leaves these questions unanswered, but there is one area that accounts for much of the situation he identifies. In large measure, the answers to those questions can be found within the policy and political processes that affect public libraries and the choices made by the library profession in relation to policies and politics.

The amount of funding and other support for a public library primarily depends on local and state policies and politics, while the parameters within which libraries operate as social institutions are heavily driven by national policies and politics. The political and policy decisions that impact public libraries are inexorably linked to the perceptions of libraries among decisions makers and members of the public, as well as the ways in which public libraries choose to represent themselves to the world around them. Public libraries tend not to fare well in the political and policy processes, for some reasons beyond their control and for some reasons that are their own creation.

Drawing on original research by the authors and a wide range of resources from across the fields of library science, governance, public policy, education, and other related areas, this book examines the complex position of public libraries within policy and politics in the United States. Traditionally, these areas have been badly neglected by library scholarship and insufficiently considered in library missions and advocacy efforts. If the public library is to continue to meet the enormous number of community needs that it now fulfills, and if it is to continue to exist as an institution of the public good that is publicly funded, the attitudes toward and depth of engagement with policy and politics must change among public librarians, professional organizations, and scholars.

In the abstract, public libraries seem like they should be in a position of greater strength than ever in terms of public perception and political support. Public libraries provide digital literacy education and guarantee access to technology and the Internet, ensuring that everyone in the community can participate in e-government (digital communications between citizens and government), online education, job seeking, and myriad other ways in which the Internet is now central to daily life for most people. In the majority of communities, the public library is the only place where free public Internet access is available. Public libraries have proven central to emergency response and recovery in communities affected by disasters all around the nation in the past decade. Public libraries are partnering with community organizations, nonprofits, and other local government agencies to create services that would never have been possible, such as programs that enable people living in food deserts to order and pick up fresh groceries at the library. Many library resources are now offered on an anytime, anywhere basis through their websites or via mobile-enabled services, with no trip to the library necessary.

And these are just examples of major innovations in what public libraries have regularly performed in the past fifteen years. Librarianship has long been one of "those professions in which change is most drastic" (Shera, 1963, p. 313), yet it has not wavered in its commitment to its communities through the changes. In fact, the past fifteen to twenty years have seen a dramatic shift in user-centered and sometimes user-created innovation. Public libraries still serve as a truly public space where community groups can meet, where children learn to love to read and learn through story hours, and where physical and digital books, reference materials, magazines, videos, music, databases, and even musical instruments, seeds for planting vegetable gardens, and cake pans for children's birthday parties, can be borrowed at no cost.

Public libraries remain a lifeline to people in need of social services, job seekers, new immigrants, and so many other populations that have few other places to turn. The economic downturn of the past five years has demonstrated the value of public libraries to their communities, particularly as they assist the public to find jobs, gain digital literacy skills, engage with governments, and access technologies and resources. As governments shrank, public libraries stepped in to fill the void—and the need—left behind by fewer resources and capacity. Governments may have shrunk, but the need for assistance in difficult economic times increased.

The results of a national survey by the Pew Internet and the American Life Project released in January 2013 demonstrate the depth of attachment that members of the public have for their public libraries. Among Americans aged sixteen and older, an astounding 91 percent believe that public libraries are important to their communities, and 76 percent say public libraries are important to their families (Zickuhr, Rainie, & Purcell, 2013). In the past year, 59 percent of respondents to the survey had visited a public library in person and/or online. The survey results also reveal a large problem for public libraries in terms of letting community members, politicians, and policy makers know what they contribute to their communities—only 22 percent of respondents were familiar with most or all of the services offered by their public library.

Having overwhelming public endorsement and successfully serving their communities' needs seem to do public libraries little good in the arena of politics and policy making. When local communities have to cut spending, libraries are usually suggested as a great place to save money as part of austerity programs. Most libraries have suffered fairly significant, permanent cuts over the past few years. Suggestions for closing them altogether abound, with Google often being identified as already having made libraries obsolete. At the national level, the federal government has been creating an array of laws that simultaneously create substantial burdens for libraries and limit the information that they can provide to their patrons. Governments at all levels have embraced a governance philosophy that emphasizes the privatization of public goods whenever possible, with those goods that cannot readily be privatized needing to demonstrate clear economic contributions. Altogether, this is not a political and policy-making environment that will likely be beneficial to public libraries.

This environment did not just spontaneously appear, however. Public libraries have done themselves no favors in the lack of attention they have accorded to policy and politics, given the enormous impact that both actually have on libraries. The insufficient efforts to explain the contributions of public libraries outside of the circles of library professionals and library patrons have not helped, either. While it is true that "it is easy for an overburdened profession, in the press of urgent detail, to forget the larger issues exist" (Wakeman, 1962, p. 348), those larger issues profoundly affect the profession whether they are confronted or not.

Publicly funded entities need the members of the public to understand and value what they do. Even people who have never had reason to call the fire department generally still appreciate its existence, understand what services it provides, and want it to be funded. For public libraries, many community members who are not library patrons have no idea about the range of services and material that libraries provide. People who don't know what the library does are less likely to lobby strongly enough for it to be supported with tax dollars. The political figures and policy makers who don't use the library and don't know what it does beyond providing books (a service on the decline) will not be overly inclined to fund it, particularly in the absence of widespread and vocal public support.

Thus, public libraries face the improbable and unenviable position of mattering more to their communities than they ever have, while also having a large portion of the community and many people in power unsure why the library continues to exist. Fortunately, a greater engagement in the arenas of policy and politics at local, state, and national levels—emphasizing advocacy strategies that actually explain the value of public libraries in terms that community members and policy makers understand—offers the ability to change perceptions about libraries and the ways in which they are treated under the law.

As a profession, we need to wake up to the need to engage meaningfully in these processes in order to effectively fight for support for these institutions that mean so much to so many. If we don't act with commitment and sense, the funding will continue to decrease, and the questions of relevance and value will grow more ominous. There are many things libraries could be doing, or doing better, to demonstrate their value to their communities and to convey policy and political outcomes that would better serve them to the people making such decisions. Crafting a new role for public libraries in the world of policy and politics will not be easy, but it is very necessary. It is a process that public libraries, individual librarians, and supporters of libraries must dedicate themselves to as an essential part of keeping services available and the doors open.

This book is intended to both explain the complexity of current circumstances and offer strategies for effectively creating a better future for public libraries. It is a data-driven examination of the intersections of public libraries, library advocacy, and the policy-making and political processes that shape libraries. Exploring and acting on these issues as an integrated whole represents the only way that public libraries will be able to engage an openly hostile political, policy-making, and economic climate to ensure that libraries can continue to meet the needs of their communities.

By tracing where we are in terms of politics and policy, how we got here, and what we can do to make things better—and using data along the way—this book hopefully will make the situation public libraries currently face less disheartening. The ideas and suggestions in this book are intended to promote reflection, discussion, and, most importantly, action. As a profession of practitioners, administrators, educators, and scholars, we all understand the vital importance of public libraries. We must learn to effectively turn our own understandings into a narrative that enables people who use the library, people who make funding decisions about the library, and people who craft policies related to the library to understand that public libraries are still the quintessence of the public good.

Acknowledgments

This book brings together a wide range of research and ideas that have arisen from many years of studies, papers, conference presentations, class discussions, library visits, friendly conversations, and quiet pondering in the garden. We are grateful to have the opportunity to share these ideas with professionals, scholars, and students who want to help public libraries grow and thrive regardless of the policy making and political ideologies of the moment.

We would like to thank foremost our editor Martin Dillon, Robert Hayunga, and the other folks at Scarecrow Press for their staunch support for this project. Martin's enthusiasm and guidance made the writing process for this book a relatively painless experience, which is quite impressive.

We're grateful for the support given by all of the other members of the staff of the Information Policy and Access Center at the University of Maryland while we were writing this book: June Ahn, Frank Bonnevier, Sarah Dammeyer, Jeff DiScala, Kristofer Dubbels, Rebecca Follman, Leahkim Gannett, Gary Goldberg, Karen Kettnich, Jessica Koepfler, Christie Kodama, Michael Kurtz, Jean Lee, Emily Likins-Hohman, Sheri Massey, Abigail McDermott, Alexis Moses, Johnna Percell, Kaitlin Peterson, Ricky Punzalan, Brian Real, Sophie Reverdy, Molly Schwartz, Katie Shilton, Beth St. Jean, Mega Subramaniam, Natalie Taylor, Kim Thompson, Amanda Waugh, Ann Weeks, Kim White, and Erin Zerhusen. Along with being a delightful group of people to work with, many of them patiently listened and willingly gave feedback on ideas as this project took shape.

We are equally grateful to our families, the assorted spouses, significant whatevers, children, parents, and pets that were supportive of our writings endeavors for the book and who also sometimes willingly gave feedback on the ideas. Special thanks to Carol Jaeger—a retired educator and Paul's long-suffering mother—for providing suggestions and edits on the completed manuscript.

Also deserving of our gratitude are the readers of the book. Thank you for spending your time with our book. We hope that the ideas and data herein provide valuable insights into the intersections of public libraries, policy, politics, and advocacy that you can act upon in working at, supporting, lobbying for, and/or studying libraries.

And to the public libraries that are so essential to their communities and the dedicated public librarians who make the libraries work—long may you run.

List of Abbreviations and Acronyms

ALA	American Library Association
APL	Austin Public Library
ATF	Bureau of Alcohol, Tobacco, and Firearms
BLS	Bureau of Labor Statistics
BTOP	Broadband Technology Opportunities Program
CIPA	Children's Internet Protection Act
CIS	community-focused information services
CTC	community technology center
DMCA	Digital Millennium Copyright Act
DOPA	Deleting Online Predators Act
E-rate	education rate
ESL	English as a second language
FBI	Federal Bureau of Investigation
FCC	Federal Communications Commission
FDLC	Federal Depository Library Council
FDLP	Federal Depository Library Program
FEMA	Federal Emergency Management Agency
FERA	Federal Emergency Relief Administration
FFL	Family Friendly Libraries
GPO	Government Printing Office
HPL	Hartford Public Library
IMLS	Institute of Museum and Library Services
IRS	Internal Revenue Service
LAP	Library Awareness Program
LGBTQ	lesbian, gay, bisexual, transgender, and questioning
LIS	library and information science
LSA	Library Services Act

LSCA	Library Services and Construction Act
LSTA	Library Services and Technology Act
MLS	master of library science
NAP	New Americans Project
NCLIS	National Commission for Library and Information Statistics
NTIA	National Telecommunications and Information Administration
OCLC	online computer library center
PLA	Public Library Association
QBPL	Queens Borough Public Library
ROI	return on investment
SOPA	Stop Online Piracy Act
TAP	The American Place
USA PATRIOT Act	Uniting and Strengthening America by Providing Appropriate Tools Required to Intercept and Obstruct Terrorism Act
USCIS	United States Citizenship and Immigration Service
WIC	Women, Infants, and Children Program
WPA	Works Progress Administration

ONE

Politics, Policies, and Public Libraries

During the recent global economic downturn, public libraries in the United States have experienced a surge in their usage. At the same time, they are undergoing a critical transformation from being places of collections to community centers that provide the assistance, resources, and technology necessary to apply for social services, seek employment, complete schoolwork, engage civically, communicate with friends and family, and find entertainment options. Public libraries have come to serve as the primary guarantor of Internet access for those with no access, with limited access, or who need help navigating online content, while also playing a key role in digital literacy instruction, e-government delivery, emergency response, and a range of other new Internet-enabled functions to serve their communities. But more significantly, public libraries engage in a range of activities that build digitally literate and inclusive communities that support twenty-first-century learning, economic development, and engagement. Most recently, libraries have become spaces for innovation through the creation of makerspaces, humanities-based programming that encourages audiences to engage, adapt, and create new materials, and the provision of resources and space for community technology enthusiasts.

These new roles are in addition to the long-established roles of public libraries, ranging from promoting early childhood literacy to supporting educated democratic participation. Public libraries can be understood as a connecting layer of society, bridging social structures and individual members of the public through the connections of print, technology, community meeting spaces, and other means of sharing knowledge (Pawley, 2009). Libraries have also begun to create innovative partnerships with other community organizations to deliver otherwise unavailable services to their communities, from providing grocery delivery in food deserts to

1

serving as comprehensive immigration centers. The contemporary public library has evolved into both a community center and a center for services to the community.

Yet, as libraries have increasingly taken on essential roles to ensure access to information and create digitally inclusive communities, library support has been slashed at the local, state, and federal levels. In a political climate centered on austerity, libraries have been targeted as an unwise expenditure of public funds. Some jurisdictions have moved to privatize their libraries and library services; some commentators claim that Google has eliminated the need for libraries; and *Forbes* magazine continues to label a master of library science (MLS) as the worst master's degree to earn. This overall denigration of the value of libraries among economic, political, and policy-making circles has accelerated since the Reagan administration in the 1980s, being driven by the widespread embrace of the principles of neoliberal economic and neoconservative political ideologies. These forces work in tandem to undermine the value accorded to public goods and public services in policy-making and political contexts by demanding that public institutions demonstrate the economic contributions of their service to the public.

In this same time frame, the number of laws and policies that directly affect public library operations has increased significantly. The ability of libraries to meet the needs of the public through the services and resources they offer is intertwined with state and federal laws that govern copyright, privacy, cybersecurity, access to telecommunications infrastructure, and censorship, among others. The resulting complex legal framework in which libraries reside, particularly in the digital realm, creates a number of challenges for libraries as they seek to serve their communities. This complexity is enhanced by the mixed messages often imbedded in these laws and policies. By way of example, a recent Federal Communications Commission (FCC) report lauded public libraries for being the primary source of digital literacy education in the nation, while simultaneously suggesting that a large portion of the federal funds currently earmarked for libraries be reallocated to provide corporate subsidies. The end result is that public libraries—perhaps the most inclusive of community institutions—are providing unprecedented levels of community and individual support as they simultaneously are bled dry financially, hedged in their services by law and policy, and turned into a political scapegoat. This counterintuitive situation has been badly neglected as an area of study in the scholarship of political science, public policy, and library science.

To engage these issues of great importance to libraries, communities, public policy, and the health of democracy, this book analyzes both the politics and the policy context surrounding public libraries in the United States. In using the term *politics*, the meaning is intended to focus on the impacts of political discourse and the positions asserted in political processes on public libraries. The issue at hand is not the promotion of the active endorsement of specific politicians or political parties by libraries. *Policy*, on the other hand, denotes the process of creating government directives to address public problems through decisions, actions, and options that will be acted on by individuals, organizations, and the government itself. Policies can be created by legislation, executive orders, agency memos, rule making, signing statements, and a range of other measures at the government's disposal depending on the level of government.

PUBLIC LIBRARIES IN THE POLITICAL WORLD

In the seventh century, Greek poet Archilocus wrote, "The fox knows many things, but the hedgehog knows one big thing." In 1953, social philosopher Isaiah Berlin expanded this notion to describe how thinkers can generally be separated into two categories: foxes, "who pursue many ends, often unrelated, and even contradictory," and hedgehogs, "who relate everything to a single central vision" (Berlin, 1953, p. 3). Simply put, intellectual hedgehogs seek synthesis, and intellectual foxes seek evaluation (Hlebowitsh, 2010). While the terms can be seen as having inherently negative connotations, Berlin meant them as equally valid approaches if applied thoughtfully, listing Aristotle, Shakespeare, Pushkin, and Balzac as foxes and Plato, Dostoevsky, and Nietzsche as hedgehogs.

Foxes are intellectual gatherers—adapting to changes, taking many approaches to a problem, seeing many possible outcomes, dealing well with uncertainty and complexity, practicing self-reflection, and examining problems in a multidisciplinary manner. In contrast, hedgehogs are intellectual predators, who frame the operation of the world in one or two very big ideas that they espouse, confidently bending new information to fit their pet ideologies. Foxes think loudly and act flexibly, while hedgehogs speak loudly and act stubbornly. The terms stem from the differences between the two animals in nature. The fox is amazingly adaptable in habit, diet, and living quarters, while hedgehogs keep to established behavior patterns. In the natural world, foxes have flourished and hedgehog populations are declining quickly. These metaphors apply not only to individual thinkers, but to organizational and governmental philosophies, with policies often reflecting a fox-like or hedgehog-like attitude toward policy objectives (Michel, 2009; Provizer, 2008). Berlin was extremely interested in the political process and the implications of these ideas for political leaders and policy makers (Hanley, 2004).

In the current political environment in the United States, the public library is a fox in a political world dictated by hedgehogs. Contemporary discourse about politics and policy are dominated by the loudest voices and the most strident opinions. The disadvantageous position in which public libraries find themselves in current political and policy-making processes stems from the simple fact that they have neither the loudest voices nor the most strident positions. As we will explore throughout this book, public libraries are heavily affected by decisions in political and policy-making realms that shape the funding, activities, and roles of libraries in society. Over the past two decades, as a result of these decisions, libraries have been tasked with fulfilling additional responsibilities in the face of increased limitations on their activities and funding sources. These decisions have occurred at all levels of government, but have been primarily driven by national debate and federal initiatives. Library discourse, however, tends to shy away from engaging the complex interrelationships that so heavily impact the services public libraries can provide to patrons and the roles that libraries can play in their communities. "For a profession that specializes in the business of information, the library profession suffers from a great paucity of research on its role in an area on which its very existence depends" (Jenkins, 1990, p. 45).

The insufficient engagement of these political and policy issues by libraries, unfortunately, hinders the ability of libraries to articulate their contributions and positions to politicians, funders, and members of the public, while simultaneously curtailing the development of advocacy, management, and research strategies to better support library goals and functions. There are many deeply rooted reasons for the failure to adequately engage these issues at the broad national level. Traditionally, public libraries have viewed themselves as primarily local entities, based on the preponderance of funding being from local and state agencies, and with many of the operational decisions being tied to local-level entities like city councils and library boards. Such relationships have been a central part of library operations since the beginning of the modern public library movement in 1876 (Wiegand, 2011).

Public libraries have also long embraced a stance of attempting to remain impartial arbiters of information, which has been unhelpfully characterized as a position of *neutrality*. While meant as a way to remain impartial in the eyes of the public, the end result is self-defeating, as this stance has far too often been interpreted as meaning that public libraries should remain bystanders in political debates that affect their ability to function. "If we don't lobby for libraries and the public's access to information, the money and support will not be there" (Abbott-Hoduski, 2003, p. 2). The assumption of a bystander position, though, is not always by choice; in many places, libraries have had limitations placed on their ability to advocate for themselves in decisions made by local governments.

The other key challenge in engaging complex national debates about policies and politics that directly impact public libraries is that such debates are frequently not couched in those terms. In the current environment where information, communication, and technology have become intertwined, many proposed laws and political debates have enormous consequences for libraries as providers of information access, technology access, and information education. But many of these debates on issues that are so important to libraries never actually mention libraries. Instead, the impacts on libraries are part of economic debates, technological decisions, and information policies. The latter, in particular, has an additional layer of complexity to the extent that information policy—the policy decisions related to information, communication, and technology—generally does not dominate political or media attention. Unlike other types of policy, it lacks a tangible component. While one can tactilely experience or at least observe the impacts of trade, education, finance, the environment, the military, and other prominent areas of policy, information remains an abstraction. Yet information policy decisions shape the creation, access, usage, management, exchange, security, display, collection, and other uses of information, with innumerable implications for public libraries.

The position of the library profession in policy and politics has been further undercut by the fact that many in the library profession have simply not wanted to engage in issues beyond the library, a theme that has been returned to repeatedly in library discourse. A classic example of the genre is Ervin J. Gaines' vitriolic article from 1980 attacking the notion that a library should do anything to serve its community beyond providing access to books, mocking movements toward "social work" and the "epidemic of outreach" (pp. 50–51). Others in the library community have not been against becoming involved in policy and politics so much as afraid to become involved. "We somehow seem to be a profession startled to find that we really do have deeply held convictions, that our words really do have meaning and consequence, and that when we act on our professional values someone actually notices" (Buschman, Rosenzweig, & Harger, 1994, p. 576).

As public libraries and library professionals tend not to be directly engaged in political and policy-making processes, the voices of public librarianship that are inserted into debates are those of a handful of small professional organizations with limited lobbying arms. The intentions of the American Library Association (ALA) and other organizations are to represent the perspectives of libraries to governments, but they are badly outmanned and outfinanced by industries and other professional organizations. If a policy decision related to information pits major technology corporations on one side and professional library organizations on the other, the practical advantages will not rest with the library organizations.

Simply put, having a limited voice in these policy and political debates is not conducive to the long-term ability of public libraries to fulfill their missions and meet the needs of their communities. "Librarians and library supporters haven't shifted their political advocacy to the aggressive stance which will provide the funds we need to stay afloat, let alone keep up with the future as it develops" (Turner, 1997, p. 5). The inescapable fact at this point is that public libraries are entities that are strongly affected by political discourse and policy making at all levels of government, with decisions shaping budgets, freedom of access, intellectual property, and management perspectives, among many other core elements that determine the extent to which libraries can successfully serve their communities.

Set against the backdrop of a global recession, the last few years serve as a microcosm for the interrelationship between public libraries, policy making, and political processes. Politicians campaign on platforms that emphasize austerity and cost cutting and aggressively cut the budgets of libraries and other institutions for the public good. All the while, earlier policy decisions that weakened the economy have led to an increasing number of people turning to public libraries for help with finding a job, applying for social services, interacting with government agencies, and learning new digital skills through the technology access and assistance provided by the library, as well as availing themselves of entertainment options for which they can no longer afford to pay (Bertot, Jaeger, & Greene, 2013; Sigler et al., 2011; Taylor et al., in press). While the president of the ALA in 2009 could state with no uncertainty that "public libraries have been America's first responders to the economic crisis" (Rettig, 2009, n.p.), this public support role has led to the foisting of many more responsibilities onto libraries with no additional funding.

Notwithstanding a growth in demand for their services, libraries are increasingly appearing in political debates as a symbol of big government by politicians who seek to curtail spending and/or limit social mobility of underrepresented populations (Bertot, Jaeger, & Sarin, 2012). Public libraries have become viewed as easy targets for budget cuts by many, as evidenced by a Fox News Chicago editorial that asked, "With the Internet and e-books, do we really need millions for libraries?" (Davlantes, 2010, n.p.). A similar sentiment was found in a Florida newspaper editorial asserting that the Internet, and Google in particular, has made public libraries redundant and that "no serious research is carried on in the library stacks" (Elmore, 2008, n.p.). These views have not spontaneously appeared but rather are the result of "50 long years of conservative framing [and] can be summed up in two words: 'tax burden'" (LaRue, 2011, n.p.).

The fact that library activities and contributions to their communities cannot be easily translated into monetary terms makes them easy targets for budget cuts, a fact that has been all too apparent throughout the prolonged economic downturn that began in 2008. Governments have been telling libraries around the country to make across-the-board cuts, reduce staffing, cut materials budgets, close facilities, reduce hours, raise fees and fines, and/or seek private funding (LaRue, 2009). Major systems—including Boston, Chicago, Detroit, Los Angeles, Miami-Dade, Philadelphia, Seattle, and Toronto—have each faced a combination of staffing cuts, service reductions, and even branch closings in some cases. In Chicago, the union representing library employees voted to accept a 10 percent pay cut and the elimination of 120 part-time positions to preserve more jobs (Pensa, 2009). In just 2012, the Miami-Dade system lost 30 percent of its budget and about 200 staff positions, while the Detroit system closed four branches and the entire Seattle system was closed for one week, during which time employees were not paid (Kelley, 2012). Some bright spots have emerged—in Los Angeles, community members rallied to limit drastic cuts imposed by city leaders that resulted in a staff reduction of 1,156 to 828 in one year and the closure of all libraries for two days a week (Kelley, 2011, 2012). Citizens of many other communities, however, have not been as successful in fighting cuts. Although most citizens support library funding and will vote in favor of ballot initiatives for library funding, the unfortunate reality is that they often do not get a chance to express their support (Dempsey, 2009, 2010).

Cuts imposed on medium- and small-sized systems—particularly systems of one library—may not be as large in real dollars, but the impact of such cuts is often proportionally greater. The Charlotte-Mecklenburg system, for example, suffered repeated dramatic cuts (Bethea, 2011). In 2006, that library system was visited by then-First Lady Laura Bush to honor it for its innovative outreach and community programs; by 2011, it had lost one-third of its staff, closed branches, cut most programs, and slashed hours in half at the remaining libraries. In Colton, California, the city manager walked into the two library branches one day in 2009 and informed everyone who worked there that they were fired and that the libraries would be closed indefinitely (Goldberg, 2009). In Jackson County, Oregon, all fifteen libraries were closed for seven months, laying off one hundred library employees in the largest library closing in the history of the United States (Battistella, 2010). By 2012, most libraries and systems of all sizes were "furiously treading water," with libraries reporting an overall average of 2.7 fewer employees than the year before (Kelley, 2012, n.p.). As this prolonged economic downturn continues, public libraries have become particularly vulnerable in terms of support. Most libraries rely on local property tax revenues for a large portion of their funding, and such revenues have fallen considerably as the housing market has collapsed. At the same time, as governments at all levels look to reduce their overall spending in reaction to falling revenues, public libraries, which continue to struggle with defining their value in economic terms, have been a particularly appealing target for additional spending reductions.

Changes in political discourse beyond economic issues have also created an electoral environment that is markedly less hospitable to public libraries than librarians of even ten years ago could have imagined.

Similarly, the explosion of federal policies related to information translates into federal policy having much greater relevance to public libraries than at any time in the past, though public libraries are rarely considered in such policy debates. In the past fifteen years or so, among many other mandates, federal policy has given public libraries the following:

- the Uniting and Strengthening America by Providing Appropriate Tools Required to Intercept and Obstruct Terrorism Act (USA PATRIOT Act) and the right of government agencies to collect a wide range of libraries' physical and electronic records and observe a wide range of patron behaviors in libraries;
- the Homeland Security Act, with its capacities for government agencies to limit government information made available and to take information out of library collections;
- the Children's Internet Protection Act (CIPA), requiring the filtering of Internet access for all library computers—and thereby reducing the information patrons can access—in order to receive certain types of funding;
- the E-rate (short for "education rate") funding program, which requires libraries to complete a byzantine application process in order to receive support for library technology;
- the Digital Millennium Copyright Act (DMCA), raising serious issues for libraries in providing electronic resources through their own services and through interlibrary loan;
- the E-government Act, which ultimately encouraged many government agencies to offload the training and support for use of their online services to public libraries; and
- the FCC's 2010 Broadband Plan, which suggests reducing funding of libraries through E-rate and using the funds to promote private-sector growth of broadband access.

For public libraries, the impacts of such policies and the impacts of politics are in many cases closely linked.

For example, despite a series of government programs that promote digital inclusion and the widespread use of mobile technologies, many populations—based on socioeconomic status, education, geography, language, literacy, and disability—experience gaps in access to the Internet and training in digital literacy skills (Jaeger, Bertot, Thompson, Katz, & DeCoster, 2012). The National Broadband Plan, the Proposed Framework for Digitally Inclusive Communities (2011) developed by the Institute of Museum and Library Services (IMLS), and the multiagency DigitalLiteracy.gov site—as well as many other government policies and statements— all rely on public library technology and training in different ways to achieve a more digitally inclusive society. Such reliance occurs because public libraries are uniquely equipped to support these efforts with hardware, Internet connections, trained staff, and significant resources avail-

able online and in print to support lifelong learning and skills development (Jaeger & Bertot, 2011; Jaeger, Bertot, Thompson, Katz, & DeCoster,
2012). In fact, this role will likely grow as reductions of funding for school
libraries result in students needing another outlet for homework resources, thereby increasing usage of the public libraries in those districts
(Resmovits, 2011). By and large, however, these digital inclusion policies
fail to adequately acknowledge the significant costs that are borne by
libraries as they strive to fill the various gaps in access (e.g., social services in many states are entirely online, and agencies refer individuals to
the public library to access and fill out forms) (Gorham et al., 2013; Jaeger
& Bertot, 2011).

Prior to this recent proliferation of policies about—or having an impact upon—libraries, federal policy discussions concerning libraries were
devoted largely to funding issues, primarily in connection with the Library Services and Construction Act (LSCA) in its various forms. In a
world of warrantless wiretaps, mandated filtering, and worries about
copyright in interlibrary loans, a focus on federal policy as a purely economic issue seems truly appealing. Unfortunately, public libraries are
now heavily affected by policy making in much more than economic
policy at local, state, and federal levels. The combination of policies and
politics of recent years has placed libraries in the position of having to
defend both the "public" and the "good" aspects of being a public good.

As John Buschman (2003) has thoughtfully examined, public libraries
have suffered considerably in society as a result of the changes in political
philosophy that were ushered in during the Reagan administration. Deregulation, changing tax and social priorities, spending cuts, and the emphasis on documentable contributions from organizations have had the
most significance for entities that were previously considered to exist
purely for the public good. Along with libraries, schools and social service providers have scrambled to do more with less support, while trying
to convince policy makers of the value of their social contributions. This
philosophy places libraries in the near-impossible position of trying to
place an economic value on knowledge and learning or on literacy and
inclusion (Jaeger, Bertot, Kodama, Katz, & DeCoster, 2011; Jaeger, Bertot,
Thompson, Katz, & DeCoster, 2012). These changes have also fueled the
trend of libraries viewing patrons as consumers, which has only served to
reinforce the notion that library functions exist for a purpose other than
the public good (D'Angelo, 2006).

As such, the tidal wave of federal policies that place new limits or
burdens on libraries has coincided with the institutionalization of a philosophy of governance and policy making that runs contrary to the notion of publicly funded entities that exist solely to benefit the public. One
manifestation of this political philosophy in policy making has been the
advent of the idea of privatization, the bidding out of government responsibilities to private-sector companies to perform the same function,

presumably at lower cost. Some public libraries in the United States, as well as in other countries that have embraced this philosophy of governance, have faced the prospect of being privatized by their local governments as early as the mid-1990s. For example, the Riverside County public library system in California, serving more than 1 million residents, was privatized in 1997, while the same year the residents of Jersey City, New Jersey, protested to prevent the privatization of their library system (Hanley, 1998). The ALA recently published a book called *Privatizing Libraries* (Jerrard, Bolt, & Strege, 2012), which begins by stating the strong opposition of the ALA to privatization.

The current situation—characterized by economic turmoil, a proliferation of federal policies that impact libraries, and a dominant political philosophy that fails to recognize public libraries' social contributions—is one in which libraries must convince an increasingly skeptical audience of their value to the communities they serve, especially politicians and policy makers who seem to be inherently skeptical about the value of libraries. Engagement in the political and policy processes therefore "has become a fundamental duty of all who believe in the very real contributions libraries make to U.S. culture, productivity, levels of literacy, and embodiment of democratic values" (Halsey, 2003, p. 1). Given the crisis mode in which many libraries find themselves operating, it is of little surprise that they have been unable to present a unified voice in the political and policy debates that have far-reaching implications for their future. Their failure to carve out a role in these ongoing dialogues, however, has equally far-reaching implications.

THE DISSERVICE OF A DISORGANIZED DISCOURSE

Library professionals, educators, and researchers have not been extremely successful in engaging in these political and policy debates that have led to the enactment of the laws described above. Often, a general misunderstanding of a law or policy has fueled a disorganized or counterproductive response, while the lack of awareness of a law or policy has resulted in a rather muted response. In both of these types of cases, the result has frequently been the institution of a law or policy that limits the ability of libraries to guarantee access and equity. Recent laws and policies that have the largest impact on libraries have been ones that typically serve to constrict the information that libraries can make available, notably CIPA, the USA PATRIOT Act, and the Homeland Security Act.

The disservice to access and equity that results from disorganized and underinformed political and policy discourse in librarianship is aptly demonstrated in the reaction to the passage of the USA PATRIOT Act. In the immediate aftermath of the passage of the law, much of the professional discourse focused on resistance to the law—advocating for wholesale shredding of physical records and deleting of electronic records, computer usage information, and patron checkout records—with some even advocating that librarians should be willing to go to jail to oppose the law. While the USA PATRIOT Act and the Homeland Security Act did raise, and continue to raise, significant issues for libraries (as discussed in Gorham-Oscilowski & Jaeger, 2008; Jaeger, Bertot, & McClure, 2003; Jaeger & Burnett, 2005; Jaeger, McClure, Bertot, & Snead, 2004), the actual impacts of the laws and the reactions to them in the library community have not been sufficiently connected. Perhaps as a result of this disconnect, the vehemently negative initial reaction a decade ago to the provisions of these laws has been replaced by an apparent lack of discussion about them.

Another example can be seen in a current policy debate surrounding the revision of Title 44 of the U.S. Code, which governs the operations of the Government Printing Office (GPO) and the Federal Depository Library Program (FDLP). With the vast majority of government information being distributed electronically through channels other than the GPO and the FDLP, policy reform that leads to changes in their missions and operations is inevitable. Notwithstanding a range of available approaches that libraries could promote in the policy debates to promote the conversion of these programs into valuable contributors in the age of e-government (as discussed in Bertot, Jaeger, Shuler, Simmons, & Grimes, 2009; Jaeger, Bertot, & Shuler, 2010; Shuler, Jaeger, & Bertot, 2010), the reaction in the field has been one of utter fragmentation, with Federal Depository Library Council (FDLC) meetings devolving into impasse and inaction. Even the presentation of potential futures envisioned for the program can lead to strong negative reactions, arguing that no change is needed in response to the advent of e-government. In all likelihood, such fragmentation will lead to a policy solution that does not effectively meet the needs of the FDLP libraries or their patrons.

The insufficient amount and breadth of policy and political analyses to serve the library profession comes at a particularly inopportune time, as policies that are introduced by both the legislature and the executive branch are becoming increasingly confrontational. Proposed policies related to copyright and telecommunications, as two examples, have become increasingly one sided in recent years. Whether due to successful pressure from certain groups, policy makers' ignorance about technologies and their implications, or a combination of both, policies related to both copyright and telecommunications have increasingly focused on the interests of only one stakeholder group rather than balancing—or at least considering—the needs of all stakeholders in an issue.

The recent tussle over the Stop Online Piracy Act (SOPA), which was ultimately withdrawn from consideration in Congress, emphatically demonstrates this trend. SOPA was strongly supported by content creators, such as the movie, television, and music industries, and it was strongly opposed by the content providers, including the large Internet companies. The proposed legislation would have benefitted content creators by giving them the right to shut down any website deemed to have facilitated copyright or trademark infringement before any such infringement is proven, thereby prioritizing the rights of one stakeholder entirely over another. A more balanced proposal would not have been so controversial and might have been passed by Congress, but it would have been out of step with the general current trend of confrontational policy making.

It is perhaps impossible to ascertain whether policy making has become inherently more confrontational due to the agendas themselves, to strong increases in partisanship in the political parties, or to a general dissipation of the traditional stakeholder-based approach to policy processes. Regardless of the reason, public libraries now face a policy environment where, if the library community wants their perspectives to be interjected into debates of policy and politics, the onus is on them to do so.

Whether or not the library community will actually take this step, however, remains an open question. Given the recent proliferation of books, articles, online discussions, and blog posts prognosticating on a perceived demise of libraries or a death of library education (e.g., Cox, 2011; Dilevko, 2009; Swigger, 2012), it is not unreasonable to wonder if the policy and political pressures on libraries are wearing on the psyche of library practitioners, researchers, and educators. The policy and political issues may loom so large that they seem too complex to fully grasp and too all encompassing to confront. The resulting response is one of quietly waiting for the end of the relevance of libraries. It does not have to be this way by any stretch of the imagination. A far more robust scholarship devoted to policies and politics that affect libraries would empower the field by imparting insights into the issues to change practices for the better, advocate for laws and policies that will support libraries, and understand the roles of libraries within the broader political and policy contexts in which they operate.

Based on the scholarship and professional literature about libraries, however, one could be forgiven for thinking that those who work in, teach about, and study public libraries are generally unaware of connections between libraries, policy, and politics (Jaeger, Bertot, & Gorham, 2013). Amazingly, no book—prior to the one you are reading at this moment—has provided a data-driven examination of the intersections of public libraries, public policy, political processes, and library advocacy in the United States. This major gap is part of a much larger lack of discourse in such a vital area—an omission made all the more surprising by virtue of the fact that, over the past thirty years, significant shifts in technology, political ideologies, and policy goals have resulted in an environment in which public libraries face the highest expectations to serve community needs against unprecedented political, economic, and policy challenges.

In David Shavit's 1986 book *The Politics of Public Librarianship*, he bemoaned the fact that the last major engagement with the intersections of politics and public libraries had been written thirty-seven years before by Oliver Garceau as part of the Public Library Inquiry. Prior to Garceau's 1949 book, Carleton Bruns Joeckel (1935) provided the first book-length examination of public libraries and government, but the focus of the book was on the optimal level of government for libraries to be part of. Currently, we are now more than fifteen years on from Edwin Beckerman's *Politics and the American Public Library* (1996), the last significant work to look seriously at the impacts of political processes on public libraries. Several books in the last twenty years have dealt with the political process as the context of lobbying (e.g., Abbott-Hoduski, 2003; Halsey, 2003; Turner, 1997), but these books have focused on lobbying activities rather than political content and forces. While a very few other books dealing with libraries and politics in more limited ways were written during this time span—such as E. J. Josey's *Libraries in the Political Process* (1980), a collection of essays about advocating for funding for libraries in thirty-six different parts of the country—there have only been the slimmest number of texts with a specific book-length focus on libraries and politics in more than seventy years.

Direct engagements with the impact of policy making on public libraries are even scarcer in larger works, and of the books focusing on information policies—those that most significantly shape the contents and functions of libraries—there appears to be a general disinclination to deal with library issues. As with books about libraries and politics, very few information policy books have been written, and many of those are the same vintage as the Beckerman book (e.g., Burger, 1993; Hernon, McClure, & Relyea, 1996). The book edited by Hernon, McClure, and Relyea, for example, includes only a single essay on the impact of information policies on public libraries. A rare exception, Wellisch, Patrick, Black, and Cuardra's *The Public Library and Federal Policy* (1974), actually examines what the title suggests it does, but it dates from nearly four decades ago. The only two recently published books on libraries and policy, respectively, focus on the United Kingdom and provide an international overview that includes a mere fourteen pages on the United States (Cornelius, 2010; Helling, 2012).

Journal articles that deal with libraries and political processes and/or policy making appear to be equally rare. A decent number of articles address certain issues of policy or politics, but rarely do they draw the policy or political issues into the broader contexts in which these issues exist. When articles do engage these issues, they more commonly seem to focus on the policy dimensions of a situation rather than the political dimensions or both. While policy research can provide data "to better

understand the political context in which programs and services operate"
(McClure & Jaeger, 2008, p. 263), it is not the same as directly investigating the political dimensions of a situation. The limited focus on issues of
policy and politics in library journals in recent years is also tied to the
constriction of outlets that publish library research, as many journals
have disappeared or rebranded themselves as information science journals, pushing library research to the margins or completely outside of the
scope of the remaining journals.

This lack of discourse evidences the uneasiness that most of the library community feels when faced with the opportunity to enter the
political and policy-making arenas. The ill-fated legal challenge to CIPA
provides a cautionary tale of what can go wrong when the library community chooses to enter those arenas. The ALA filed suit to block implementation of the law on grounds of infringement of intellectual freedom
in the abstract. After a series of mixed decisions through the courts, the
Supreme Court ultimately ruled against the ALA, revealing an utter lack
of understanding of the goals of libraries and the contributions of libraries to their communities (Gathegi, 2005; Jaeger, Bertot, & McClure, 2004).
In hindsight, a more robust policy and politics discourse in the field
would have better prepared librarians to advocate for a different approach in the law while it was being written and enabled them to develop
a strategy for challenging the law if and when such action was deemed
necessary.

The places in which librarians have dared to discuss the impacts of
policy decisions on public library funding are primarily in the newer
forms of publication, including social media (especially Twitter), in the
myriad of blogs published by and for librarians, to some extent at library
conferences, and on library listservs. Bloggers like Andy Woodworth
(http://agnosticmaybe.wordpress.com), for example, actively engage in
less than popular discussions of the impact of policy decisions on funding for libraries, especially in his home state of New Jersey. It is important
to note, however, that these discussions

1. Take place among fellow librarians and most often do not engage
   with outside stakeholders—most certainly not with policy makers.
2. Occur on publishing platforms that are not yet, especially in the
   minds of policy makers, professional or scholarly in nature, and
   may in their minds hold less weight than a scholarly article or
   book.
3. Often create tension within the library profession. Librarians who
   have dared to speak openly about these kinds of issues are revered
   by some in the profession, but reviled by many, who see frank
   discussions of these kinds of issues as either not part of the role of
   librarians or as airing dirty laundry in a public setting.

At a more philosophical level, a greater discourse on the policies and politics that shape public libraries would help library educators and researchers more clearly see to the need for consistent, direct engagement and advocacy as a part of scholarship and teaching. Along with providing data and analyses, however, this discourse must also create support mechanisms for finding and engaging the policy materials, as well as for understanding the political processes, that determine support of and responsibilities for public libraries and that shed light on the roles that libraries play in society as a whole.

To return to the earlier discussion about the economic climate currently facing public libraries, as local and state government budgets have dwindled in the prolonged economic downturn, most public libraries have received proportionally decreased funding. The decreased funding fits within a new governance perspective of treating public goods as consumer enterprises. And the same economic downturn has led more people to visit libraries for help with applying for government benefits, searching for jobs online, and finding free entertainment. This particular confluence of policy and politics has enormous consequences for public libraries, library professionals, and patrons, but these political and policy-making decisions also have powerful long-term consequences for society as a whole.

Reduced funding means fewer hours, fewer resources, fewer services, and fewer staff members able to provide assistance and education in the library and also means that libraries will not be able to provide the level of service to the public that they both need and have come to expect. The paucity of digital literacy training and free Internet access within certain communities has sizeable implications for people with limited literacy and access, resulting in growing disparities in access to education, civic, social service, health, employment, and other forms of information, while simultaneously reducing opportunities for many members of society to become equipped to participate in the digital age and digital economy. These policy and political consequences are not just felt within the four walls of public libraries; they reverberate throughout the entire nation. In the face of such policy and political decisions, an important foundation for empowering library faculty, students, and practitioners in the current environment is an ongoing rich discourse on these issues of policy and politics.

GOALS AND STRUCTURE OF THE BOOK

The subsequent chapters of this book will address the issues discussed above in much greater detail, drawing on two decades of original research conducted by the authors, as well as existing research about the intersection of public policy, political discourse, and public libraries. This book is a culmination of a series of papers by the authors seeking to understand the origins and implications of the current standing of public libraries in public policy and political discourse, issues that some of the authors have been examining for more than a decade. The book covers key issues such as the

- contributions of public libraries to their communities and the impacts of policy and politics on these contributions;
- history of the treatment of public libraries in public policy and the history of the funding of public libraries;
- development of the political and economic ideologies that frame current policy and political approaches to public libraries;
- current policy and political environment surrounding public goods and public service, including the laws and policies related to information and libraries;
- impacts of current public policy and politics on the funding and function of public libraries;
- impacts of movements of privatization and commercialization on the funding and function of public libraries;
- political and advocacy efforts on the part of public libraries over time, from traditional stances of neutrality to sporadic attempts by the library profession to engage in political activities; and
- efforts to demonstrate the value of libraries in the face of the political and economic ideologies that currently dominate public policy.

Building upon the discussion of these key issues, the book offers proposals for professional, policy-making, and political strategies that can strengthen, rather than undermine, the public library and its ability to meet the needs of individuals and communities. The discussion and analysis in the book draws upon data and real-world examples from the many studies that the authors have conducted on related topics, including libraries' outreach to increasingly diverse service populations and efforts to meet community needs through innovative partnerships.

In an effort to encourage direct public policy and political engagement about libraries by all involved stakeholders, the book

- establishes an overarching framework and themes necessary for successful support of public libraries through public policy and political discourse;
- provides guidance on incorporating relevant data, analysis, and representations into public policy discussions about libraries;
- proposes approaches for professional organizations, for policy makers, and for political figures that will focus on the divergent individual and community needs met by libraries;
- offers value demonstration frameworks for use by libraries in policy and political discourse; and

- connects these public policy issues related to public libraries in the United States to both other types of libraries in the United States and to libraries in other nations facing similar policy issues, such as the United Kingdom.

As this intersection of politics, policy, and libraries has grown in importance and complexity in recent years, the need for a book on interrelationships of policy, politics, and libraries is long overdue. Many examples of past and current policies and political issues will be used throughout the book to explain where we are and how we got here, but the book is not a catalogue of all the current policies related to libraries. The intent is to ensure the book is able to serve as a learning tool to prepare for the future and avoid being time-locked in the past.

Echoing Douglas Zweizig's famous distinction between "the library in the life of the user" and "the user in the life of the library" (1973), chapters 2 and 3 present "the library in the life of policy" and "policy in the life of the library," respectively, to illuminate the complexity of the historical developments that have led to the current political and policy context encircling public libraries. Chapter 2 focuses on the evolution of public libraries in the United States in two important, interrelated ways. First, the historical contributions of public libraries to their communities are explored. Moving from the early days of prescriptive readings and limited collections through the embrace of inclusive collections and use to the current Internet-enabled, open environment, this chapter helps readers to understand the important content and service changes undertaken by public libraries over time. Second, this chapter focuses on the ways in which these changes in perspective have led the ALA and its members to craft the Library Bill of Rights and become an advocate for social inclusion, freedom of expression, and civil rights, and how this perspective resulted in increasingly diverse patron populations. Reviewing the history of the development of the public library into an essential public good is necessary for understanding the ways in which policies and politics have treated libraries in historical and contemporary contexts.

Chapter 3 examines the very significant changes over time in government actions toward public libraries and how these actions impact libraries and their communities. For many years, local and state policies and politics were the only ones with a direct impact on libraries. This local nature has often emphasized the contents of the collection, operational issues, and library funding. However, after many years of limited involvement in public libraries, the federal government has become a major influence on public libraries through crafting policies and framing political debates in ways that have significant impacts on how libraries can serve their communities. Particularly since the advent of the Web, laws and policies—such as CIPA, the USA PATRIOT Act, the DCMA, the Telecommunications Act, and many others—have heavily shaped the funding of public libraries and the contributions public libraries are able to make in their communities.

In a large part, the much greater intervention by the federal government in public libraries, both in terms of influencing service and determining funding, has coincided with the rise of the neoconservative political ideology and the complementary neoliberal economic ideology, which are the focus of chapter 4. Despite the opposite-sounding names, these two ideologies work in tandem to restrict the freedom and support of entities of the public good, such as libraries, while at the same time they have given far greater freedom to corporate entities. Coming to prominence in the United States with the election of Ronald Reagan, these ideologies now dominate the political discourse and policy-making processes for both political parties. After detailing the development and nature of these ideologies, this chapter examines the ways in which they frame the current policy and political environment about public goods and public service. This chapter also explores the specific impacts of neoconservative governance and neoliberal economic ideologies on public libraries. With major influences on the public policy and politics of the funding and function of public libraries, these twin ideologies have worked to simultaneously increase government intrusion into library operations and reduce financial support of libraries. They have also allowed for other activities that undermine the social roles of public libraries, such as turning the support of libraries into a highly partisan issue and facilitating the movements of privatization and commercialization of libraries. This chapter also examines the misconceptions about public library use, services, and patrons frequently evidenced within political discourse by politicians and the media, and how these misrepresentations have been promoted by neoconservative governance and neoliberal economic ideologies. The significant shifts in political and economic ideologies that have so greatly impacted public libraries in the United States are not isolated, either by nation or by library type.

Paralleling the time frame of the influence of neoconservative governance and neoliberal economic ideologies on public libraries, there has been an evolution in terms of both the patrons seeking assistance in libraries and the needs of the communities that libraries serve. In the past twenty years, as chapter 5 details, library collections and services have become predominantly Internet enabled, with digital literacy and help with online activities like job applications, social services, distance education, e-books, and many others becoming primary functions of libraries. The Internet-enabled capacities have also brought communities to rely on public libraries in new ways, such as guaranteeing e-government access, facilitating immigration, and supporting emergency response and recovery. Concurrent socioeconomic changes have made the library an increasingly important part of the lives of patrons without access to or the ability to use the Internet-enabled technologies necessary to participate in contemporary education, employment, or government. These changes have led to dramatic increases in patron usage of public libraries. Simultaneously, libraries are serving increasingly diverse populations and communities as the racial, ethnic, and linguistic composition of the United States rapidly evolves. The impacts of policy and politics on the ability of libraries to serve these populations and meet their needs, and the ways in which these activities influence the way libraries are treated in policy and politics, are examined in this chapter.

Chapter 6 focuses on engagement in the political process and policy making by public libraries and their organizations. While libraries have always advocated for funding, they have long held to a stated stance of political neutrality. This stance has often not been matched by their actual activities, from openly and actively censoring collections during the world wars, to maintaining a policy platform with assertions about nonlibrary issues (e.g., global warming, military spending), to sporadically engaging in opposition to certain proposed laws. Along with exploring the political and policy consequences of these efforts at political engagement, this chapter will also discuss the primary response of library organizations to the current predominant political and economic ideologies. As public services are expected to prove their value as a prerequisite to receiving funding in the current political climate, public libraries have faced the difficult challenge of quantifying the value of education and community support. Most libraries and national organizations have unhelpfully fallen back to assertions—rather than data-driven demonstrations—of library value. This chapter examines the policy and political impacts of adopting this approach, laying the groundwork for an in-depth discussion of alternative approaches to demonstrating value.

Employing a wide range of data sources and current practices, chapter 7 offers a set of proposals for public libraries to advocate for support through data-driven demonstrations of value to their communities. As public libraries have been a significant target for reductions in funding in spite of their dramatic usage increases in the past five years, libraries are in desperate need of better strategies to continue to fight for financial support. This chapter provides guidance and suggested best practices on incorporating relevant data, analysis, and representations into public policy discussions about and advocacy of support for public libraries at local levels and beyond. Arguing that public libraries need to be portrayed as a unique community good, the chapter provides conceptual and factual themes necessary for public libraries to successfully advocate for financial support in light of contemporary political and economic ideologies. Based on data about public libraries and their impacts, this chapter fosters the ability of libraries to use their contributions to the advancement of major political goals—such as digital literacy and digital inclusion—as a primary advocacy tool.

Chapter 8 draws these large-scale discussions of policy, politics, and advocacy down to the community level. This chapter wraps together the ideas introduced in the book and examines the future directions of these concepts, emphasizing the long-term reasons for data-driven advocacy and value demonstration and the long-term potential consequences of failing to adequately respond to contemporary political and economic ideologies. Ultimately, the future of public library support through funding and through policy is at the local level, with the public library serving as a cornerstone of community-based governance. This chapter meditates on the ways in which the effective engagement of public libraries in policy making and political discourse can serve to increase equality and social progress in the information society, with sensible politics and policies about libraries at the local level serving to shape the national discourse.

Across these chapters, the main message is that there is a pressing need for public librarians and other supporters of public libraries to be:

1. aware of the political process and its implications for libraries;
2. attuned to the interrelationships between policy and politics; and
3. engaged in the policy process to articulate the need for policies that support public libraries.

This book has been written to be both scholarly and accessible to general readers, with the goal of it being useful to students, educators, researchers, practitioners, and friends of public libraries in library and information science (LIS). Everyone working in or supporting public libraries needs to be aware of and engaged in the topics addressed in this book.

Given the interdisciplinary nature of the topics of this book, it also seeks to be of interest to the fields of public policy, government, economics, and political science interested in the relationships between public libraries, public policy, and political processes. This book has liberally incorporated research from these fields, which has hopefully both strengthened the arguments and increased the utility of the ideas it presents. But the core goal of this book is to serve the roughly 17,000 public libraries and the tens of thousands of library professionals in the United States. This book addresses a topic that all librarian professionals—particularly library administrators—need to be familiar with to ensure that public libraries continue to thrive in a political and policy climate increasingly hostile to the notion of the public good.

DATA SOURCES

Before diving into the arguments of the book, it is important to discuss the origins of much of the data used in this book. This book draws heavily on the findings from a series of national surveys of public libraries that

began in 1994 as the Public Libraries and the Internet survey and continued until 2006 through various funding sources. From 2006 to 2012, the
survey was part of the Public Library Funding and Technology Access
study (http://www.ala.org/plinternetfunding), funded by the ALA and
the Bill and Melinda Gates Foundation. In 2013, the survey became a
stand-alone study again, funded by IMLS. Through the changes in names
and funders, the survey has been conducted annually or biennially with
the purpose of identifying public library Internet connectivity and usage
as a basis for (1) proposing and promoting public library Internet policies
at the federal level; (2) maintaining selected longitudinal data as to the
connectivity, services, and deployment of the Internet in public libraries;
and (3) providing national estimates regarding public library Internet
connectivity. Through 2004, the surveys were conducted roughly every
two years and enabled longitudinal data collection through ad hoc funding from various sources. Beginning in 2006, the surveys switched to an
annual data collection cycle through funding by the ALA and the Bill and
Melinda Gates Foundation.

Though the primary goals of the survey have remained consistent, the
survey evolved over time, experiencing three clear shifts in data collection, methodology, and approach:

- Prior to 1998, the surveys collected data at the system level (e.g.,
  total number of workstations across all library branches, if appli-
  cable).
- Between 1998 and 2004, the surveys collected data at the building/
  outlet level (e.g., number of workstations in a particular branch,
  speed of connectivity at the branch), as well as system-level data
  (e.g., E-rate applications).
- Beginning in 2004, the surveys expanded to collect data at the state
  and national levels, and included both building/outlet-level and
  system-level data.
- Beginning in 2002, the survey offered participants a fully online
  version of the survey as well as a printed version of the survey to
  complete. Each year, more surveys were completed online, and in
  2009, the survey became an online-only survey.

Throughout these shifts, the survey has maintained core longitudinal
questions (e.g., numbers of public access workstations, bandwidth), but
consistently explored a range of emerging topics (e.g., jobs assistance, e-
government, emergency roles). A further evolution of the study began in
2013, with the content of the studies focusing more heavily on the issues
of digital literacy of certain individuals and groups that are becoming
increasingly central to the missions of public libraries. A complete chronicle of the evolutions of the study can be found in Jaeger, Thompson, and
Lazar (2012).

Due to its continued record taking, longitudinal quality, and matchless data, figures from the surveys have appeared over the years in congressional testimony; filings with the FCC; filings with the National Telecommunications and Information Administration (NTIA), particularly NTIA documents regarding the recent Broadband Technology Opportunity Program (BTOP) grant program; evidence cited in the U.S. Supreme Court decisions on CIPA; U.S. Senate hearings on the E-government Act; Pew Internet and the American Life reports; and many other critical policy venues. State librarians also have used the results in state legislative testimony and in a range of state policy documents and initiatives. Local libraries have used the data to lobby for funding and other forms of support from local governments. In short, the data and findings from the surveys are used by a number of stakeholders in a wide range of ways.

The Internet access, services, training, and assistance provided by public libraries are vital to both serving the needs of individual patrons and their communities and supporting national initiatives for digital literacy and digital inclusion, particularly in light of the extraordinary circumstances of the prolonged economic downturn. Without the Public Libraries and the Internet and Public Library Funding and Technology Access studies, these and many other central roles of public libraries would be inadequately documented. All of the Public Libraries and the Internet and Public Library Funding and Technology Access reports are also available in electronic format at http://ipac.umd.edu. Unless otherwise noted, all data about public libraries and technology are from the Public Libraries and the Internet and Public Library Funding and Technology Access studies; the most recent study data can be found in Bertot, McDermott, Lincoln, Real, & Peterson (2012).

TWO

The Development of Public Libraries as a Public Good in the United States

In 1949, the forward-thinking library scholar and educator Jesse Shera observed that "the objectives of the library are directly dependent on the objectives of society itself" (p. 248). Perhaps no truer summary of the essence of public libraries has ever been articulated. Since the beginning of the modern public library movement, libraries have never been about the materials. Today, public libraries are community spaces, meeting places, and study areas that offer printed materials, electronic resources, audio and visual materials, computers, story time, information literacy and technology literacy training, job-seeking help, social services of many types, e-government, and so much more. And yet they are not defined by any of these elements. The public library now stands as the quintessence of the public good; it fills most information-based needs of its community, particularly through the use of Internet-enabled technologies and resources.

How public libraries reached this point is essential to understanding public libraries in the political arena because this history reveals the decisions that have led to both the magnificent achievements of public libraries and the challenges they currently face in policy and politics. The ways in which public libraries have developed into the embodiment of the public good ineluctably have led to the ways in which politics and policies impact public libraries.

THE REALLY LONG TAIL

Libraries have existed for millennia, having gone through many permutations, functions, and levels of availability, with many early libraries

23

having religious or scholarly functions (Cossette, 1976; Jackson, 1974; Krummel, 1999; Lerner, 2009). As social institutions, they "have evolved in response to certain problem situations and have been shaped by countless, relatively independent individual decisions" (Swanson, 1979, p. 3). The most famous early library is the Library and Museum of Alexandria, founded circa 300 BCE by Ptolemy I, which was the center of learning in the ancient world for several hundred years (El-Abbadi, 1990).

In many subsequent centuries, libraries were confined to educational or religious settings, with the Middle Ages in Europe being the low point for libraries as scientific knowledge became equated with paganism (Manchester, 1993). After the invention of the printing press, it became possible for wealthy individuals to build personal libraries. Few of these libraries offered any opportunities for the general public to access the works, and literacy was far from common until the 1800s (Jackson, 1974). In the most dramatic sense, these libraries were intended for a very small group of patrons, collecting materials to fit the specific needs, norms, and tastes of the specific small group of individuals who used them.

The first popular libraries were commercial subscription libraries, formed in towns around the United Kingdom and the colonies in the early 1700s (Davies, 1974). Commercial types of libraries, such as subscription libraries and circulating libraries, tended to specialize in popular novels of the day, with the massive popularity of Samuel Richardson's 1740 novel *Pamela* driving up enrollment in many of these libraries (Jackson, 1974). At the beginning of the American Revolution, nearly a hundred libraries existed in the colonies; one hundred years later, there were more than 3,500 libraries in the United States (McMullen, 2000).

Though 1876 is considered the beginning of the modern library movement, Americans had founded thousands of libraries before then—social, circulating, subscription, academic, church, hospital, asylum, government, military, commercial, law, town, scientific, literary and philosophical society, mechanics, institute, athenaeum, and lyceum libraries, among others (Davies, 1974; Green, 2007; McMullen, 2000; Raven, 2007). Some of these were fairly well stocked with titles; for example, in 1701, the bishop of London shipped thirty-five boxes of books to Maryland for a religious library (DuMont, 1977). Church libraries were often an important supplementary source of reading materials in many communities, in which church libraries and Sunday school classes "inducted children into a culture of literacy and prepared them to participate in a world centered on print" (Pawley, 2001, p. 128). Some of these institutions also continued to exist well after the establishment of public libraries. The Boston Athenaeum, founded in 1807, is a subscription library that continues to thrive today (Wolff, 2009). In 1850, Harvard University had the oldest and largest library in the country with 84,000 volumes, the Library of Congress had 50,000, and the total number of volumes in the United States was around 2,000,000 (Curley, 1990).

At this time, access to books was also becoming linked to the goals of social movements—suffrage, assistance to the poor, better working conditions, and the abolition of child labor—to improve the lives of the underclasses of nineteenth-century society (Ditzion, 1939). "Born of a democratic impulse, or at least a reform-minded one, this right to read is associated with national issues of intellectual freedom and freedom of expression" (Graham, 2001, p. 1). Many of these same groups, particularly women's progressive groups, became advocates for free public libraries (Stauffer, 2005; Watson, 1994). These links to progressive movements focused on social uplift helped shape the vision for the roles of public libraries in their communities.

The first law allowing for the creation of public libraries was passed by New York State in 1796 (Halsey, 2003). American towns and counties began passing their own legislation to create tax-supported school libraries in the 1830s and public-use libraries in the 1840s, with states beginning to pass similar legislation a decade later (Davies, 1974; DuMont, 1977). Public libraries developed at a similar pace in the United States and the United Kingdom, with legislation for public funding of libraries becoming commonplace at nearly the same time (Conant, 1965; Davies, 1974; Gerard, 1978). In 1833, the first taxpayer-supported public library opened in Peterborough, New Hampshire (Wellisch et al., 1974). In 1838, New York State established an annual budget of $55,000 to establish and maintain school libraries, with most other states following soon after (Wellisch et al., 1974). In 1847, Boston established the first taxpayer-supported public library in a major city in the United States (Wolff, 2009).

It is important to remember that the funding of public libraries in the United States was a series of decisions by taxpayers actively opting for "taxation of the community for this public good" (McCook, 2011, p. 14). Sometimes taxpayers were not enthusiastic to pay increased taxes in exchange for a public library. For example, Iowa passed a state law enabling the establishment of public libraries in 1870, but only four libraries had been established five years later (Goldstein, 2003). By the time the ALA was founded in 1876, there were 188 free public libraries and many more school libraries in the United States (Daniel, 1961). Many early public libraries were established with support from philanthropists, none more prominent than Andrew Carnegie, who bestowed more than $41 million to 1,420 towns to establish public libraries between 1886 and 1919 (Davies, 1974). In comparison, the Parliament of the United Kingdom passed its first bill authorizing public libraries in 1850 (D'Angelo, 2006).

The intended clientele of public libraries were originally elite intelligentsia who promoted the establishment of public libraries to ensure access to the reading materials they were interested in, while secondarily serving to promote self-education of the working classes (Pungitore, 1995). The books in these libraries included dictionaries, grammars, books on political and moral issues, as well as books on practical sciences like agriculture, anatomy, astronomy, biology, chemistry, geometry, and mathematics (DuMont, 1977). As with the first libraries, early public libraries tended to focus on the information needs and values of one specific community group. They also were developed in certain areas to encourage order—public libraries were introduced in territories to help prepare the residents for statehood and the accompanying expectations for behavior and social order (Helling, 2012; Stauffer, 2005). At the time of the founding of the ALA, "librarians wholeheartedly embraced the role of dedicated promoter of democratic values and responsibilities" (Halsey, 2003, p. 18). With the then-recent establishment of public schools across the country, a steady growth of per capita income, increasing leisure time as a result of the labor movement, and increased suffrage, social and economic forces were in place to support this type of institution (Borden, 1931).

However, these narrow views of the role of libraries were not universal. From the beginning of the American republic, some leaders saw the library as a social institution that could simultaneously diffuse knowledge to members of society and prevent the wealthy and socially elite from having hegemonic domination over learning and education. Benjamin Franklin—founder of several libraries himself—was the first prominent political leader to advocate the development of libraries to provide political and educational resources to members of society (Gray, 1993; Harris, 1976). Franklin's Library Company of Philadelphia chose a Latin motto that translated, "To pour forth benefits for the common good is divine." Nine signers of the Declaration of Independence were members of the Library Company. Many of the other framers of the government of the United States, including James Madison, Thomas Jefferson, and George Mason, saw great value in official publishing of information produced by the new government and distributing these publications for easy duplication through newspapers and collection in other public institutions (Hernon, Relyea, Dugan, & Cheverie, 2002). In 1813, Congress passed the first act to ensure the dissemination of printed legislative and executive materials to selected state and university libraries and historical society libraries (Morehead, 1998).

Franklin's belief that the public library should have the primary function of promoting equality and raising the quality of national discourse was, however, somewhat unusual for several generations (Augst, 2001). Well into the twentieth century, many more civic and political leaders believed that public libraries could provide a civilizing influence on the masses and be a means to shape the populace into adhering to social norms (Augst, 2001; Harris, 1973, 1976). Libraries were "supported more or less as alternatives to taverns and streets," and librarians "viewed themselves as arbiters of morality" (Jones, 1993, p. 135). The information values and goals of public librarians were often expressed in "broadly religious terms," as if it were the library's mission to save the lost masses

(Garrison, 1993, p. 37). This attitude was reflected in public library selections of materials for the public betterment and attempts to be social stewards of the general population (Augst, 2001; Harris, 1976; Heckart, 1991; Morehead, 1998; Wiegand, 1976, 1996).

The "felt cultural superiority of librarians led them to a concept of the library as a sort of benevolent school of social ethics" (Garrison, 1993, p. 40). Andrew Carnegie's philanthropic library-building activities between 1886 and 1917 further enhanced this role by making public libraries a means for improving the corporate and industrial skills of members of the public (Garrison, 1993; Van Slyck, 1995). During the period of prescriptive roles for public libraries, leaders of the library profession were greatly opposed to social change and feared the labor rights movement and other forces reshaping American society. Library leaders even generally felt that the growth of newspapers and increased availability of fiction were a threat to the prescribed social order, of which public libraries considered themselves an important part (Garrison, 1993; Lerner, 2009; McCrossen, 2006; Preer, 2006).

At the first ALA meeting in 1876, "most agreed that the mass reading public was generally incapable of choosing its own reading materials judiciously" (Wiegand, 1976, p. 10). Civic and political leaders believed that public libraries could provide a civilizing influence on the masses and be a means to shape the populace into adhering to hegemonic social norms (Augst, 2001; Garrison, 1993; Harris, 1973, 1976). This attitude was reflected in the elitist and paternalistic attitudes of most public libraries in selecting materials for the public betterment and in attempting to be social stewards of the general population (Augst, 2001; Heckart, 1991; Wiegand, 1996). In 1928, Charles Compton, the director of the St. Louis Public Library, suggested that "in the far distant future—we shall have a public that will be sufficiently intelligent to select its own reading" (quoted in Luyt, 2001, pp. 451–452). Thus, even as libraries were becoming accessible to greater numbers of community members, librarians generally held to narrow understandings of information value and appropriate social norms and attempted to enforce information needs of a single population across all of the groups in their communities.

These attitudes were quickly starting to change, however. Well before 1900, many city libraries had established a wide range of educational and cultural activities as part of their regular operations, offering everything from tutoring for schoolchildren to classes teaching creative arts and practical skills for adults (Davies, 1974; DuMont, 1977). Simultaneously, libraries provided exhibits, lectures, and meeting spaces for community groups of all types and began to develop services to reach their patrons across multiple community groups—such as reference services, children's services, and adult education services (DuMont, 1977). Further, libraries were also starting to model practices to improve life in communities. In cities, libraries were often among the first public institutions to adopt modern technologies and approaches for lighting, ventilation, and reducing the spread of disease (Musman, 1993).

World War I tested the burgeoning inclusiveness of public libraries, with mixed results. During World War I, public libraries actively supported the war effort by opening up facilities for use by government agencies, created war-related exhibits, promoted books about the war, served as collection agencies for bond and saving stamp drives, disseminated information provided by government agencies, promoted food conservation, and collected books to create libraries for military camps (Wiegand, 1989). They also actively engaged in censorship of their own materials—removing all kinds of German-language, pacifist, and labor-associated materials (Wiegand, 1989).

INCLUSIVE COMMUNITY ANCHORS

By the 1930s, public libraries more firmly began to turn away from their previous roles as agents of social control. It took the rise of fascism and a world war, but ultimately public libraries created and adopted a new primary social role as the veritable marketplace of ideas, offering materials that represented a diversity of views and interests, while opposing censorship and other social controls (Gellar, 1974; Heckart, 1991). Many libraries had begun to take on a social service mission in the early 1930s, a change appearing earliest in public libraries in urban settings, where working with largely immigrant patron populations meant that active engagement with multiple community groups became part of libraries' daily activities (Fiske, 1959). In these years, libraries tried to straddle both educating foreign-born patrons and helping them to adjust and build new lives, while also trying to make American citizens out of them (Barrett, 1992; Jones, 1999). This dramatic change in social roles "emerged in an environment in which the concept of the public library's social responsibility was itself changing radically" (Gellar, 1974, p. 1367).

Numerous factors affected this reorientation, but a key change was the effect fascist governments were having on public access to information in many parts of the world in the late 1930s, specifically through lethal suppression of expression, closing of libraries, and public book burnings (Gellar, 1984; Robbins, 1996; Stielow, 2001). In reaction to these global events, the ALA passed its Library Bill of Rights in 1939 and began the swing toward the modern ideal of the public library as society's marketplace of ideas (Berninghausen, 1953; Gellar, 1984; Robbins, 1996). A central component of this new stance was the unswerving assertion that voters must have access to a full range of perspectives on all significant political and social issues (Samek, 2001). Public libraries actively participated in voter registration and participation drives to increase voter turnout in the 1952 presidential election, firmly establishing the modern concept of the public library as a reliable "community source for serious, nonpartisan information on a central issue of the day" (Preer, 2008, p. 19).

After World War II, American libraries were so secure in their role in working with various community groups and promoting democracy—through supporting continuing education, serving the information needs of poor and recent immigrants, having special events for children, providing education to the working classes, opening branch libraries, and other forms of service—that a major history written at the time was proudly titled *Arsenals of a Democratic Culture* (Ditzion, 1947). These increasing commitments to their communities coincided with, and were likely fueled by, a time of robust increases in economic support of public libraries by local communities. The post–World War II economic boom that continued into the 1960s led to communities passing sales taxes, property taxes, and local income taxes as means to support public library expansion (Chatters, 1957). In fact, between 1936 and 1955, funding for libraries in the seventy-six largest cities in the United States grew at a rate far greater than rates of growth for total city expenditures (Chatters, 1957). Libraries also began to better serve larger communities by integrating into city- and county-level public library systems in many places (Leigh, 1957).

The path to a professional commitment to serving communities was not always smooth, however. Even after the passage of the Library Bill of Rights in 1939, many public libraries still banned John Steinbeck's *The Grapes of Wrath* for its political views (Samek, 2001). Other major writers that there were contemporaneous attempts to censor in libraries included Theodore Dreiser, Warwick Deeping, George Eliot, Thomas Hardy, Nathanial Hawthorne, and Sinclair Lewis (Berninghausen, 1948a, 1948b). In the 1940s and 1950s, some public libraries were still uncomfortable with the idea of equal access to all, while, in sharp contrast, others took a clear lead in the civil rights movement (Robbins, 2000, 2007). Public library "read-ins" were important to breaking down segregation not only in southern libraries, but also in other public institutions in southern communities (Graham, 2001). The decision across the profession to actively support access in the face of attempts to censor collections at the local and broader levels has come to define the commitment of libraries to standing up for the needs of their communities. Nevertheless, the collections of many libraries were directly and indirectly influenced by the politics of the McCarthy era, often leading to the silencing of unpopular viewpoints in many library collections (Richards, 2001).

One writer, in 1953, made clear that libraries needed to hold to this then-new stance of providing diverse information from numerous perspectives because "a democratic society has need for all the information it can get" (Berninghausen, 1953, p. 813). This commitment to diversity of perspectives and to battling censorship was reinforced in society when public libraries actively resisted government intrusions into library col-

lections and patron reading habits, particularly during the McCarthy era
(Jaeger & Burnett, 2005). Not only did the commitment to providing a
diversity of information resources apply to the kinds of political materials typically targeted during the McCarthy era, but it also covers materials more related to entertainment and other interests that may be considered by some to be of limited importance or lacking in the kinds of depth
and purpose that marked the goals of many early libraries. Materials
including fiction and entertainment-oriented works are now important
parts of library collections; the social importance of such materials can be
seen in the fact that they have been challenged by those who would
constrain people's access to information at least as often as more overtly
political materials. In Iowa in the 1950s, public librarians even successfully fought efforts to censor what could be sold in local bookstores and
drugstores (Taylor, 2013).

The first major government effort to monitor reading in libraries was
an Internal Revenue Service (IRS) program encouraged by the Bureau of
Alcohol, Tobacco, and Firearms (ATF) to check, without warrants, on
library patrons who had been reading books related to explosives and
guerilla warfare. The encouragement quickly spawned the Federal Bureau of Investigation's infamous Library Awareness Program (LAP), a
two-decade-long FBI program fishing for anything interesting in library
records (Foerstel, 1991, 2004). These efforts were part of a larger FBI
culture obsessed with collecting information about U.S. citizens, driven
by the efforts of its longtime director, J. Edgar Hoover. For example, in
1921, Hoover had files on 450,000 people, an amazing feat in an era before
computers; by 1974, the FBI fingerprint division had prints of 159 million
people, which included most of the population of the United States (Ack-
erman, 2007).

Though various censorship efforts have continued to affect public libraries since the McCarthy era, such as the LAP and the USA PATRIOT
Act of 2001, the public library has solidified its position as a place devoted to a diversity of ideas and inclusion of diverse communities, one
that is open to all through its active support of widespread public access
to information (Foerstel, 1991, 2004; Hartman, 2007; Jaeger & Burnett,
2005). Beyond the resistance to laws that limit the ability of patrons to
meet their information needs, public libraries and their organizations
have taken a wide range of stances to support civil rights and human
rights for many populations in the United States and abroad over the past
several decades.

The development of the public library through the nineteenth and
twentieth centuries strengthened the library's social position and has
created certain social roles for public libraries, maturing from a simple
repository of texts to a place where a wide variety of community groups
can not only find information but can also have a voice (Heckart, 1991).
The idea that the public library will provide equal access to a wide range

of information and views in numerous formats, often in a variety of languages representing a diverse array of perspectives on social and political issues, has thus become a solid social norm across different populations in society (Jaeger & Burnett, 2005). For people with limited or no other access to published and electronic materials, the expected social function of public libraries is to ensure access to newspapers and periodicals, books of nonfiction and fiction, the Internet, music, movies, community meeting places, and much more. The public library is now seen as a social and virtual space where all ages and walks of life can mix, exchange views, access materials, and engage in public discourse (Goulding, 2004; Jaeger & Burnett, 2005). Due to their inclusive stance, public libraries are even viewed as a safe community space for members of diverse and underrepresented populations who may otherwise feel less than accepted in general society (Rothbauer, 2007).

Public libraries have further cemented their position through the development of partnerships with other government agencies, nonprofit organizations, and others to provide services that they cannot provide individually (Bertot & Jaeger, 2012; Gorham et al., 2013; Jaeger, Taylor, et al., 2012; Taylor et al., in press). These partnership programs vary across the country, meeting unique local community needs. In Baltimore, Maryland, the public libraries work with the City Health Department to ensure the availability of fresh groceries to those living in food deserts by providing opportunities for patrons to order their groceries through library computers and have the food delivered the next day to the library. In Alachua County, Florida, the Alachua County Library District, working with the local office of the state's Department of Children and Families, the Partnership for Strong Families, and Casey Family Programs, opened up a new facility, the Library Partnership, a 4,500-square-foot space devoted to the library and housing approximately forty nonprofit organizations and local government agencies that provide social services focused on child welfare, greatly facilitating the ability to work with all of the interrelated agencies to get needed support as quickly as possible. These are but two notable examples of a great many across the nation, as nearly one-third of public libraries have established partnerships to meet community needs (Bertot, McDermott, Lincoln, Real, & Peterson, 2012).

While it may not always work perfectly in practice, the public library remains committed to serving the needs of the full spectrum of community groups, from the individual, to different groups in the community, to the entire service population. Whereas many traditional public spaces in communities—the town square, the public gardens, the community market, and other places that serve to foster interaction among community members—have become less visible or ceased to exist, the public library continues to be an extremely important physical public space (Given & Leckie, 2003; Leckie & Hopkins, 2002). With so few physical manifestations of the public good remaining, the public library may be "the nearest thing we have . . . to an achieved public sphere" (Webster, 2002, p. 176).

As an example, the evolution of the public library into inclusive community anchor institutions can be viewed through the perspective of evolving services to immigrants. Services to immigrant populations have long been a core function of public libraries in the United States. New immigrants can turn to public libraries for information on citizenship, employment, education, social services, health, safety, housing, and learning English, as well as materials in their native languages, programs, services, and referrals (Cuban, 2007; McCook, 2011). In many communities, the public library is the most important institution available to immigrants in adapting to their new lives and new communities, while also helping to preserve identities and connections to original cultures (Cuban, 2007; Lukenbill, 2006). Such services have been central to public libraries for well over a century.

Public library outreach and services for immigrants date back to the early years of the public library movement in the late 1800s and early 1900s (Burke, 2008; Jones, 1999). Before World War I, public libraries were particularly focused on providing services to immigrant children and first-generation Americans (Larson, 2001; McDowell, 2010, 2011). A range of materials and services were provided for young patrons as individuals and in reading and social groups focusing on a range of subject matters—literature, arts, economics, politics, and employment—with a heavy emphasis on enculturation and acclimation to the United States (Larson, 2001). These services for children were also seen as a way to reach their parents and help Americanize them (McDowell, 2011). Such services were provided in a climate "indifferent and at times even hostile" to the educational needs of young immigrants and first-generation Americans (Larson, 2001, p. 225).

By the time America entered World War I, immigrant services had been widely accepted as a key function of public libraries in urban areas, as the country was absorbing many more immigrants from a wider range of places than previously (Wiegand, 1976, 1989). The ALA began programs to promote the socialization of these new waves of immigrants and assistance in the transition from immigrant to citizen through public library services (Burke, 2008; Jones, 1999; Wiegand, 1976). The increasing focus on the needs of immigrants led to a stronger focus on the needs of other disadvantaged groups, playing a significant part in the maturation of the public library into a progressive community institution (Jones, 1999).

As a result, public libraries have a long history of helping immigrants with personal needs, like employment and housing, and with community engagement through social connections and civic participation (Caidi & Allard, 2005). In libraries in urban areas of North America, Western Europe, and Australia, services to immigrants are now a major function of their community service (Lerner, 2009). Public libraries regularly provide immigrant communities in their service areas with information about life in the new country and other materials in native languages, English as a second language (ESL) courses, computer training, civics education, job-seeking help, and other resources for acclimation (Varheim, 2010). As a result of these targeted programs and services, immigrant populations typically perceive the public library as a place of building social networks, learning about their place of residence, meeting new people in the community, staying connected to their native cultures, and learning to trust social institutions, in addition to the information resources and language services available (Audunson, Essmat, & Aabo, 2011; Chu, 1999; Varheim, 2010). Inclusive services to immigrant populations is also a topic that is part of the curriculum of many library schools (Jaeger, Subramaniam, Jones, & Bertot, 2011).

The advent of the World Wide Web has provided new opportunities for public libraries to provide innovative services to immigrants. Many libraries across the country, for example, are playing a pivotal role in helping immigrants attain citizenship. Over the past several years, public libraries in several regions with high levels of immigration have partnered with other social agencies to provide wide-ranging assistance through the immigration process, with a few libraries even becoming the immigration centers for their regions (Gorham et al., 2013).

PUBLIC LIBRARIES, THE INTERNET, AND THE EVOLUTION OF THE PUBLIC GOOD

The public library is a social creation and agency that binds members of a community—with its constituent community groups—together, with its roles in the community evolving to reflect the changes in the society it serves (Shera, 1970). The meaning of the library as a place within communities has varied across cultures, nations, and times (Buschman & Leckie, 2007). Libraries have served a range of societal needs throughout history, functioning as repository, information provider, educational institution, and social advocate (Reith, 1984). Similarly, the philosophies associated with librarianship and the principles of educating librarians have evolved over time (McChesney, 1984; Rogers, 1984). Clearly, libraries have been adaptive and changing organizations as they attempted to fill the needs of their communities and serve the public good.

These efforts have certainly been noticed by members of the public, who rate public libraries as the most-trusted social institution and "seem almost immune to the distrust that is associated with so many other institutions" (Public Agenda, 2006, p. 11). In the past two decades, the evolution of library services has been defined by the explosion of the Internet and the move of countless personal, educational, civic, governmental, employment, and other activities online. Long-standing trust in public libraries has extended to reliance on them for support in the new virtual environment by many members of their communities.

Technology is a significant part of the changing nature of libraries. From the time public libraries began to organize around professional associations and develop professional standards in the late 1800s, technology has been important in shaping libraries and the profession of librarianship. Melvil Dewey in particular was keenly focused on the creation and novel employment of technology to improve library operations (Garrison, 1993; Stauffer, 2006; Wiegand, 1996). As new means of electronic dissemination of information—such as radio, movies, and television—entered wide use, libraries reacted by eventually incorporating many of them into the services and types of materials they provided (McCrossen, 2006; Pittman, 2001; Preer, 2006). The invention of many home-use entertainment technologies led libraries to begin to include new types of media—videocassettes, CDs, DVDs, CD-ROMs—in the mission to offer patrons a diversity of materials with many perspectives (Pittman, 2001). Jesse Shera (1964), in addition, foresaw that computers would greatly reduce manual tasks performed by librarians. The progression of modern information technology has been a major influence on what libraries have tried to provide to their patrons and what patrons have in turn expected from them.

Shera (1970) asserted that technological evolution "will have tremendous importance for services which the library can offer, the ways in which it can offer these services, the advances it can make in its own technology, and in the whole underlying theory of what librarianship is" (p. 70). The specific changes eventually brought by the Internet proved, however, hard for librarians to foresee, in part because of the speed with which the Internet grew. For example, the White House Conference on Library and Information Services of 1979 anticipated the time when technology would simultaneously reduce the costs of running a library and expand the services available (Seymour, 1980). Conversely, around the same time, one library scholar asserted, "The users' perceptions of the public library, as reflected in the types of services they recognize, raise grave doubts as to the desirability of the large-scale adoption of electronic gadgetry" (DuMont, 1977, p. 128). Such a suspicion of technology was still, in 1996, a central factor in the San Francisco Public Library controversy, in which some community members raised loud objections to giving more space to computers in the library building (Baker, 1996; Kniffel, 1996). More recently, librarians and citizens of New York City protested a proposed renovation plan to the New York Public Library's main branch location. Library administrators proposed that much of the research collection be moved into storage in a nearby New Jersey facility in order to make way for computers and modern work stations (Adler, 2012).

In a collection of essays written by librarians in the early 1990s envisioning the library of the twenty-first century (Lancaster, 1993), no mention was made of the Internet or the World Wide Web as part of the library's future, though CD-ROMs received considerable attention; while, given the stage of the Internet's evolution at that point, such an omission is perhaps not entirely surprising, it does seem, in retrospect, somewhat shortsighted. At the opposite extreme—though perhaps equally shortsighted—some were predicting in the 1960s that computers would wholly replace libraries before the new millennium (e.g., Kermeny, 1962; Licklider, 1965).

The rise of the Internet in public libraries has been dramatic and swift, transforming communities' expectations and perceptions of information value and behavior, radically altering what patrons expect from libraries, with Internet access now being an essential service for many patrons. As the Internet rapidly gained social prominence and significance in the 1990s, public libraries began to offer Internet access and a range of new services through numerous media that provided patrons with exposure to a wide expanse of information and ideas. Such services now function as a natural extension of the established social roles of libraries. By providing new avenues by which to access information and by providing access to many materials the library could not otherwise provide for reasons of cost, space, or scarcity, the Internet can be considered a robust source of diverse, and often otherwise unavailable, information for patrons (Bennett, 2001; Kranich, 2001a).

The Internet—with its vast information resources, global interconnectivity, and means of community participation—has allowed libraries to finally achieve the vision of becoming true information centers for all needs of the community, and to become important bridges between the local needs of specific communities and far-flung information resources. Public libraries were written about as community information centers as early as William Learned's *The American Public Library and the Diffusion of Knowledge* (1924) and *Libraries and Adult Education* (1926). The technological changes brought by the Internet have not only made the library one of the last true physical entities of the public good, but have also allowed libraries to serve patrons around the world through digital reference and chat services and the provision of online databases and resources. However, since the Internet has become commonplace in libraries, its true impact has been downplayed or underestimated in some quarters of the library profession, ironically paralleling how libraries initially resisted periodicals.

In the early 2000s, many librarians viewed the Internet as primarily a basic reference tool that also had entertainment and communication capacities (Fourie & Dowell, 2002; Shuman, 2001). Perhaps echoing the early perceptions of the information value of libraries that saw their goal as moral arbiters and suppliers only of certain kinds of "important" information outlined earlier in this chapter, some have argued that the focus on the Internet displays a confusion of purpose that undercuts more traditional information provision activities (Baker, 1996, 2001; Brophy, 2007; Brown & Duguid, 2002; Tisdale, 1997). Given the mission of libraries to serve these needs—from the mundane to the essential—of multiple social groups, however, such concerns may in fact dangerously constrain libraries' potential.

Other fears are rooted in perception. Some argue that the increasing centrality of computers to libraries makes libraries appear too removed from the traditional perceptions of libraries and their reason for existence. Rows of computers and video game collections make some feel that "at this historical moment, the changes that libraries are undergoing makes them appear to be complicit with other contemporary forces that are eroding access to history and unraveling the connections of past and future generations" (Manoff, 2001, p. 374). A further factor may be that libraries have historically been considered refuges in times of social change (Rayward & Jenkins, 2007), but these social changes—in the tangible form of computers in the library buildings—reach into the essence of the library itself. "We subconsciously know that libraries are more complex than information centers" (Dowell, 2008, p. 42). For many librarians, though, the presence of computers may make libraries seem too much like information centers only. However, the integration of the Internet into basic library services might in fact serve both functions: it simultaneously situates libraries as important information centers *and* reflects the fact that they serve more complex needs than that designation may appear to suggest (Jaeger & Burnett, 2010).

Resistance to or fear of the Internet and its impacts are hardly unique to libraries, of course. The Internet reaches into virtually every dimension of a technologically advanced society. Ben Shneiderman (2008) has even suggested that the technological revolutions of the past twenty years are so all encompassing and significant in shaping society that traditional scientific methods need to be reconceptualized. The public library is far from alone in rethinking its meaning as a social institution. Yet this issue seems to be particularly hard for certain quarters in public libraries.

Many of the problems faced by libraries in dealing with new technologies and information sources through the years are similar to those faced now in relation to the Internet in that they force a reconsideration of the roles the library wants to play in society (Preer, 2006). As examples among countless others, the digital age has forced libraries to redefine the meaning of intellectual freedom in libraries and the meaning of the library as public forum (Dresang, 2006; Gathegi, 2005). The new technologies that have become central to librarianship have also greatly increased the ethical dilemmas in providing access to information, including intellectual freedom, privacy, confidentiality, filtering, and Internet access (Alfino & Pierce, 1997; Hauptman, 2002).

Whatever the various reasons behind the resistance to Internet-enabled roles and expectations, as demonstrated above, the public library has a long tradition of adopting new technologies to meet user information needs. In the past century, it has adopted and absorbed many different technologies to continue to expand its services, remain relevant to patrons across information worlds, and build trust in communities (Jaeger & Fleischmann, 2007; McCrossen, 2006; Pittman, 2001; Preer, 2006).

Libraries have long served as a physical public entity of the public good, with places and spaces for different community groups to meet and for members of different community groups to interact and exchange information and gain exposure to new perspectives. Regardless of the technologies and types of information, libraries are still serving as a hub of public engagement and spreading information throughout their communities. Now, public libraries are "perhaps even the last true public spaces" due to their physical presence in communities and their guarantees of access to all (Leckie, 2004, p. 233). However, the Internet and related social networking technologies are also allowing the library to become a central part of the virtual public good, where members of society gather together via social networking technologies.

Instead of being a technology that involves the one-way transfer of information, the Internet features many types of multidirectional interaction and information exchange through social networking technologies, allowing for the creation of new communities online (Stephens, 2007). In June 2007, the Online Computer Library Center (OCLC) reported that the top three Internet sites already were social networking sites—YouTube, MySpace, and Facebook—attracting an astounding 350 million patrons that month (OCLC, 2007). These participatory technologies opened up new opportunities for library services. In the most practical sense, many libraries already offer virtual reference and chat services, online databases, and other virtual forms of traditional services. The more challenging use of social networking technologies will be to cultivate the interactions of different groups online and to create a meaningful virtual public good. At this point, "libraries have a chance not only to improve service to their local communities, but to advance the field of participatory networks" (Lankes, Silverstein, & Nicholson, 2007, p. 32).

Libraries already play a vital role in ensuring the health of online communities—providing free Internet access to those who would not otherwise have it. Beyond providing access, the library already takes a major role in ensuring participation in some online activities. Federal, state, and local governments increasingly rely on the public library as an access point through which all members of society can reach e-government websites, with many government websites and publications even directing people to go to the public library for assistance in filing taxes, welfare requests, immigration documents, and numerous other essential government forms (Bertot et al., 2006a, 2006b). At the same time, a significant proportion of the U.S. population—including people who have no other means of access, people who need help using technology, and people who have lower-quality access—rely heavily upon this access and trust the e-government assistance available through public libraries (Jaeger & Fleischmann, 2007). Some difficulties with respect to such new responsibilities, which entail libraries trying to reach across communities and populations to diverse individual patrons, are not surprising. Long before the advent of the Internet, the goals of providing service to all created a great and increasing number of obligations to meet with thinly spread library resources (Conant, 1965; Gerard, 1978).

Another linkage of traditional library service with new technology capacities has been intended specifically to reach otherwise underserved populations. One omnipresent example of this among public libraries is the provision of information literacy and technology literacy—usually discussed in conjunction as "digital literacy"—classes that enable patrons to use computers and the Internet on their own to accomplish online tasks, as well as the informal assistance always available to patrons using the Internet. In many communities, the public libraries have become the only available source of formal or informal digital literacy education for members of the community (Jaeger, Bertot, Thompson, Katz, & DeCoster, 2012).

A less common example of such efforts is known as community-focused information services (CIS), which focus on using new media technologies to enable patrons to create and share content about themselves and their communities (Bishop, Bazzell, Mehra, & Smith, 2001; Durrance & Fisher, 2002; Fisher, Durrance, & Hinton, 2004). CIS projects have developed around the globe and involve not only preservation and access to information resources, but also promotion of community participation and engagement (Srinivasan, 2006a, 2006b, 2007). These CIS efforts both reassert the public library as a vital community asset that can help connect patrons to find locally relevant information and provide new means through which to bring library services to underserved populations within diverse communities (Becvar & Srinivasan, 2009; Boast, Bravo, & Srinivasan, 2007; Caidi & Allard, 2005; Lyons, 2007; Mehra & Srinivasan, 2007). The Chicago area provides two key examples of CIS projects. NorthStarNet (http://northstarnet.org) is designed to link people from diverse populations across the various suburbs of Chicago's urban sprawl, while SkokieNet (http://skokienet.org) not only focuses on current community members' interests—such as community revitalization, child care, jobs, and housing—but offers resources to new immigrant populations in their native languages, including Indian, Korean, and Assyrian, among others.

Clearly the contributions of public libraries to their communities remain significant in the age of the Internet. Symbolically, public libraries have great social meaning as social institutions that are trusted to provide a range of information, education, technologies, and perspectives, as well as places for different community groups to interact. National surveys have repeatedly shown the public library to be the most trusted public or government institution in the country, primarily because they serve the public good and change to meet new public needs (Lukensmeyer, 2012). Further, libraries, by ensuring information access and information literacy, contribute significantly to the health of the community, promoting interaction and sharing of physical and virtual spaces with different groups in the community. While patrons may not always rub shoulders in the physical library, they can separately use library resources to create perspectives that they can share in other forums across their local community or across cyberspace (Jaeger & Burnett, 2010). The vital roles of public libraries in contemporary society of building and supporting communities and civic engagement are evidenced by the large amount of support that they receive from major private foundations, such as the Gates, Knight, and MacArthur Foundations. These organizations would not be continuing to make such investments if they did not see public libraries as central to education, economics, and participation (Ellis, Jacobs, & Stasch, 2012a, 2012b).

The historical changes that have led to the public library as the provider of a vast range of physical and virtual services attempting to reach the information, technology, and related educational needs of all groups in a community have occurred in less than a century. The evolution of the public library as perhaps the most durable agency of the public good encapsulates many of the rapid major physical and virtual social changes that have shaped the society in recent decades, as well as the varying reactions to these changes. Throughout these changes in community needs and available technologies, public libraries have continued to reflect and reinforce their commitment to serving all members of their communities in an equitable and inclusive manner and to promoting freedom of expression in both physical and virtual contexts. This evolution by which public libraries are serving their communities more and more through computer-related activities has paralleled a time in which the political and policy pressures on public libraries have increased notably, as will be explored in the next chapter.

THREE

The Evolution of Policies Affecting
Public Libraries in the United States

While libraries have long viewed themselves as a pillar of democracy by supporting an informed, educated, and engaged citizenry, political and policy decisions have treated libraries in a number of different ways, ranging from neglect to direct intervention. Building on the historical development of public libraries described in chapter 2, this chapter examines the very significant changes over time in government actions toward public libraries and how these actions impact libraries and their communities. The chapter also explores the reactions of public libraries to these new expectations and their attempts to engage large policy issues in the national political and policy-making processes.

For many years, local and state policies and politics were the only ones with a direct impact on libraries. This local nature has often emphasized the contents of the collection, operational issues, and library funding. However, after many years of limited involvement in public libraries, the federal government has become a major influence on public libraries through crafting policies and framing political debates in ways that have significant impacts on the ways in which libraries can serve their communities. Particularly since the advent of the Web, laws and policies have heavily shaped the funding of public libraries and the contributions public libraries are able to make in their communities.

Tracing the development of the relationships between libraries, policy, and politics at local, state, and national levels over time, this chapter posits that these relationships have passed through four distinct phases. Understanding these phases and incorporating these understandings into library advocacy and perspectives in political and policy discourse will allow libraries to better assert the contributions of libraries to democracy, the reasons for the stances they take, and the importance of political and policy decisions that support and adequately fund libraries.

PUBLIC LIBRARIES AND POLITICS

Public library professionals and scholars have long articulated the value of public libraries as being central to democracy, giving rise to such oft-repeated phrases to describe public libraries as arsenals of democracy and marketplaces of ideas. The power of this association can be seen in the title of a book published in 2001: *Libraries and Democracy: The Cornerstones of Liberty* (Kranich, 2001b). This equation of the public library as foundational to democracy holds "near-mythic status" (Dervin, 1994, p. 369) and serves as "the alpha and the omega" (Buschman, 2007a, p. 1483) of the profession. When the ALA created a document entitled "12 Ways Libraries Are Good for the Country," support for democracy was the first reason presented on the list (ALA, 2000).

Public libraries are indeed fundamentally public institutions that serve to inform the public and alleviate social problems, which clearly can support a healthy democratic society (Buschman, 2009, 2012). Libraries support democracy as transmitters—they are filled with "resources and channels of information" that provide "a wide range of knowledge and opinion" to support the literacy and intellectual growth of community members (Line, 2003, p. 386). They are "inextricably bound up with the life of a community" (Foskett, 1962, p. 7), serving as advocates for their patrons and their communities (Clark, 2009).

However, even if libraries are important in a democracy, libraries have never *demonstrated* that they are central to democracy or based in democratic functions (Danton, 1934). That assertion from 1934 remains true to this day. The case for the democratic role of libraries has been one of assertions of value rather than demonstrations of value. This difference is enormous in terms of the political and policy-making processes. When discussing political processes and involvement in the United States in a book published in 2012, John Buschman suggests that library discourse "really has not gone beyond some of the very earliest of formulations at the beginnings of modern democracy" (p. 10). This complements a telling observation made two decades before that library discourse makes many large assumptions that libraries and the information to which they provide access have "implications for democratic political processes and participation," but these assumptions are generally neither well developed nor empirically supported (Lievrouw, 1994, p. 350).

Instead, public libraries have relied upon "assertions and rhetorical claims" when seeking support through the political process, rather than actual evidence or data to make the case for their democratic contributions and for increasing the level of funding to support these contributions (DeProspo, 1977, pp. 197–198). Thus "librarians have been unable to make a claim for social relevancy which has generated the kind of administrative support needed to make an impact on the nation and the Congress" (Shields, 1980, p. 9). Instead public libraries have opted to "rely on simple comparisons—letting people draw untestable conclusions" (Wheeler, 2011, p. 48). Tellingly, a 350-page report on public libraries and federal policy published in 1974 listed many contributions to society by libraries—including availability, familiarity as a landmark, ability to meet the changing and wide-ranging needs of the largest number of people, dedicated public servants—but did not list support for democracy as one of those contributions (Wellisch et al., 1974).

Part of the library community's lack of ability to demonstrate the value of being a foundation of democracy ties to the lack of attention the concept receives in scholarship. The field of LIS only averages four refereed journal articles published yearly that deal with democracy in any way since the mid-1960s (Buschman, 2007a). That average represents an overall decline from earlier years of that time frame. While never robust, focus on social and political issues within librarianship has fallen off from a higher period of interest in the late 1970s and early 1980s (Kajberg, 2011).

As a result, a disconnect exists between the way libraries see themselves as arsenals of democratic culture and the limited ability of library discourse to convey clear connections to actual democratic political processes. Serving as an arsenal of democracy is a central pillar of the narrative that libraries use to justify their funding and support. Perhaps some of the political weakness of public libraries in contemporary funding debates is tied to relying on an argument that cannot be well articulated, especially in times of fiscal austerity. If public libraries cannot show their importance in the overall political culture and their tangible support of civic values and democratic engagement, they will be more vulnerable to being treated with indifference—or not considered at all—in politics and policy.

Oftentimes, the policy and political discussions related to libraries are based on a historical perspective in which libraries are viewed merely as book warehouses and places where children participate in story time. Ask the average person (or policy maker) about their local public library, and chances are they will mention getting books there as a child or as an adult, and they will not know about the myriad of other resources and services that libraries provide. Almost never will they mention the role libraries play in educating citizens of a democracy. While such focus on the urgency of the present is hardly unique to considerations of policy and political processes in library discourse, it is problematic when a foundational aspect of the argument is based on the notion that libraries are central to the arc of democratic progress.

EVOLVING DYNAMICS OF POLICY AND LIBRARIES

One step toward being able to better articulate the roles of libraries in democracy as part of policy and political discussions is to spend more time considering the historical relationships between libraries, policy, and politics in a democracy. It is a story that can be considered in four phases:

1. the entirely local years, when decisions of funding and policy that impacted libraries were truly limited to local and state governments;
2. the years of the world wars and the early Cold War, when libraries became involved in national political issues to try to support democracy and/or government objectives;
3. the years in which federal government interest in public libraries focused primarily on providing funding to increase access and service; and
4. the current period of direct government intervention in public libraries through a range of laws and policies that shape library activities (Jaeger, Gorham, Sarin, & Bertot, 2013).

As much of general library history from these periods—particularly the first two—is covered in the previous chapter, this chapter will focus on the political and policy side of the story.

During the years that public libraries were entirely shaped by local political and policy decisions, the range of influences was far more knowable, and the avenues of engagement with these processes were much clearer. Over time, all of the local issues have continued to be considerations for public libraries, but they now coexist with an enormous range of political and policy-making pressures at the national level.

From the beginning of the modern public library movement, the local community has played a huge role in the operations of the public library. Even today, regardless of the size of the population served by the library, the local government provides at least three-quarters of its funding, as shown in figure 3.1.

When libraries were established by communities, it was often a large commitment to build the library, staff it, and build the collection, given the size and funding base of many agrarian American communities in the late 1800s. Yet a public library was seen as a great source of pride for a community, a sign that the community had arrived and was significant (Wiegand, 2011). In most communities, the perceived status of the public library and the proportionally large amount of funding it required led to a great deal of local political involvement in decisions of operations, hiring, and collection development. Many library governing boards were comprised of the people who were already local community and political leaders.

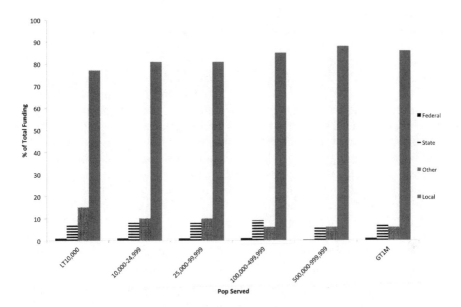

Figure 3.1.   Source of Funding (2011) *Source:* **IMLS, Public Libraries Survey, Fiscal Year 2011.**

Though different communities have different structures of governance, public libraries since their establishment have needed sufficient engagement in the political process to continue to receive funding. "Local politics are crucial to public libraries because they can affect their quality, if not their very existence" (Shavit, 1986, p. 22). The amount of funding made available to the library by the local government is the most immediate determinant of its ability to meet community needs. As long as most libraries have existed, they have simultaneously had to navigate the politics of local government that shapes their funding and the policy making of local library boards that places parameters on the activities of the library.

This local nature of public libraries leads to a great deal of flexibility in the ways in which libraries can identify and respond to local needs. However, it also contributes to the disparities between library funding and services in different areas, particularly in those areas serving minority and marginalized populations that most strongly need a vibrant public library. To limit such disparities, many European nations enact national goals and standards for public libraries, including minimum funding and service standards (Helling, 2012). Without such established national goals and standards, most public libraries in the United States historically have been, and remain to this day, heavily beholden to the whims of local politics and policy that can heavily impact their ability to meet their community needs.

Even in the local years, public libraries navigated other key challenges in relation to politics and policy. Ensuring that the majority of community members have a positive impression of the library is of great importance. As voters influence the decisions of local politicians both by what they say and who they vote for, too many community members upset at the local library will likely negatively impact funding. A manifestation of this is the constancy of potential objections to materials that are made available in the library by members of the public or local government officials. As a truly public institution, libraries have faced challenges to materials spanning the novels of Horatio Alger in the early twentieth century (for supposedly giving children too much hope) to more recent challenges to the Harry Potter novels (for allegedly promoting witchcraft). As noted earlier, since the adoption of ALA's Library Bill of Rights, libraries have had a professional policy to defend the rights of patrons to access materials that certain community members find objectionable. But, realistically, libraries also have to account for the tastes and standards of their individual communities when selecting materials.

The local nature of public libraries also includes a role for the state. While states generally provide only a small portion of library funds, they have long had a role in standardizing and coordinating the public libraries in each state. In some states, virtually as soon as the library was built, representatives of the state were there to give opinions on the collections or the operations of the library (Wiegand, 2011). While state libraries clearly can advocate for public libraries in the state, the public libraries must also account for the opinions of elected state representatives and the staff of the state library.

The desire to serve their communities and support government agendas led to some very divergent library initiatives during the years of the world wars and the Cold War. On one hand, as detailed in the previous chapter, World War I offered libraries a chance to take a clear role in providing educational materials for a democracy at war and otherwise actively supporting the war effort (Wiegand, 1989). Yet public libraries also actively engaged in censorship of their own materials by removing German-language, pacifist, and labor-associated materials, and a similar dichotomy of efforts was evidenced during World War II (Wiegand, 1989). However, these activities represented the first concerted efforts of public libraries to be a part of the national political agenda.

Between the world wars, public libraries received their first support from the federal government level. In the 1930s, public libraries received a small amount of federal support during the Depression through the Works Progress Administration (WPA) and the Federal Emergency Relief Administration (FERA), which used its programs to pay unemployed individuals to work in libraries, primarily doing maintenance, book repair, inventories, and odd jobs (Novotny, 2010; Shields, 1980). This support was so limited, and so many libraries opted to limit or halt purchasing new materials to conserve funds, that most library collections were nevertheless in tatters at the end of the Depression (Kramp, 1975). The voracious appetite of the public for reading materials even overwhelmed the Library of Congress, which featured usage rates doubling every few years and thousands of patrons looking for reading materials every day (Aikin, 2013).

However, the WPA funds represented the starting point of the federal government beginning to envision a direct role for itself in the public library. Also in the late 1930s, President Roosevelt's Advisory Committee on Education considered potential federal funding for state libraries as a way to support public education, but no actual support resulted from the idea (Shavit, 1985). The 1940s saw the establishment of the Washington Office of the ALA, which then made concerted efforts to lobby for federal support for public library funding. For several subsequent decades, however, the ALA would focus on the best interests of libraries as institutions rather than the interests of library professionals, patrons, or communities (Curley, 1974; Raber, 2007; Raymond, 1979).

Following their involvement in World War I efforts, libraries pursued a similar path during World War II. They provided materials for military libraries, offered patriotic books on the home front, and limited access to materials sympathetic to the other side or by authors from enemy nations. By working to be active supporters of the war efforts, public libraries earned a great deal of political capital and recognition, giving rise to the phraseology of the "arsenals of democracy," which was originally expressed by President Franklin Roosevelt in acknowledgment of their wartime support. Yet libraries were not deemed central enough to the war effort to be granted extra funding for their activities (Halsey, 2003).

Over the next few decades, these federal roles were primarily expanded in terms of an interest by federal law enforcement and intelligence agencies in the reading habits of certain Americans. During the "Red Scare" of the 1940s and 1950s, the federal government encouraged libraries to limit access to—or to entirely remove from their collections— books that were seen as sympathetic to socialist and communist ideas (Doyle, 2001). These initial efforts were soon systematized as the LAP. The LAP and other actions undertaken to monitor reading materials and other information activities of many library patrons represent the main interest of the federal government in libraries during the early years of the Cold War, creating many tensions between libraries and government agencies. The ostensible purpose of the LAP was to enhance national security by thwarting attempts by foreign spies to collect unclassified information available in U.S. public libraries. Librarians, however, vehemently opposed this so-called counterintelligence effort by the FBI to coerce them into monitoring library usage, a practice that violated their "commitment to the principle that unrestricted access to and dissemination of ideas are fundamental to a democratic society" (U.S. House Committee on the Judiciary, 1998, p. 5). The potential for abuse was great—the LAP, having been created within the FBI's bureaucracy, operated within a gray area: "It was authorized by no federal law, nor did it represent any clear violation of federal law" (Foerstel, 2004, 35).

The library community, led by the ALA, played a critical role in calling national attention to the LAP, which ultimately led to congressional hearings to investigate the legality of this program. In the aftermath of their experience with the LAP, the ability—and willingness—of libraries to speak out (both for and against) federal policies that impact them began to take center stage, as the focus shifted from the funding of libraries to more concerted government intervention in their policies and practices. However, a project of libraries during this same time opened up the possibilities of greater federal government support of public libraries.

After World War II, there were concerns about participation in elections. To help increase voter turnout in the 1952 presidential election, public libraries across the country sponsored voter registration, education, and participation drives and created large displays of political materials from both parties and objective analyses of candidates, issues, and positions written by commentators and scholars. These efforts helped to measurably increase voter turnout and establish the modern concept of the public library as a reliable "community source for serious, nonpartisan information on a central issue of the day" (Preer, 2008, p. 19). This experience was not a comfortable one for library leadership, as many felt it represented too much engagement in the political process; their support of the democratic process through information and education, however, helped encourage federal interest in financial support of public libraries. It could be accurately observed in 1974 that "there has not been a clearly or consistently articulated federal policy" toward libraries (Wellisch et al., 1974, p. 203), and the same holds true today. However, the 1950s marked the initial discovery of libraries by federal policy makers, allowing libraries to make their first meaningful appearances in the national political process.

In 1956, the federal government passed the Library Services Act (LSA), the first program of federal assistance for libraries, emphasizing library services in rural underserved and unserved areas, as well as the improvement of existing libraries in rural areas. This law was a controversial one, as many members of Congress felt that libraries should be a purely local matter (Raber, 1995). Proponents of this departure from the established history of local funding crafted arguments that played to the geopolitical tensions of the time, tying public libraries to the democratic ideal of an informed citizenry (U.S. Senate, 1956). Members of Congress were also swayed by testimony from the first director of ALA's Washington Office, Paul Howard, who explained that about one-third of the U.S. population at the time (35 million out of 132 million) lacked access to a public library (Fuller, 1994). The purpose of this initial injection of federal funding into libraries, however, was limited in scope, in terms of both the dollar amount ($7.5 million per year) and the duration (five years). The LSA was not intended to fundamentally alter the local nature of libraries, as evidenced by the express statement in Section 2(b) that this act was not to be "so construed so as to interfere with State and local initiative and responsibility in the conduct of public library services."

The LSA, which was subsequently extended, improved library services for more than 40 million people within the first seven years (Wellisch et al., 1974). Amendments to the LSA expanded the law's focus to include assistance for urban areas, construction, interlibrary cooperation, and certain target populations (e.g., institutionalized persons), culminating in the law being renamed to the LSCA in 1964 (Shavit, 1985). Reauthorization of the LSA, and later the LSCA, provided numerous opportunities to revisit the debate on federal funding of libraries. Both the Nixon and Carter administrations openly wanted to curtail federal funding for public libraries (Fuller, 1994). Opponents of federal funding made two somewhat contradictory arguments: (1) that the amount of money made available through the existing program was not significant enough to make a difference, and (2) that federal funding was no longer necessary because the primary goal of extending library service to all parts of the country had been largely achieved.

Proponents of continued federal funding pointed their fingers at local and state governments, asserting that these entities generally undervalued, and thus provided insufficient support for, libraries (Congressional Research Service, 1984). The ALA, in one of its first major engagements with national political processes, became a key player in this debate, actively lobbying for greater appropriations under both the LSA and the LSCA. When the Nixon administration tried to halt the release of LSCA funds, the ALA filed a lawsuit against the administration, leading to the release of $52 million in LSCA funds (Halsey, 2003). The ALA's lobbying for financial support annoyed the Nixon administration so much that they had the IRS audit ALA as an intimidation tactic (Shields, 1980).

Ultimately, proponents of federal funding for libraries prevailed and the LSCA was reauthorized on multiple occasions. Over time, it incorporated support for library services, library construction, interlibrary cooperation, literacy programs, foreign language materials, and library services for American Indians. The LSCA was, however, a measured success. The limited amount of funds actually made available under the LSCA in real dollar terms was far less than the Carnegie grants of fifty years before (Lee, 1966). In fact, in the first twenty-five years of federal contributions to library funding, the total support amounted to less than the cost of two aircraft carriers (Josey, 1980). Moreover, attempts to create a national library policy and a more consistent funding structure proved futile. The National Library Act, introduced in 1979, was intended to promote universal library service and minimum standards of service nationally, moving away from the notion of a public library as a purely local institution, in line with changes in perceptions of public schools. This piece of legislation, however, never made it out of the congressional committee stage (Shavit, 1986).

INTERVENTION AND THE CURRENT POLITICAL APPROACH TO LIBRARIES

Although the past quarter century has seen a significant increase in attention paid to libraries at the national level, this increase has not been accompanied by a meaningful increase in federal funding to libraries. Both the Reagan and George H. W. Bush administrations actively worked to have LSCA and all federal funding for libraries eliminated as part of a governing philosophy emphasizing smaller federal government and decreased support for public services (Fuller, 1994). While these efforts proved unsuccessful, they foretold the increasingly hostile political environment in which public libraries find themselves.

In the mid-1990s, the LSCA became the Library Services and Technology Act (LSTA) in order to emphasize the importance of libraries as access points for computers and the Internet. Funding for programs, however, was shifted to other entities or disappeared entirely; literacy program funding, for example, moved to the Department of Education (McCook & Barber, 2002). The E-rate program, authorized as part of the Telecommunications Act of 1996, provides financial support to some libraries for Internet connections and wiring. The National Commission for Library and Information Statistics (NCLIS) was created to provide national data on libraries and to provide policy guidance regarding libraries, but it was subsequently closed. NCLIS also brought attention to key issues related to libraries and public policy, becoming involved in issues such as access to government information, literacy, services to older adults, and the creation of the Federal-State Cooperative System for Public Library Data (Wall, 1990).

When it was discovered that the entire budget of NCLIS was going to personnel costs, NCLIS was soon closed down and library program management was transferred from the Department of Education to IMLS. Though a small federal agency, IMLS offers policy guidance regarding libraries, manages the LSTA funding, is in charge of collecting and reporting national public library data, and funds library research and innovative education programs. Yet, in spite of these programs, federal contributions to public libraries are still well below 1 percent of total library funding and have not succeeded in ensuring equal availability and quality of library services around the country (Jaeger, Bertot, et al., 2007; Jaeger, McClure, & Bertot, 2005).

The scarcity of federal funding, however, should not be construed as a return to the first historical phase, referred to here as the "local years." On the contrary, in recent years, policy making and political processes at the federal level have ushered in an unprecedented level of intervention in libraries at the national level. Some of these policy decisions have been aimed directly at libraries, while others have impacted libraries collaterally. Looked at collectively, the impacts of these decisions are significant. After hundreds of years of primarily being left alone by federal policy and politics outside of the contexts of war, this change is radical in both size and scope. Given the number of laws that now directly affect libraries, their services, and their patrons, the federal intervention in libraries which we are now witnessing may continue for the foreseeable future.

In many of these interventions, the library has been the direct target as a result of its ability to collect information on people's reading habits or to influence those reading habits. The post-9/11 period gave rise to laws like the USA PATRIOT Act and the Homeland Security Act, which enhanced government agencies' ability to collect a wide range of libraries' physical and electronic records and to observe patron behaviors in libraries, while also limiting the government information available through use of zealous classification standards and permitting information to be removed from library collections (Jaeger, Bertot, & McClure, 2003; Jaeger & Burnett, 2005; Jaeger, McClure, Bertot, & Snead, 2004). In voicing opposition to these laws, librarians once again cast themselves in the role of defender of their patrons' rights of privacy and freedom of expression. As with the LAP, librarians were forced to reevaluate how they handle patron information.

This time, however, librarians also found themselves at the center of lengthy legal proceedings as they challenged the constitutionality of Section 505 of the USA PATRIOT Act, which greatly expanded the FBI's authority to issue national security letters (Gorham-Oscilowski & Jaeger, 2008; Matz, 2008). Having thrust themselves into the middle of the post-9/11 debate about the appropriate balance between national security and individual liberty, librarians then had to grapple with the uncomfortable glare of the political spotlight as the attorney general of the United States even questioned their patriotism for objecting to the intrusive and extensive nature of these laws. Many librarians took this issue extremely seriously, with *American Libraries* even publishing an editorial titled "Who Wants to Be the First to Go to Jail?" (Kniffel, 2002). Many libraries developed strategies to inform patrons that their activities in the library might be monitored by the government.

During this same time period, Congress repeatedly sought to address the issue of pornographic and other indecent content online, and as in the national security realm, libraries became vocal advocates for their patrons' First Amendment rights. While the first two laws passed by Congress were thrown out by the courts, the third—CIPA—survived legal challenges by ALA that went all the way to the Supreme Court. CIPA requires the filtering of Internet access for all library computers in order to receive certain types of federal funding. These filtering mechanisms are highly imperfect, often blocking far more content than is covered by the law; the mechanisms in the law for requesting unfiltered access can be very slow and are entirely optional; and, most significantly, the requirements are far more broad than they need to be, covering all patrons and staff, regardless of their age (Gathegi, 2005; Jaeger, Bertot, & McClure, 2004; Jaeger & McClure, 2004; Jaeger & Yan, 2009; Jaeger, Bertot, McClure, & Langa, 2005).

The primary federal funds covered by CIPA, those available through the E-rate funding program, are relied on by many libraries to support library technology and Internet access, giving many libraries no choice but to comply with CIPA's requirements. Here, by virtue of their long recognized contributions to the development of an informed citizenry, libraries find themselves in a difficult position. Libraries do not create the online content that CIPA seeks to regulate, but they nevertheless have become a target in the federal government's effort to protect children from it, forcing them to juggle several different legitimate interests, namely, their need for federal funding, their commitment to providing unrestricted access to information, and their desire to limit children's exposure to potentially harmful content.

Other laws have impacted libraries in a less direct way. The DMCA and other recent copyright reforms created serious issues for libraries. Extensions of copyright protection to such incredible lengths—such as the life of the author plus eighty years—create many questions of ownership, and these extensions create significant tensions with the increase in access to information brought about by the Internet and electronic files. The exceptions carved out in an attempt to address these issues, such as the fair-use exemption and the exemptions for use in distance education, only serve to make the issues murkier, leaving many libraries uncertain of their legal positions (Butler, 2003; Travis, 2006). Digital copies of orphan works—older works where the copyright owner is untraceable— became virtually unusable, even by the libraries that own the items (Brito & Dooling, 2006; Carlson, 2005). Libraries struggled mightily with previously much clearer issues of interlibrary loan, electronic resources, and services to remote patrons, while universities had to determine how to try to provide resources to distance education students (Allner, 2004; Carrico & Smalldon, 2004; Ferullo, 2004; Gasaway, 2000).

Yet another type of intervention has occurred through the offloading of federal government responsibilities onto libraries. Some of this offloading has been more the result of incompetence than intent, such as the dramatically increased roles of libraries in emergency response and recovery during the 2004 and 2005 hurricane seasons (Bertot et al., 2006a, 2006b; Jaeger, Langa, et al., 2006). While the actions of public libraries in the devastated areas, as well as the areas to which the refugees had evacuated, earned them enormous respect among residents, politicians and federal government employees downplayed these roles because the success of libraries in helping communities made the federal response seem all the more incompetent (Jaeger & Fleischmann, 2007).

The more deliberate offloading of federal government responsibilities on public libraries—without any accompanying support—is best demonstrated through e-government. The E-government Act of 2002 encouraged government agencies to move as much information, services, and communication as possible online. Agencies soon realized that it was easier and cheaper to send patrons to public libraries for help understanding and using e-government than to do it themselves, leading them to offload the training and support for use of their online services to public libraries (Bertot et al., 2006b; Jaeger & Bertot, 2009, 2010). Given their public-access infrastructure, libraries are capable of serving as an instrumentality through which this particular federal information policy is carried out, and local, state, and federal governments quickly realized the opportunity to shift cost and effort onto public libraries. Public libraries and e-government delivery are so interconnected at this point that not only is e-government heavily shaping public library activities, but the way in which public libraries provide access has also impacted the format of e-government (Jaeger, Taylor, et al., 2012). This role, however, has emerged at a time when public libraries are faced with budgetary constraints and forced to provide more services with fewer resources.

A related area that has devolved to public libraries is the provision of access to government documents in a more traditional sense. As public law libraries have closed or become less open to the public and academic libraries have dropped out of the FDLP, public libraries in many regions are the only public-access points for physical government documents and other materials (Jaeger & Bertot, 2011). However, most public librarians are not trained to function as government document librarians, putting a further strain on their ability to effectively serve patrons.

The expectations related to government information, and e-government in particular, are part of a growing problem for public libraries in terms of perception. There is increasing pressure for public libraries to have available all types of information, based on the misconception that public libraries can be like Google (Waller, 2009). Public libraries have built a reputation on being able to provide trusted information sources and guidance using those sources, while Google, in presenting all information it can find without any sense of evaluation other than the number of hits a page receives, is the antithesis of the approach and skills of public libraries. Google may ultimately become the only backup that public libraries have in providing public access to government information, however, as there is no other organization or constituency to which to transfer public library information services. Public libraries are, in a sense, the last line of defense for e-government services and resources in communities, having picked up increased roles and responsibilities as government agencies, academic libraries, and law libraries reduced their public services.

Broadband policy, a priority of the current administration, is yet another area that has enabled the federal government to intervene in public libraries. Similar to e-government, libraries serve as an instrumentality through which broadband policy is carried out, as many have been able to obtain federal funding through BTOP to improve their public-access infrastructure. Here, however, the federal government views libraries as one of many instrumentalities that can help it further its broadband policy goals. For example, the FCC's 2010 Broadband Plan contains a seemingly enormous contradiction—while acknowledging the contributions of libraries, it also suggested defunding libraries to promote private-sector growth of broadband access. Yet in markets with low demand for Internet access and services, increases in demand are more likely to result from consumer outreach and digital literacy than from more infrastructure (Jayakar & Park, 2012). Service providers typically lack incentives to invest in outreach and literacy programs, as they fear greater usage of the Internet will reduce profits from other services, such as phone and cable television (LaRose, Strover, Gregg, & Straubhaar, 2011). Even when service providers do provide information literacy tools and outreach, such actions are often simply a means to bring in customers who will ultimately pay for more expensive services. Comcast, for example, offers $9.95 Internet services, dubbed Comcast Essentials, for qualified low-income customers who have children. However, service speeds are slow enough to make it almost necessary for patrons to purchase more expensive service options (Randall, 2013).

And in yet another derivation of federal government intervention in libraries, libraries are now much more commonly used as a blatantly political tool. They have become a symbol of public-sector spending in political debates, with proponents of austerity now emboldened to belittle support for public libraries to accomplish political goals, such as the reduction of public spending and the elimination of public-sector unions (Bertot, Jaeger, & Sarin, 2012). The main economic arguments for austerity were based on poor assumptions with data, incorrect math, and data errors in spreadsheets that resulted in wildly incorrect results—and such errors and invalid assumptions have been widely documented by economists—yet these demonstrably incorrect results continue to be used in many conservative arguments for cutting back on public goods to save money (Herndon, Ash, & Pollin, 2013).

In addition, there are ongoing policy developments, proposals, and regulations that can have substantial impacts on libraries as information access providers. The continued debate over network neutrality—the free flow of content over the Internet—can directly affect the provision of digital content to library patrons. The debates over digital content piracy culminated in SOPA. Though not passed into legislation, SOPA affected libraries through its focus on content providers on which libraries depend. And more broadly, efforts to reform Title 44 to account for the increasingly digital context of library service can have an impact on the GPO and the FDLP. In short, the policy and political environment is not static and continues to spawn legislation and regulation that can have significant consequences for libraries both as content creators and as content providers.

In a relatively short period of time, the means used by the federal government to intervene in public libraries has evolved from the post-9/11 focus on libraries as a direct target of federal information policies to the use of libraries as both an instrumentality and a tool, depending on the particular information policy or political goal at issue. In light of these shifts, it is difficult to make predictions with any certainty as to how the federal government will intervene in public libraries in coming years. However, given the extent to which the services provided by public libraries have become increasingly intertwined with various federal information policies, there is little doubt that intervention will continue in some form or another.

NEUTRALITY AND THE POLITICAL WORLD

The ways that public libraries are affected by the policy-making and political processes are also heavily shaped by a stance of their choosing. By taking the stance of a neutral profession—specifically the intentional distancing from the political and policy processes—the public library has made it more difficult for its own perspective to be articulated and heard in political and policy-making processes over the years. As federal policies make greater and greater intrusions into public library operations, this stance becomes increasingly detrimental to public libraries.

The goal of neutrality has been a point of contention in library discourse for many years. Neutrality manifests itself in two keys areas of librarianship: (1) trying to create collections that present as many different viewpoints as possible, and (2) trying to remain apolitical to the greatest extent possible. One of the staunchest defenders of library neutrality summarized the position as the responsibility of the library being to "select materials from all producers, from the whole world of published media, to build balanced collections representing all points of view on controversial issues, regardless of their personal convictions or beliefs" (Berninghausen, 1972, p. 3675). In contrast, criticisms of neutrality have been stated just as starkly: "The basic question for librarians to face is whether or not, individually or collectively, they wish to exert their influence in defense of freedom outside of the libraries where freedom is being assaulted. I hope we will not stand like chickens, waiting for our turn on the block" (Ellsworth, 1948, p. 58).

While both of these areas of neutrality are a source of controversy, the latter point is central to the discussion at hand. Some present an apolitical posture as an act of service to patrons, while others see the commitment to a plurality of opinions in library collections as mitigating against political engagement by the field (Byrne, 2003; McMenemy, 2007). "Neutrality is the wrong word—we aren't neutral, we just suppress our feelings as an act of discipline while at work and protest on our own time" (White, 1990, p. 73).

In practice, though, neutrality is at best a modernist ideal from a bygone age. In a time before the embrace of cultural diversity and postmodernist perspectives, the idea of a rational, unbiased actor in any profession would have seemed far more plausible than it is today. Critics of neutrality have noted, among other issues, that

- the work of libraries as community institutions means that they must adopt the normative standards of the community, meaning neutrality does not exist for libraries (Cornelius, 2004; Floridi, 2002);
- materials themselves are not neutral, so no collection of materials can ever be neutral (Alfino & Pierce, 2001; Budd, 2006; Burton, 2009);
- many libraries carry the names of private and corporate benefactors, undermining any image of neutrality (Graham, 2003);
- presenting all sides of an issue as having equal moral weight is engaging in moral relativism and misleading patrons (Good, 2006);
- decisions made in resources to acquire, programs to present, and services to offer are based on the class position and outlook of the librarians and their communities (Durrani & Smallwood, 2006);
- abundant information available through the Internet makes neutrality impossible if librarians are to also promote digital literacy (Graham, 2003; Jaeger, Bertot, Thompson, Katz, & DeCoster, 2012);
- those who challenge access to materials in libraries seek "to regulate and control what others read," which is an inherently political act (Knox, 2013, p. 200);
- public libraries are government entities, benefitting some groups more than others based on policy-making decisions (Shavit, 1986); and
- perhaps most significantly for the discussion at hand, public libraries are publicly funded institutions whose fate is determined by local, state, and national politics (Burton, 2009).

Even if neutrality is treated as an aspiration rather than an achievable goal, these difficulties with neutrality challenge the very notion of it as a driver of the profession.

The challenges presented by neutrality are reflected in the professional literature time and again as new social and political issues arise. At various points in the last quarter century, arguments have been made for abandoning neutrality to promote educational equality, challenge antiterrorism laws, combat privatization, and advocate for multiculturalism, among many other issues (e.g., Berry & Rawlinson, 1991; Blanke, 1989; Durrani & Smallwood, 2006; Jerrard, Bolt, & Strege, 2012; Kniffel, 2002; Stoffle & Tarin, 1994). One could certainly argue that the positions taken by librarians against the intrusions of the LAP, the USA PATRIOT Act, CIPA, and other laws already constitute a clear abandonment of neutrality on at least these issues.

The largest challenge to librarianship by neutrality, however, can be found in the way it limits the ability of libraries to advocate for themselves, their patrons, and their communities:

> By offering neutral responses in the increasingly partisan cultural atmosphere, the librarian denies him or herself the opportunity to definitely reverse the tide of negative educational trends which have seen the diminishment of the influence of the library in American society. . . . If the librarians cannot be motivated to take a stand on pressing social issues out of a sense of moral duty, certainly the librarians should break his or her neutrality in the name of self-interest. (Good, 2006, p. 28)

As there are fewer resources available for public services and more responsibilities being placed on public libraries, the failure to actively engage politically threatens the ability of the library to function and perform its vital educational functions.

Public libraries are not the only social institution that has tried to remove itself from politics. As public schools became standardized and professionalized, they originally pursued a strategy of being apolitical as well. However, the movement to change their stance began in the 1950s (Eliot, 1959). While the implications of this change for public schools have been both positive and negative, politicians, policy makers, and members of the public certainly are more aware of the implications of decisions on public schools than they are for libraries. And all of those populations have a much clearer sense of the roles of schools than they do of libraries in society.

By continuing to hew to this neutral stance, public libraries have boxed themselves in as far as the ability to advocate for their own needs. "It is often the case that the librarian's role as advocate is often undermined not merely by society but by librarians themselves" (McMenemy, 2007, p. 178). By simultaneously declaring themselves central to democracy and above the world of politics that all other public institutions inhabit, public libraries have "evolved into a paradox" (Shavit, 1986, p. 3).

Political and policy decisions shape what libraries can do, but libraries commonly say they want nothing to do with politics and policy.

Nevertheless, these proclamations of neutrality are not truly representative of the reality of the activities of the library profession. Across the Library Bill of Rights, the Code of Ethics, the ALA Policy Manual, and other ALA documents are many direct and indirect declarations of stances on political issues related to information—freedom of expression, privacy, censorship, inclusion, and literacy being prominent themes among them. Some of these documents stray well beyond information issues, however. The ALA Policy Manual (2012a) focuses mostly on information, but also includes pro-disarmament, pro-environmentalism, and pro–nuclear freeze provisions in the section titled "National Information Services and Responsibilities." These are clearly political stances, including some that have no rational relation to librarianship.

In spite of the profession's adoption of various political stances—information-related and beyond—it has yet to abandon its overall stance of neutrality. Ironically, in practice, libraries have never been neutral in their collections or programming, emphasizing mainstream information sources, privileging them over alternative sources, and shaping collections to both fit perceived community standards and the wishes of library boards, local governments, and professional organizations (Samek, 2001; Wiegand, 2011). Not only has the value of neutrality been problematic in terms of how it has been implemented and mobilized in public libraries since the 1960s and 1970s, but also it is perhaps impossible to ever achieve in reality (Scott, Richards, & Martin, 1990).

The result is a self-imposed voicelessness on many important issues with dramatic impacts on libraries. "Public librarians have, for the most part, kept quiet" (Kent, 1996, p. 212). Such quietness, and related assertions of neutrality, have not served libraries well in policy and politics thus far, and it will only become more problematic as the ideology of austerity more significantly dominates decisions about funding and policy. Trying to be quiet and apolitical when one exists in a starkly political world is not a good survival strategy.

The combination of a stance of neutrality and a limited amount of research demonstrating the contributions of libraries to democracy frequently places libraries in the position of having major political and policy decisions happen to them, with their voice basically unexpressed, unheard, or ignored (Jaeger & Bertot, 2011; Jaeger, Bertot, & Gorham, 2013). For example, the self-imposed voicelessness of libraries in the political process has made it much easier for governments to offload the significant e-government and emergency response duties discussed above to public libraries in the past few years (Jaeger & Bertot, 2011).

Perhaps the most telling example of the considerable downside of relying on apolitical positioning and assertions of value to democracy was the court case over CIPA. The intent of the law was very popular—to protect children from harmful materials online. Yet by requiring the placement of filters on all computers, rather than only those accessible to children, the law is clearly unnecessarily broad. The library community's decision to challenge the law on its face, as opposed to waiting for it to be implemented, was ill advised. By challenging the law on its face as an infringement of intellectual freedom, they relinquished the opportunity to make their case based upon either actual incidents in which people were unable to reach information due to the expansiveness of the law or actual incidents of problems with filters overblocking content to demonstrate its overreach. Instead, the Supreme Court was able to rule entirely in the abstract and produce an opinion that evidenced a lack of comprehension of both technology itself and of the operations of libraries (Gathegi, 2005; Jaeger, Bertot, & McClure, 2004; Jaeger & McClure, 2004). Had libraries been prepared to demonstrate value to democracy as engaged participants in political discourse and thereby been able to articulate a very different case to the courts, it is not hard to imagine that the end result of the legal challenge may have been different.

The disengagement with the political process not only has consequences for libraries; it also limits the attention paid to library-generated perspectives on and solutions to issues of policy that would benefit other groups. One legal scholar recently labeled libraries as possessing "compelling answers" to current major policy problems, such as privacy and intellectual freedom, but bemoaned the disinclination of libraries to engage these issues in the political arena (Richards, 2013, p. 689).

POLICY, POLITICS, AND IDEOLOGY

In spite of the federal government's limited funding of and more considerable interventions in public libraries, they remain a resolutely local institution, and most of the everyday political issues are local ones. The early efforts to control collections are different than those today, but library board members, local political leaders, and community members still challenge existing materials and try to shape acquisitions. Battles over budgets almost entirely occur at the state and local levels. However, the spiraling interventions of the federal government in libraries during the recent past represent a seismic shift in the relationship between politics, policies, and libraries.

Though various federal efforts now affect public libraries in profound ways, the public library still maintains the position adopted in the early twentieth century of being open to all through its active support of widespread public access to information (Foerstel, 1991, 2004; Jaeger & Burnett, 2005; Hartman, 2007). With the widespread opposition to the intrusions of the USA PATRIOT Act, the costly legal challenges to CIPA, and the willingness to provide e-government services and resources, as three prominent examples, a steadfast belief in democracy clearly drives public libraries at a deep level. Yet public libraries have difficulty expressing their actual roles in the democratic process.

The self-perception of a library "conditions the kinds of choices the library makes and the way it acts" (Beckerman, 1996, p. 11). Hopefully greater attention paid to the long view of the impact of politics and policies on public library history will give public libraries a clearer self-perception of their intended roles in democracy and how the political and policy environment has responded to and shaped their actions. "History is not an occasional or partial affair" (Shera, 1952, p. 251), and this disconnect between public libraries and the historical impacts on them by public policy and politics has devastating consequences. The ability of libraries to better articulate their role in democracy as part of the policy and political discussions that will shape the future of the library depends heavily on their ability to express how political and policy decisions impact them—and how they wish for these decisions to impact them. However, as the next chapter details, greater engagement in the political and policy-making processes is only the first step, as public libraries now face a situation in which they need to work against major ideological currents of politics and economics that have taken hold in the United States over the past several decades.

FOUR

Prevailing Governance and Economic Ideologies

In 2012, political commentator E. J. Dionne suggested that the current levels of elevated partisanship and political gridlock stem from the disjunction between two political visions of the essence of the United States: the strong-sense individual freedoms enumerated in the Constitution and communitarian beliefs necessary to support the social infrastructure that enables individual freedoms. Dionne argued that an overemphasis on individualism impairs the ability of the American system to function (2012). The luxury to lead a life of individualism, though, is entirely dependent on a strong state to protect individual rights and a community agreement to respect individual rights, while a stable society relies on a certain level of equality between individuals (Gutmann, 1995; Stiglitz, 2012; Wolin, 1993). Such tensions between individualism and communitarianism are far from new, though, as much of American politics since the election of President Nixon in 1968 have been focused on moving away from the support of public goods (Perlstein, 2008).

Historians often refer to the middle of the twentieth century as the "great consensus," as so much of the political activity and policy making of governments at all levels was focused on building communities, rights, and infrastructures. The period is typified by the political emphases of presidents in that time span, from the New Deal social support, civil rights, and building programs for social institutions of Franklin Roosevelt and Harry Truman, through the focus on physical infrastructure of Dwight Eisenhower, to the Great Society social investments and civil rights programs of John Kennedy and Lyndon Johnson. The unraveling of the great consensus during the later years of the Johnson administration ushered in a new political landscape centered much more strongly on the individual than the community.

While Nixon the candidate and Nixon the president deftly played to
the interests of the individual voter as a means to attain power and control, the political and economic ideologies to solidify the move away from
public goods were firmly entrenched by the administration of Nixon's
one-time protégé, Ronald Reagan (Perlstein, 2008). While the neoliberal
economic ideology and the neoconservative political ideology sound like
they would be diametrically opposed, they in fact have served as the
central defining characteristics of American governance for the better
part of fifty years, moving from defining federal governance down to
defining most state and local governance in the United States and significantly shaping the stances of the Republican and Democratic political
parties.

Public libraries, as the living definition of the public good, do not fare
well under these ideologies. Unfortunately, the terminology and advocacy of public libraries in this time have only served to make their position
worse. While the venerable statement that "new policies create a new
politics" (Schattschneider, 1935, p. 288) often holds true, it has not in the
case of public libraries. Public libraries have never played a major part in
policy making at the local, state, or federal levels—they are typically
affected by policy decisions made without their input—or input that
shapes the policy outcome. Even major successes of public libraries in
recent years—e-government, emergency response, digital literacy, technology access, and community partnerships, among others—have not
given them a greater role in the policy process. Regardless of libraries'
demonstrations of success and contributions, their lack of voice is predetermined in part by governance ideologies that are based on the belief
that public goods are always inferior to private efforts.

THE AMERICAN NIGHTMARE

One political scientist has labeled the governance that has resulted from
the confluence of the neoliberal economic ideology and the neoconservative political ideology as an "American nightmare" (Brown, 2006, p. 690).
If so, it is a nightmare widely embraced by most politicians, regardless of
where they stand on the political spectrum. It is not a uniquely American
nightmare, however, as both the liberal and conservative political parties
in the United Kingdom have embraced the same ideologies since the
election of Ronald Reagan's spiritual twin Margaret Thatcher as prime
minister. During her years as prime minister, Thatcher oversaw the evis-
ceration of public library funding in the United Kingdom, with her suc-
cessor John Major continuing her policies. Libraries in that nation have
yet to recover from those two decades, and the economic downturn has
worsened the situation (Helling, 2012).

The neoliberal economic ideology is an approach to the economy that extends beyond economic policy, mandating that decisions of governance be based on what is best for markets, as free markets are seen as being dependent on all decisions reinforcing their freedom. Under this approach, economic, political, and social decisions are driven by market concerns and organized by the language and rationality of markets. It is "consistently hostile to the public realm," seeking to replace public goods with "the rule of private interests, coordinated by the markets" (Clarke, 2004, pp. 30–31). As president, Reagan liked to frequently repeat the joke that the nine scariest words in the English language were "I'm from the government and I'm here to help." The erosion of the public good through economic decisions in the United States actually began after World War II, when the vast majority of infrastructure funds distributed by the federal government went to housing, education, and development in the newly created suburbs rather than urban areas. In this transition, many of the agencies of the public good found in urban areas—cafes, museums, bookstores, lecture halls, and parks—did not follow the population to the suburbs in large numbers (Cohen, 2003).

In 1987, after being elected prime minister for a third consecutive term, Thatcher stated, "There is no such thing as society," but instead "the great driving engine, the driving force of life," is individuals and groups wanting to make money (Thatcher, 1987). This statement was perhaps the clearest window into the thinking of adherents of neoliberalism. Without society, nothing can be the fault of society, alleviating government of the need to look after members of society who are in need of help. Without the need to support members of a society, institutions of the public good become utterly superfluous. Now there are at least three different major arguments that society does not exist, all emanating from the neoliberal economic ideology and being united by a central premise that rejects any central structure binding people together beyond economics (Dean, 2013).

Many major policy changes since Reagan's election can be understood as clear articulations of the neoliberal economic ideology. The deregulation of the private sector is based on strengthening the ability of corporations at the expense of individuals, based on the assumption that the market will find ways to protect individuals through options. The widespread use of school choice, charter schools, and school vouchers stems from the neoliberal belief that the market will provide better options than government, even if many of the new educational options are not particularly successful at providing an education. The past several decades have provided numerous other examples of this approach, with many previously common functions becoming ones of self-care couched in the language of consumerism. A famous example of this was President George W. Bush's ultimately unsuccessful proposal to change Social Security to individual retirement accounts, under which citizens would have been left to fend for themselves in the market.

The movement for all government functions to justify themselves in economic terms may be the essence of the neoliberal economic ideology, with many public goods being assessed as cost calculations. Al Gore spent much of his eight years as Bill Clinton's vice president spearheading efforts throughout government—known collectively as National Performance Review studies—to focus on efficiency, productivity, and profitability rather than good governance or the public good. A little-remembered part of the early development of e-government was that some government officials initially advocated for it as a revenue stream for government, making citizens pay for searches, transactions, and interactions with government that they would only be able to do online.

The notion that all government functions can and should have a clear economic value has led to dwindling investments in and support of education, physical infrastructure, benefits, workplace safety, environmental safety, and public libraries, among many other government functions. Many public institutions have thus been driven to act more like corporations, as can be seen in public schools being underwritten by corporate sponsorships and vending machine contracts (Buschman, 2012). It is intriguing to note that, prior to the widespread embrace of the neoliberal economic ideology by politicians, sociologists and historians had made clear that degrading the public sphere in favor of the private sphere serves to undermine the value of both the public and private spheres as elements to support a functional society (Sennett, 1974).

The neoconservative political ideology is based on the idea that the state should exercise power as moral authority rather than through representative governance. A neoconservative state is strong and willing to use that strength to accomplish policy goals that may be driven entirely by moral evaluations, such as "wars of choice." The moral basis of governance is embraced by elected officials. George W. Bush famously spoke of his decisions in terms of "political capital" that he had earned and could spend as he saw fit rather than in terms of trying to represent the interests and perspectives of the governed.

Many of these values are rooted in support of what is seen as the "traditional" family unit and "pro-family" perspectives that are part of the neoconservative narrative, resulting in promotion of certain gender roles and opposition to rights for certain disadvantaged populations through politics and policy (Burnham, 2010; Gaffney, 2013). Neoconservatism is designed to appeal to the upper and middle classes, creating a narrative that they, as the wealthy, hegemonic majority, are besieged by minority groups and the disadvantaged who are trying to change their way of life. The neoconservative political ideology has succeeded in getting much of the middle and upper class to believe that it needs protection from the government, rather than focusing on the reality of receiving the considerable benefits of the government that accrue to advantaged populations (Burnham, 2010).

Neoconservatism also belittles educational institutions, like schools and libraries, as serving to erode the values of the supposed majority. The field of education was far more attuned to the ways in which neoconservatives were framing education than the field of librarianship, with assessments of the impact of neoconservatives already appearing in education discourse before Reagan was elected (Park, 1980). Libraries certainly did everything they possibly could to reinforce the narrative in the minds of neoconservatives—and much of the general public—that they were actively threatening community values based on the way ALA's challenges to CIPA played out in the courts.

As state steerage of the economy is central to the neoconservative approach, its economic dimensions have simply become the same as the neoliberal economic ideology. Under the combination of these two ideologies, economic discourse now "prescribes the form that 'problems' have to be given before they can be acted upon, the kinds of 'choices' that exist, and the meaning of 'rationality'" and frames the discussion and choices in "virtually every sphere of public activity, from health care, social welfare, and education to weapons systems, environmental protection, and scientific research" (Wolin, 1981, pp. 26–28). This approach to policy encourages divisions and promotes inequalities in availability and funding of public services (Wolin, 1993).

Curiously, as the neoliberal economic ideology has greatly decreased regulation of the corporation, the moralistic aspect of the neoconservative political ideology has increased the regulation of the citizen. Limitations on previously established rights, such as limiting women's access to the services of reproductive choice as a way to curtail the ability to seek an abortion, amount to moralistic regulations on citizens. When failed Republican presidential nominee Mitt Romney stated that "corporations are people too" in a 2012 campaign speech, it was no mistake, though under the combinations of these two ideologies, corporations are likely able to act more freely than citizens.

Corporations are also much more likely than individuals to garner political support and funding for the infrastructure on which they depend. Big business lobbies for the infrastructure that supports business activities—roads, railways, shipping, and power and other utilities—and the government always meets these corporate infrastructure needs. "What is missing is investment in such things as public libraries, parks, city streets and sidewalks, urban mass transit" (Galbraith, 1998, p. 207). This disjunction was evidenced in the spring of 2013 when Congress passed legislation to stave off cuts from the Federal Aviation Administration (FAA) budget that would have led to delays in airplane flights as a result of mandatory furloughs for air traffic controllers. Complaints from business made this cost-saving measure disappear immediately, while the many larger cuts to public services that do not impact businesses remain in place, such as major reductions to Head Start preschool programs, Meals on Wheels programs for older adults, and health care for the poor.

Since the combination of these ideologies swept into common usage under the Reagan and Thatcher administrations in the United States and the United Kingdom, the result has been radical change through reductions in tax rates, spending cuts for public services, deregulation, and erosions of social support for the public good. In a public discourse in which every public good can be questioned and required to demonstrate a tangible value, economic terminology began to dominate. Yet, as with librarians and library collections, economics and economic analysts are not neutral. By treating political and moral questions as being interchangeable with economic ones, these ideologies have allowed for political discourse and policy-making processes to question anything to which it is hard to assign a tangible value or that does not comply with a strict moral vision of the government. Being a public good is no longer sufficient. "The whole idea of human rights has lost some of its romantic appeal and moral authority" (Moyn, 2012, n.p.).

The omnipresence of these ideologies at the federal level has resulted in their widespread adoption in lower levels of government as well. At all levels of society, political problems have been transformed into individual problems with market solutions (Brown, 2006). Unfortunately, the market and the government provide services in very different ways. Public goods can deliver many kinds of contributions, supporting democratic equality, social efficiency, and social mobility (Labaree, 1997). In supporting the public good, governments can provide services, distributions, and stabilization of the market, none of which the market itself can provide as effectively, or at all in many cases, as it focuses on monetizing discrete services to individuals provided by different companies (Ver Eecke, 1998, 1999). Further, many elements of the public good are not easy to monetize, so decreasing government support to them will not easily be replaced by support from the market. Public libraries, while they contribute enormously to their communities, are not likely to turn a profit for a company. As a result, they are coming to stand as "a symbol of the impoverishment of the public domain" (Newman, 2007, p. 905).

In the recent years of the prolonged global economic downturn, the emphasis on the value of public services has been extended under the new buzzword of *austerity*. While clearly an intentionally ambiguous term, austerity provides a means to justify deeper cuts into public goods and services that cannot articulate an economically quantified value and/or that are deemed morally objectionable under the neoconservative ideology. As the language of value is based on economic contributions rather than public good, the terms of austerity are clearly biased against educational and cultural institutions like public libraries.

FEAR AND LOATHING IN THE PUBLIC LIBRARY

The public library is an important social institution that provides much-needed resources—education and training, job search resources, and Internet access for applying for jobs and social services, among many other services—for patrons and communities (Sigler et al., 2011; Taylor et al., in press). In library literature, public libraries are seen as providing value to their patrons and communities through services and resources related to information, education, literacy, economic regeneration, culture, diversity, and recreation in a public space that is welcoming of all community members (Bourke, 2005; Debono, 2002; Given & Leckie, 2003; Hafner, 1987; Hillenbrand, 2005; Kerslake & Kinnell, 1998; Leckie & Hopkins, 2002; Webster, 1995; Williamson, 2000).

The sheer number and presence of libraries suggests that they may have greater cultural value than community members, policy makers, or librarians themselves realize (Buschman, 2007a, 2007b). However, the "value of a good library—like good teaching—is extraordinarily difficult to quantify" (Buschman, 2005, p. 1). The bounty of information provided by the Internet has made demonstrating library value even more complex, as many commentators see libraries as needing to be more like or to be replaced by Google (Waller, 2009). Others have argued that the library is diminishing its own value through the focus on Internet-based services and reducing the emphasis on more traditional information provision activities (Brophy, 2007; Brown & Duguid, 2002; Buschman, 2003; Tisdale, 1997). Most of the contributions made by public libraries to patrons and communities are very hard to put in economic terms, and attempts to do so are hampered by the fundamental incompatibility of this approach with the premise, activities, and goals of libraries.

While some attempts have been made to express public library value in the terminology of business or purely economic terms, such efforts are limited by the actual activities and goals of libraries, which are not inherently business functions. The field of education, on the other hand, has worked to change the parameters of value applied to it—from purely economic terms to their own metrics of teacher evaluations, standardized testing, and a focus on components and types of education—through advocating in the public discourse for how education should be measured and valued. By being engaged directly in political and policy-making processes, the field of education has been able to establish the narrative of how they will be judged in terms of productivity, efficiency, and economic metrics. While policy makers and educators are still debating what forms of assessment are the best measures of progress and learning outcomes, the fact remains that these forms of tangible assessments exist and the debate continues. This lesson is an important one for all other cultural institutions.

No matter how the public library tries to demonstrate its myriad contributions, however, a political climate dominated by the neoliberal economic ideology and the neoconservative political ideology may prevent it from successfully arguing for its continued relevance. Neoliberalism targets professional groups, as their specific knowledge bases threaten the assumption that markets know more than other social actors (Clarke, 2004). This has led to conflicts with many unions, particularly those of government workers and teachers, due to their specialized knowledge bases that cannot be easily replicated by the market. While librarians are a much smaller population than either of those groups, it is a workforce that is particularly associated with knowledge due to the nature of library work. Simply put, the neoliberal economic ideology wants libraries to fail. Not surprisingly, President Reagan believed that information was central to the future of the country and decided to support businesses working in the information sector to facilitate economic success with information while actively trying to suppress library funding and their focus on information as an educational tool (Harris & Carrigan, 1990).

The job losses of the Great Recession clearly reflect the negative attitudes toward public-sector jobs and unions that have been most clearly impacted by the Great Recession. Based on recent Bureau of Labor Statistics (BLS) data, 680,000 public-sector jobs in the United States were lost between June 2009 and August 2012, or roughly 3 percent of the local, state, and federal government jobs that existed before the prolonged economic downturn began. In previous recessions, public-sector employment has traditionally increased (Hatch, 2004). According to the Center on Budget and Policy Priorities, state budget shortfalls have ranged from $107 billion to $191 billion between 2009 and 2012, and current projections place state budget shortfalls at $55 billion for 2013 (http://www.cbpp.org/cms/index.cfm?fa=view&id=711). Some states—Florida, Nevada, and Arizona, for example—have fared much worse. This current situation stands in stark contrast to other recessions of the past several decades, during and after which the number of public-sector jobs actually increased. Certain public-sector areas have been hit particularly hard in this prolonged economic downturn, with 20 percent of the public health workforce losing their jobs since 2009 (Kliff, 2012).

State and public libraries have not been untouched in these cuts. According to the 2012 Public Library Funding and Technology Access Study, public library funding has stagnated or declined since 2009, resulting in a reduction of operating hours and staff at some libraries. In addition, 40 percent of states reported reduced state aid funding for public libraries over the last three years. In the most recent annual library budget survey conducted by *Library Journal*, overall state funding fell 8.3 percent, with 44 percent of respondents observing a decrease in state funding (Schwartz, 2013). In at least one state (Texas), state aid was completely cut, which if not reinstated in the next legislative session will result in a loss of federal LSTA funds. Overall, budgets for public libraries, public schools, public health services, and other state and local government agencies devoted to the public good have been cut substantially since the recession began, greatly limiting their ability to serve their communities in many cases. In fact, hundreds of thousands of government jobs have disappeared across the country during the prolonged economic downturn and are not coming back.

The public library is also an affront to the neoconservative political ideology in many of its positions. The public library is associated with a diversity of viewpoints and intellectual openness, both of which run contrary to the neoconservative narrative of "traditional" values and social structures. In the United Kingdom in the 1980s, public libraries were bizarrely attacked in the political discourse by some conservatives for the crime of "daring to order books in the name of the public" (Webster, 2005, p. 283). Many challenges to materials are rooted in neoconservative values conflicting with public library values, such as the incessant challenges to *And Tango Makes Three*—a 2005 children's book in which a couple made of up of two male penguins adopts a penguin chick—for threatening the "traditional" family unit. The public library is also an institution that serves all classes in society, and it is particularly supportive of the needs of the marginalized and minority populations that neoconservatism portrays as threatening the values of the middle class (Jaeger, Subramaniam, Jones, & Bertot, 2011).

This neoconservative ideology also has manifested in organized national efforts to control access to materials in public libraries, most notably Family Friendly Libraries (FFL). Created in 1992, FFL is a "profamily" conservative organization to try to limit access to lesbian, gay, bisexual, transgender, and questioning (LGBTQ) materials and other materials the group perceived as a threat to "traditional families"—a mother and father raising children together in a Christian household—in public libraries (Gaffney, 2013). Most pro-family organizations are conservative Christian organizations opposed to LGBTQ rights, reproductive rights, public education, and/or science education (Diamond, 1998; Kintz, 1997; Wilcox, 2011). "Pro-family activists target public institutions themselves as the problem, believing that schools and libraries abuse their professional trust by attacking religion, promoting 'liberal causes' such as gay rights, and ultimately denying conservative parents their right to inculcate their religious and political beliefs in their offspring" (Gaffney, 2013, p. 188).

Attacking the ALA as being antichild and anticommunity, FFL argued that commitments to diversity and access had no place in public libraries. While their focus was initially on books, the FFL turned all of its attention to online materials in the late-1990s, leading the movement to pressure Congress into passing CIPA and also campaigning for the wildly overreaching Deleting Online Predators Act (DOPA) that never even left committee. The group has been less active in the years since but continues to argue for enforcement of CIPA standards in public and school libraries (Gaffney, 2013). These various types of attacks on public libraries in policy and politics are intrinsically tied to larger debates about culture and society. "When the cultural discourse is contested, the institutions charged with the transmission of culture become arenas in the contest" (Robbins, 2000, p. 161).

On the other side, arguments in favor of support for public libraries in national policy and politics have typically relied heavily on basic liberal ideology, offering aspirational assertions of the importance of public libraries as a social equalizer and the moral imperatives of education for all (Harris & Carrigan, 1990; Molz, 1976). Not only do these types of arguments in favor of libraries have no chance of success in the current political climate; they serve to further antagonize the sensibilities of the neoconservatives that dominate current political discourse.

The strong political and policy currents flowing against public libraries in the United States and the United Kingdom are hardly universal. Many nations, particularly in northern Europe, have expanded the official roles of public libraries in recent years and have increased support for them to parallel these new responsibilities. Nations like Sweden, Denmark, and Finland have used the growth of the Internet and the increasing number of government services available online as an opportunity to bolster the centrality of the public library as a social institution by expanding funding, resources, services, and access to government agencies in public libraries (Helling, 2012). It is worth noting that such support has been accomplished in nations with very different policy-making structures—Denmark has a more centralized government and library policies are addressed in politics, while Sweden has a more decentralized government and library policies are addressed at local levels (Landoy & Zetterlund, 2013).

A 2012 article in *Forbes* magazine declared that a master's degree in LIS is the worst type of master's degree based on career earning potential (Smith, 2012). Despite the designation by *Forbes*, librarians are not poorly paid. Within the realm of public-sector occupations, the BLS gives a higher median annual wage for librarians than for social workers, dispatchers, firefighters, kindergarten teachers, elementary school teachers, middle school teachers, secondary school teachers, school counselors, and special educators, among others. While librarians are paid less on average than police officers, nurses, and college faculty, librarianship involves less danger than the first two and requires less education than the third. Put in the public-sector perspective, librarianship is not a poorly paying career choice, especially for people who want to serve the public good.

E-mail lists, as well as blogs and other social media, reacted to the *Forbes* piece, with many librarians responding with an emphasis on noneconomic reasons to earn an MLS—the desire to have a job focused on public service, the fact that they did not get an MLS to become wealthy, and the widely acknowledged high levels of career satisfaction among librarians. These same themes were central to the official response posted by the ALA on its website and the editorial written by former ALA president Maureen Sullivan in the *Washington Post* in July 2012 (Sullivan, 2012). However, it is a critical mistake to see the *Forbes* piece as anything but political in nature (Bertot, Jaeger, & Sarin, 2012).

Steve Forbes, who has guided *Forbes* magazine as editor in chief and its parent corporation as president and CEO, is one of the popularizers of the ideologies of neoliberal economics and neoconservative governance. Through his magazine, Forbes has influenced the thinking of the moneyed classes about public services and the public good. The magazine has made numerous direct assaults on the value of various public goods over the decades. For example, a 1997 *Forbes* article attacked the idea of providing a public education for children with disabilities as "a costly failure," "an unmonitored mess," and "a scandalous waste of money," ultimately arguing that most children with disabilities did not deserve to be educated (Gubernick & Conlin, 1997, p. 66). Seeing these types of assertions in print in a magazine like *Forbes* can have an enormous reinforcing effect on readers who are already skeptical of the importance of public goods. Neoconservative media measurably increases the likelihood of voting and measurably shapes the positions taken by voters (DellaVigna & Kaplan, 2007). As most readers of *Forbes* likely already favor neoliberal economic and neoconservative governance ideologies, these types of articles strengthen their existing beliefs, making it more difficult for information representing other perspectives to have an impact (Hoff & Stiglitz, 2010; Rabin & Schrag, 1999).

Steve Forbes ran for the Republican presidential nomination in 1996 and 2000 on a platform that was definitional of neoliberal economics and neoconservative governance. Though his campaigns failed, elements of his platform have been inspirational to the George W. Bush administration, the Tea Party, and the austerity movement through slashing public services to yield substantial reductions in tax rates. In the 1996 campaign, Forbes advocated for a greatly reduced flat tax system of 17 percent on earned income above $36,000 and complete exemption of any investment or inheritance income. Such a plan would eviscerate the federal budget and public services. He also campaigned on allowing opt-outs of Social Security and other government social programs, while promising to eliminate virtually every federal agency related to social, cultural, environmental, and educational concerns. By his next campaign, Forbes had even expressed support for the repeal of the Sixteenth Amendment, which allows the federal government to collect taxes. Across the views expressed in his campaigns and other political activities, Forbes demonstrated the neoliberal/neoconservative belief that cultural, educational, and social service agencies are unnecessary, and even unwise, tax expenditures.

It is important to note that the 2012 *Forbes* article only rated thirty master's degrees. With many politicians treating public libraries as easy targets for cost-saving initiatives—through cutbacks in funds and hours of service, privatization, suggestions of all-volunteer staffing, and other means—it would hardly be surprising if the MLS was predestined to be named the worst master's degree by that publication. Also curious is the fact that the source of their data on average incomes by degree came from a private, nontransparent vendor. The fact that the vendor data cited in the *Forbes* piece indicates a higher average salary ($57,600) than that listed by the BLS (2012) (listed as $54,500) is especially curious. It is not unreasonable to question the validity of the data used, as other publicly available data seem to contradict, at least in part, some of the article's conclusion. What is not in question, however, is the political agenda driving the conclusion of the *Forbes* piece.

LIBRARY SERVICES IN THE AGE OF AUSTERITY

In a different political climate, perhaps the same employment data could be interpreted not as showing that the MLS is the worst master's degree, but that libraries are heavily undervalued and librarians are underpaid for all that they do for society. The current political realities, unfortunately, make such a scenario pure fantasy. For libraries, the limitations on serving their communities due to budget cuts and other austerity measures are a particularly acute problem, even among agencies of the public good. While it is deeply unlikely that the neoliberal economics and neoconservative governance movement would ever be able to reach a crescendo in which the nearly 17,000 public libraries in the United States were all shut down or privatized, the thousand paper cuts of austerity unquestionably will undermine the myriad ways that public libraries have developed to support their communities.

The contemporary public library is a mix of community center and community service center, with librarians simultaneously acting as information experts, educators, and social workers to serve the unique needs of their community. In fulfilling these roles, public libraries are generally the champions of "interest groups of less influence," which has dramatic consequences in the political process (Landoy & Zetterlund, 2013, p. 106). The wealthier members of society do not frequently need these types of resources and therefore can easily be unaware of the importance of the library in the lives of so many Americans—especially as the U.S. population continues to become more demographically and culturally diverse. With only the image of the library of their childhood from thirty or forty or fifty years ago, the advantaged view the library as completely dispensable with Google always at hand. Unfortunately, these individuals are also the people working as politicians and policy makers and the ones contributing the majority of money to political campaigns that support neoliberal economics and neoconservative governance. The view of the library as an antiquated institution that people only use by choice, rather than out of necessity, has even led to assertions by some in positions of power that libraries should be funded exclusively through private donations, just like museums (Holt & Holt, 2010).

As a result, all of the existing and innovative services that public libraries are providing to their communities to help them through the long-term economic crisis have resulted in the untenable pairing of dramatically rising usage and precipitously declining funding. Public libraries have long experienced that economic downturns lead to increased usage of the library and its services, with references to this relationship dating back to as early as 1880 in library discourse (James, 1985). This relationship is now known as the Librarian's Axiom and has been demonstrated to be true through numerous studies and, more importantly, many years of library operation during times of economic crisis (Davis, 2009, 2011; James, 1986; Lynch, 2002). During the Great Depression, library services and materials were "eagerly sought" and "contributed something to the lessening of social ills during a difficult period" (Herdman, 1943, p. 334). The demand for library books and for reference services skyrocketed; between 1930 and 1932, circulation at libraries around the country jumped by 25 to 30 percent annually, though those averages were down to 14 percent by 1935 as libraries had fewer intact materials left for patrons to borrow (Waples, Carnovsky, & Randall, 1932; Herdman, 1943).

The increased demand coupled with budget decreases left many libraries with decimated collections by the end of the Depression (Kramp, 1975). The needs of patrons during this time also led to expansions of services for unemployed adults and of children's services, creating "a broader concept of community service" that continues to this day (Ennis & Fryden, 1960, p. 253). Yet a lack of funds drove libraries to stop buying materials and hiring new employees—a whole generation of library school graduates had to take jobs without pay simply to be able to work in their chosen fields (Shera, 1933). Subsequent recessions have increased demand for library services, though even in the best of economic times, libraries are a vital resource for individuals in economic distress (Berman, 1998; Nyquist, 1968).

This current Great Recession has been no exception. Libraries in communities with long-term economic difficulties typically have more limited resources for patrons (Constantino, 2005). Yet, between 2006 and 2008, the number of Americans with library cards increased by 5 percent, in-person library visits increased by 10 percent, and library website visits increased by 17 percent (Davis, 2009, 2011). "These increases in use translate into 25 million more in-person visits, 11 million more uses via computer, and about 4 million more uses by telephone" (Davis, 2009, p. 13). On average, circulation in libraries rose 5.6 percent between 2007 and 2008 alone (Hoffert, 2009). In 2009, more than 14 million people were considered regular patrons of library computers for Internet access (C. Hill, 2009a).

These increases in usage are not uniform across socioeconomic strata. As compared to higher-income households, those making less than $50,000 a year, and especially those making less than $30,000 a year, are far more likely to use the library and consider it important to their families (Zickuhr, Rainie, & Purcell, 2013). In 2012, 30 percent of American households lacked home Internet access, and, unsurprisingly, public libraries are the primary option for Internet access among those who do not otherwise have access (NTIA, 2013). In individual libraries, the impacts can be overwhelming, with some systems seeing a 25 percent increase in visits in one year or a 500 percent increase in computer usage in a recent three-year period (N. M. Hill, 2009).

In a typical public library, this has translated to an increased usage of books, audiobooks, and DVDs for entertainment, as well as the Internet, with patrons primarily searching for employment, unemployment benefits, and social services (Holland & Verploeg, 2009; Martell, 2009). In 2012, 73 percent of unemployed and 52 percent of underemployed Internet users went online to look for work (NTIA, 2013). Such increases should not be surprising as jobs are scarce and, according to a 2009 survey, 63 percent of people have reduced their entertainment spending during the Great Recession (Gibbs, 2009).

In addition, parents working longer hours and having fewer funds for after-school activities equates to more children, tweens, and teens coming to the library for entertainment and a safe haven (Farrelly, 2009). People also see libraries as a place where patrons can get information from librarians on using the Internet to help save money (Porter & King, 2009). Past president of the ALA Maureen Sullivan recently stated that "while libraries have long been refuges for the down and out, anecdotal reports underscore that [libraries] are dealing with more people than ever before with mental health issues and basic needs such as food and shelter" (Nieves, 2010, n.p.).

The need for use of technology to access social services is particularly acute. In the United States, millions of people were relying on government-provided social services to meet basic needs even as the long-term economic downturn took hold: Medicaid (57.8 million people in 2006); food stamps (over 33 million in 2009); the Women, Infants, and Children (WIC) program (9 million in 2009); Social Security (over 7 million in 2009); and many others (U.S. Centers for Medicare and Medicaid Services, n.d.; U.S. Office of Retirement and Disability Policy, n.d.; U.S. Supplemental Nutrition Assistance Program, n.d.; U.S. Women, Infants, and

Children Program, n.d.). In addition to these federal services, each state provides a range of local services that cover health, family, employment, and other social services.

With one in six Americans living in a household where there is difficulty feeding the members of that household and nearly half of older adults facing poverty, many Americans who have never previously applied for social services now find themselves seeking government support (Chen, 2010; Reuters, 2010). However, most of these support services must now be applied for online (Bertot & Jaeger, 2012; Jaeger & Bertot, 2011). Because public libraries are so well positioned to offer e-government services, use of public library computers for this purpose is high, especially among patrons who have no other access to the Internet outside of the library (Becker et al., 2010). Thus, the economic downturn, by both exacerbating the digital divide and increasing the volume of applications for social services, is strongly driving public library usage (Bertot & Jaeger, 2012; Gehner, 2010; Holt & Holt, 2010; Kinney, 2010).

In short, despite the strong political and policy headwinds that they face, public libraries are vital centers of information, education, social services, resources, and technology access that have only grown more important since the prolonged economic downturn began. While chapter 6 will turn in detail to strategies to articulate the value of all of these contributions to politicians, policy makers, and members of the public who do not regularly use libraries, the next chapter focuses more deeply on the evolutions of public library offerings and usage since the advent of the Web. In these past two decades, the innovative education, services, resources, partnerships, and technology access that public libraries are able to provide to their communities have made them even more important to their communities than they have been in the past. In striking contrast to the narratives of neoliberal economics and neoconservative governance, public libraries are increasingly central to the lives of patrons without access to or the ability to use the Internet-enabled technologies necessary to participate in contemporary education, employment, and government.

FIVE

Changes in Public Libraries and Changes in Communities

Following the advent of the Internet in the 1990s, public libraries quickly became the leading provider of free public Internet access in communities across the country. By 2002, almost every public library was offering public access (Bertot, McDermott, Lincoln, Real & Peterson, 2012). Ten years later, the importance of this role has not diminished; according to the most recent Public Library Funding and Technology Access survey data, 62.1 percent of responding libraries indicated that they were the sole provider of Internet access in their communities (Bertot, McDermott, Lincoln, Real & Peterson, 2012). Through the provision of this vital service, libraries are therefore acting as a bridge over the often discussed "digital divide," defined as "the gap—whether based in socio-economic status, education, geography, age, ability, language, or other factors— between Americans for whom Internet access is readily available and those for whom it is not" (Jaeger, Bertot, Thompson, Katz, & DeCoster, 2012, p. 3).

The concept of access, however, is not as simple as it may appear, as it involves the provision of both hardware and Internet connectivity (physical access); a user's ability to effectively navigate the online environment (intellectual access); and the user's ability to make sense of the technology and the information it provides within their existing frames of reference (social access) (Burnett, Jaeger, & Thompson, 2008). Physical access is a basic and familiar concept—the ability to reach something, in this case technology and information. Physical access to information is generally viewed as access to the document or other form embodying information, be it conveyed through print, electronic, verbal, or another means of communication—literally the process of getting to the information that is being sought (Svenonius, 2000). The vast majority of discourse on information access tends to focus on physical issues, such as the physical structures that contain information, the electronic structures that contain information, and the paths that are traveled to get to information (Jaeger & Bowman, 2005). While it is a necessary prerequisite, mere physical access is not sufficient for full access. "It is a common, but mistaken, assumption that access to technology equals access to information" (McCreadie & Rice, 1999, p. 51). The ability of a user to get to information and the ability of that user to employ information to accomplish particular goals are very different (Culnan, 1983, 1984, 1985).

The next level of access is intellectual access—the ability to understand the information. Intellectual access can be understood as the accessing of the information itself after physical access has been obtained (Svenonius, 2000). Intellectual access to information "entails equal opportunity to understand intellectual content and pathways to that content" (Jaeger & Bowman, 2005, p. 68). Issues of intellectual access involve understanding how the information is presented to people seeking it, as well as the impact of such presentation on the process of information seeking; intellectual access to information includes the means through which the information is categorized, organized, displayed, and represented.

Social access is the most advanced level of access—the ability to communicate and use the information in social contexts (Burnett, Jaeger, & Thompson, 2008). Such social contexts can range from personal communication for entertainment purposes to educational and work settings to democratic participation. Gaining and understanding information without the ability to communicate that information inhibits social engagement through the information. People also have a stronger sense of community and belonging in situations in which they can exchange information in social contexts (Johnson, 2010; Williamson & Roberts, 2010). Social access is now heavily dependent on information technologies for communication in many contexts. The social access depends both on an individual user's attitudes toward information technologies and on the ability of the user to employ information technologies to engage in social interactions.

Libraries risk compromising their ability to bridge the digital divide and to promote digital inclusion if they fail to pay adequate attention to any of these facets of access. Even the one that is arguably the easiest to keep abreast of—the provision of physical access—creates challenges for libraries as they struggle to meet the demands posed by the increasing number of patrons coming to the public library to obtain this access. A significant percentage of public libraries are seeing increased usage of both public Internet workstations (60.2 percent) and wireless Internet access (74.1 percent) (Bertot, McDermott, Lincoln, Real, & Peterson, 2012). Libraries are responding to this growing need by augmenting both the number of public terminals they offer and their connectivity speeds. Fig-

ure 5.1 shows the growth in the average number of public-access terminals over the past fifteen years. After a number of years of modest increases in this area, the average number of public-access terminals increased from 14.2 to 16.4 public-access computers over the last two survey cycles. Moreover, an increasing percentage of public libraries are
reporting connectivity speeds greater than 1.5 Mbps (69.7 percent, up
from 60.3 percent in 2010–2011 and 51.8 percent in 2009–2010), and in
some cases greater than 10 Mbps (31.2 percent, up from 24.9 percent in
2010–2011).

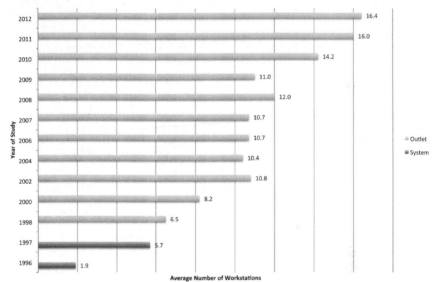

Figure 5.1. Average Number of Public-Access Workstations, 1998–2012
Source: Public Library Funding and Technology Access Surveys, 1998–2012
(http://ipac.umd.edu).

Notwithstanding these improvements, public libraries' existing resources are not always sufficient to keep up with the public's steadily
growing demand. Though libraries reported increases in public-access
computers and bandwidth, 41.4 percent of libraries (down from 44.9 percent in 2010–2011 and 45.1 percent in 2009–2010) reported that their connection speeds are insufficient some or all of the time, and 65.4 percent of
libraries (down from 76.2 percent in 2010–2011 and 73.5 percent in
2009–2010) reported that they had fewer public-access computers to meet
demand some or all of the time. Tables 5.1 and 5.2 demonstrate these
recent trends in the adequacy of Internet connections and public-access
terminals to meet patron needs.

Table 5.1.   Internet Connection Adequacy, 2010–2012 (percent)

	2010	2011	2012
Insufficient to meet patron needs	14.7	13.3	13.0
Sufficient to meet patron needs at some times	30.4	31.6	28.4
Sufficient to meet patron needs at all times	54.4	54.6	58.3

Source: Public Library Funding and Technology Access Surveys, 2010–2012 (http://ipac.umd.edu).

Table 5.2.   Public Workstation Adequacy, 2010–2012 (percent)

	2010	2011	2012
Insufficient to meet patron needs	18.2	17.1	13.4
Sufficient to meet patron needs at some times	55.3	59.1	52.1
Sufficient to meet patron needs at all times	26.5	23.8	34.6

Source: Public Library Funding and Technology Access Surveys, 2010–2012 (http://ipac.umd.edu).

Libraries reported cost factors (77.9 percent, similar to the 78.8 percent reported in 2010–2011 and down slightly from 79.8 percent reported in 2009–2010) as a challenge in maintaining, sustaining, and enhancing their public-access technology infrastructure. An additional challenge facing many libraries is that staff members must juggle issues that arise in connection with public-access technology along with any number of other roles they play within their libraries. Technology support is most frequently provided by the library director (50.4 percent) or public service staff (37.6 percent), and the absence of dedicated technology staff leads to frustration among patrons as updates and repairs are not made as quickly or as frequently as they would like. Unfortunately, as few libraries (a mere 9.2 percent) have seen recent increases in the number of full-time employees, it appears unlikely that a significant number of libraries will be able to remedy this particular situation.

Maintenance of a robust public-access infrastructure, however, is only one component of the Internet-enabled services provided by libraries. Public libraries currently contribute to the creation of digitally inclusive communities in four critical areas (Bertot, Gorham, Jaeger, & Taylor, 2012):

- access to online content and resources,
- technology training in various formats,

- assistance with employment-related needs, and
- e-government support.

These four areas clearly overlap and cannot be understood in isolation from one another. Technology training, for example, may very well be necessary before a user can effectively use an e-book, apply for a job online, or navigate a government's website. Accordingly, discussion of *how* public libraries promote digital inclusion should preface any discussion of the particular Internet-enabled services they are providing to their communities.

The terms *digital divide, digital literacy,* and *digital inclusion* are well entrenched within current policy discussions pertaining to libraries, yet their importance is not always clearly stated. "If the digital divide and digital illiteracy are the problem, digital inclusion is the proposed solution, representing the ability of individuals and groups to access and use information and communication technologies" (Jaeger, Bertot, Thompson, Katz, & DeCoster, 2012, p. 6). Public libraries therefore are the means through which the proposed solution can be implemented, stemming largely from their commitment to and experience with digital literacy training.

As currently understood, digital literacy is closely linked to "twenty-first-century literacy," an overarching term that weaves together the threads of technology literacy, information literacy, media creativity, and social competence and responsibility (Adeyemon, 2009). As explained in the National Broadband Plan:

> Though there is no standard definition, digital literacy generally refers to a variety of skills associated with using [information and communication technologies] to find, evaluate, create and communicate information. It is the sum of the technical skills and cognitive skills people employ to use computers to retrieve information, interpret what they find and judge the quality of that information. It also includes the ability to communicate and collaborate using the Internet—through blogs, self-published documents and presentations and collaborative social networking platforms. (FCC, 2010, p. 90)

Digital literacy, by promoting access to information, is closely tied to the ideals of civic engagement, educational success, and economic growth and innovation (Scott, 2011). Public libraries' long-standing commitment to these very ideals makes them particularly well suited to engage in "an evolving national dialogue about how we marry robust access to technology resources with the twenty-first-century literacy skills necessary to ensure digital opportunity for all" (Clark & Visser, 2011).

The National Broadband Plan characterizes public libraries as "venues for free Internet access" where "reluctant and new users [can] begin to explore the Internet, become comfortable using it and develop the skills needed to find, utilize, and create content" (FCC, 2010, p. 176). Recent data confirms the accuracy of this characterization—82.7 percent of libraries offer informal point-of-use assistance, 44.3 percent offer formal technology training classes, 34.8 percent offer one-on-one training, and 29.5 percent provide online training materials. Only 9.8 percent offer no technology training at all, lending further support to the notion that libraries are making a significant contribution to the development of digitally inclusive communities. In offering technology training, libraries are providing an in-demand service: 36.3 percent of public libraries reported increased use of these services over the last year (up from 27.6 percent in 2010–2011 and 26.3 percent in 2009–2010).

As with all technology-related matters, however, the need to constantly evolve is strong. Whereas a few years ago it was enough for a library to offer basic computer classes, this is no longer the case, and there is a growing consensus that libraries must now focus on implementing initiatives that take a broader view of digital literacy (California ICT Digital Literacy Leadership Council, 2010; Clark & Visser, 2011; Jaeger, Bertot, Thompson, Katz, & DeCoster, 2012). The increasingly diverse types of formal technology training classes that libraries are now offering demonstrate this evolution. While the most frequent offerings are general computer skill classes (87.0 percent), general Internet use classes (86.5 percent), general online and Web searching classes (75.6 percent), and general software use classes (73.3 percent), it is worth noting that

- 49.2 percent offer online job-seeking and career-related information classes, and
- 39.4 percent offer social media (e.g., blogging, Twitter, Facebook, YouTube) classes.

As libraries begin to offer training in more specialized areas, it raises an interesting question: If their goal is to promote digital inclusion, how do they know which services they should provide in furtherance of this goal? Given the resource and budgetary constraints currently faced by many libraries, the choices they make regarding services provision require careful consideration based upon a nuanced understanding of the communities they serve (Scott, 2011). At this time, two areas have been identified—e-government support and employment-related assistance—that libraries have embraced as central to the development of digitally inclusive communities. These two areas are characterized by Bertot, Gorham, Jaeger, & Taylor (2012) as "critical needs." As discussed below, however, there are challenges to overcome in providing services in each of these areas.

SUPPORTING E-GOVERNMENT

As government information at local, state, and federal levels has become increasingly available online, public libraries often find themselves serving as the primary, or only available, access point for e-government, training, and assistance (Bertot & Jaeger, 2012). At just the level of local government, the most common e-government activities in public libraries include finding court proceedings, submitting local zoning board information, requesting planning permits, searching property and assessor databases, registering students in school, taking driver's education programs, applying for permits, scheduling appointments with government officials, paying fees and taxes, and completing numerous other local government functions online (Jaeger, 2009).

Serving as the guarantor of e-government access, along with access to government information, is a somewhat natural extension of the established social roles of the public library. "The public library is one place that is culturally ingrained as a trusted source of free and open information access and exchange" (Jaeger & Burnett, 2005, p. 487). Notwithstanding this history, public libraries—particularly early on—often struggled with the provision of e-government services. The difficulties were due largely to the fact that government agencies were directing users with questions about their websites to public libraries without providing adequate notice or guidance to libraries regarding their new responsibilities (Bertot et al., 2006a, 2006b).

Three developments then occurred in tandem that made it all the more important for public libraries to step into this role: (1) due to the Great Recession, an increasing percentage of the population became eligible for a variety of state and federal social services (Taylor et al., 2012), (2) government information and services have increasingly become available exclusively online, and (3) government agencies have reduced the number of "frontline" personnel who are available and equipped to field e-government-related inquiries from the general public. The first development led to an increasing number of people being directly affected by the latter two developments.

By way of example, the Florida Department of Children and Families reduced the number of caseworkers and assistance providers by over 3,000 positions due to its implementation of the AccessFlorida online application system, resulting in a near complete lack of available agency staff from which users could seek assistance (Gibson, Bertot, & McClure, 2009). In the time since these developments transpired, government agencies have come to rely on public libraries to provide patrons with assistance in completing e-government applications and forms and locating government information online (Jaeger, 2009; Jaeger & Bertot, 2009).

E-government access, assistance, and training are now one of the largest demands on staff time and technology resources, saving federal agencies huge amounts of money and greatly taxing the infrastructure of public libraries (Jaeger, Bertot, Thompson, Katz, & DeCoster, 2012; Jaeger, Taylor, et al., 2012). Recent survey data highlight the many facets of the e-government service role that public libraries are now playing:

- 96.6 percent of libraries reported providing assistance to patrons applying for or accessing e-government services (up considerably from 80.7 percent in 2010–2011 and 78.7 percent in 2009–2010);
- 70.7 percent of libraries reported that staff provide assistance to patrons for completing government forms (up from 67.8 percent in 2010–2011 and 63.3 percent in 2009–2010); and
- nearly all public libraries—91.8 percent—reported providing assistance to the public for understanding how to access and use e-government websites (up from 89.7 percent in 2010–2011 and 88.8 percent reported in 2009–2010).

The Opportunity for All study (Becker et al., 2010) reveals that library patrons are taking advantage of these services: "More than 26 million people used public library computers to get government or legal information or to access government services. Of these, 58 percent downloaded government forms, such as Social Security paperwork, tax forms, and Medicare enrollment documents. Nearly half of these people wound up submitting a government form using a library computer" (p. 4).

There are various factors at play, however, that complicate the provision of e-government services. Library patrons are often ill equipped to engage in e-government. What has become more evident in recent years is that there are a number of "prerequisites" to being able to use e-government services and, more importantly, that public librarians should not assume that their patrons have met all of these prerequisites. Lack of access to computers and the Internet is but one reason why members of the public turn to libraries for e-government assistance. Additional reasons include the following:

1. a lack of technical skills to use the online services and resources;
2. a lack of understanding of civics that renders them unable to discern between federal, state, and local government services and/or which agencies are responsible for which e-government services;
3. discomfort with engaging in online interactions without guidance;
4. inability to engage in e-government services due to the lack of accessibility and usability of government websites in general and e-government services in particular; and
5. a range of social barriers to the access and use of e-government services such as trust, language, and culture (Bertot et al., 2006a, 2006b; Heanue, 2001; Jaeger, 2009; Jaeger & Bertot, 2009).

Each of these reasons alone can impede successful e-government interaction. The difficulties are amplified, though, in those situations in which users present with two or more of these impediments (e.g., recent immigrants with limited English-language skills may be unfamiliar with the structure of government in this country). Librarians find themselves having to resolve these issues before they can focus their attention on the specific e-government need that the user has presented, all of which requires the devotion of additional time and resources.

Moreover, the nature of e-government itself presents a challenge. From a librarian's perspective, much of the complexity inherent in providing e-government services can be traced to the fact that government agencies in this country have yet to adopt a uniform e-government approach, forcing them to familiarize themselves with many different systems, technologies, and forms as well as to remain informed about which agency or agencies are responsible for providing a given service. Notwithstanding this complexity, the decision facing most libraries now is not *whether* to provide e-government services but rather *which* e-government services to provide. Ultimately, the local service context—comprised of elements such as the library's budget and community needs—should drive these decisions. Given the fluidity of these elements, as well as the ongoing evolution of e-government driven by government agencies' growing preference for online engagement with members of the public, libraries must regularly revisit such decisions and redefine the parameters of their e-government service roles whenever necessary.

SUPPORTING EMPLOYMENT

Just as the Great Recession has increased the number of people coming into the library looking for assistance in applying for social services, it has also ushered in a wave of sustained unemployment. According to the Current Population Survey, a monthly survey of households conducted by the BLS, the annual unemployment rate peaked in 2010 at 10.6 percent, remaining above 8 percent until September 2012. Public libraries continue to feel the effects of this slow and halting recovery today as they seek to offer assistance to those who are struggling to find their way back into the workforce.

Public libraries have a long history of providing services to individuals who are out of work and looking for a job (Taylor et al., 2012). What makes this current period of economic turmoil somewhat different, however, is the extent to which advancements in information and communication technologies have shifted much of the job search process online. In the current job market, therefore, digital literacy skills are often critical, rather than merely beneficial:

> While the most obvious benefit of the Internet to job seeking is the ability to access online-only job postings and job applications, hidden advantages include the ability to research the background of compa-

nies, access salary averages for the position one is seeking, and find resume and interview tips. These are benefits that many without access to the Internet would not think to search for and would have trouble finding offline without significant time commitments. (Taylor et al., 2012, p. 197)

Due to these developments, the range of services that libraries provide in this area has greatly expanded. The 2010 Opportunity for All study estimated that 30 million people had used library computers and Internet access to search for employment, with 3.7 million people actually being hired for a position they applied for through the library computers (Becker et al., 2010). The latest survey data reveals that

- 92.2 percent of libraries reported providing access to jobs databases and other job opportunity resources (up from 90.1 percent in 2010–2011 and 88.2 percent in 2009–2010);
- 76.0 percent of libraries reported providing patrons with assistance in completing online job applications (up from 71.9 percent in 2010–2011 and 67.1 percent in 2009–2010); and
- 77.5 percent of libraries reported offering software and other resources to help patrons create resumes and other employment materials (up from 74.5 percent in 2010–2011 and 68.9 percent in 2009–2010).

As evidenced by this data, the employment-related services that public libraries provide are particularly important for those who do not have high-speed Internet or computer access in the home or who lack critical digital literacy skills. Furthermore, inasmuch as public libraries are often open evenings and weekends, they are able to more fully meet the needs of individuals who cannot access other employment services that are only available during the workday.

COMMON CHALLENGES

The ability of public libraries to effectively provide both e-government and employment-related services, however, is dependent upon adequate public-access infrastructure and the presence of sufficient staff to take on these additional responsibilities. The fact that too many libraries must make do with an insufficient number of public-access computers and slow Internet connectivity was discussed above, but these deficiencies create particular challenges for individuals who come to the library for e-government or employment-related services—slow connectivity speeds may make the completion of bandwidth-heavy government forms and job applications onerous (particularly during times of peak usage), and libraries may impose time limits on computers, which may operate to preclude patrons from completing lengthy forms and applications.

The lack of adequate staff and staff with sufficient expertise also presents challenges in both of these areas. At a time when budgetary issues have resulted in across-the-board staff reductions for many libraries, the availability of librarians to walk patrons through often-complicated e-government and employment processes—much less the availability of a librarian with expertise in one of these areas—is not guaranteed. With respect to staffing issues, 49.8 percent of public libraries reported that there was insufficient staff to effectively help patrons with their job seeking, while 44.9 percent of libraries reported similar challenges in meeting the e-government needs of patrons. In both areas, however, survey data reveals a gradual downward trend in the number of libraries reporting staff-related challenges, suggesting that libraries are increasingly accepting the provision of these services as a core component of the role they play within their communities (Bertot, McDermott, Lincoln, Real, & Peterson, 2012).

This brief review of public libraries' e-government and employment-related service roles highlights a growing tendency to broadly define these roles so that the provision of these services extends well beyond providing library patrons with the means to access the Internet. The value of the library's services in this area derives largely from the guidance and expertise of staff members who guide patrons through often complicated processes, ranging from applying for government benefits (e.g., Medicaid, WIC) to building a resume through an online job portal. There are other related areas in which public librarians find themselves functioning as an intermediary, such as emergency response and disaster recovery (Jaeger et al., 2006; Jaeger & Bertot, 2011); and, as the amounts and types of information and services available online continue to grow, one can envision the continued expansion of libraries' current Internet-enabled service roles.

NEW SERVICE PARADIGMS

As important as it is to reflect on changes in the types of services being provided by public libraries, it is equally important to examine how libraries have evolved—and continue to do so—with respect to the manner in which they provide these services. Two major developments in particular—(1) the emergence of Web 2.0 and mobile technologies, and (2) increasing collaboration among public libraries, community organizations, and government agencies—have shaped how public libraries are now providing key services.

Emerging Technologies

As quickly as free Internet access has become ubiquitous in libraries throughout the United States, libraries are embracing a range of technologies that expand upon this access, seeking to offer more services to those patrons who are physically present within their buildings as well as to connect with patrons (and potential patrons) online. A growing number of libraries now offer their patrons various means to access Internet-enabled resources; recent statistics indicate that 49.0 percent of public libraries provide access to mobile devices (e.g., laptops, netbooks), and 39.1 percent provide access to e-readers (e.g., Kindle, Nook), evidencing the degree to which mobile technologies are becoming central to people's daily lives. According to an April 2012 Pew Internet and the American Life report, 57 percent of adults age eighteen and older have a laptop, 19 percent own an e-book reader, and 19 percent have a tablet computer (Zickuhr & Smith, 2012). During the same period in which these devices have been growing in popularity, there has been a decline in the ownership of desktop computers. In offering access to these devices, libraries are thus demonstrating their awareness of their patrons' shifting preferences.

The surge in the use of mobile devices is also striking—63 percent of adults now go online wirelessly with a mobile phone, laptop, e-book reader, or tablet computer (Zickuhr & Smith, 2012). As such, in addition to providing access to mobile devices, libraries are increasingly designing and offering services that "promote and expand their existing services by offering mobile access to their websites and online public-access catalogs; by supplying on-the-go mobile reference services; and by providing mobile access to e-books, journals, video, audio books, and multimedia content" (Vollmer, 2010, pp. 2–3). Specifically,

- 36.1 percent of urban libraries (as compared to 9.3 percent of rural libraries) optimize their website for mobile device access;
- 31.9 percent of urban libraries (as compared to 6.5 percent of rural libraries) use scanned codes (e.g., QR codes) for access to library services and content; and
- 27.8 percent of urban libraries (as compared to 3.7 percent of rural libraries) have developed smart phone apps for access to library services and content.

Given that populations traditionally excluded from broadband and computing access in the home are gaining Internet access via mobile phones (Rainie, 2010), the provision of mobile device–specific services enable libraries to connect with members of the public who would otherwise have no access to their online services.

Similarly, public libraries' growing use of Web 2.0 technologies—"a variety of Web-based platforms, applications and technologies which exploit the Internet's connectivity to support the networking of people and content" (Reddick & Aikins, 2012, p. 1)—demonstrates their willingness to connect with patrons via nontraditional means. As with mobile devices and technologies, libraries are both providing patrons with access to Web 2.0 technologies and using those very technologies to connect with patrons who may never step foot inside their doors. Nearly 62 percent of libraries indicate that they provide access to a range of social media services and resources. These services and resources are in demand—according to a January 2013 Pew Internet and the American Life report, of the 26 percent of Americans that reported accessing the Internet through a library's computer or wireless network, 35 percent visited social networking sites (Zickuhr, Rainey, & Purcell, 2013).

In addition to providing access, libraries are increasingly using Web 2.0 technologies in their outreach efforts:

- 70.7 percent of public libraries report using social networking tools (e.g., Facebook) to connect with library patrons, the general public, and for marketing purposes;
- 45.6 percent of public libraries report using communication tools (e.g., Blogger, WordPress, Vox, Twitter) to reach the public;
- 37.3 percent report using photography sites (e.g., Flickr, Zoomr); and
- 27.5 percent use video sharing tools (e.g., YouTube, Vimeo, Openfilm).

Given that 66 percent of online adults use social media platforms (Smith, 2011), the decision to conduct outreach in this manner appears to be a sound one. Libraries' willingness to engage in social media has a positive impact on public trust (ALA, 2012b), as their ability to embrace new means of communication highlights their ongoing commitment to promoting the open exchange of information.

Partnerships

Through ongoing research, the authors have been able to identify libraries across the country that have entered into partnerships with community organizations and government agencies to provide both e-government and employment-related services. The growth of partnerships was born, at least in part, out of necessity. The public is increasingly relying upon the libraries in their communities to deliver these additional services at a time when these very institutions are contending with budgetary constraints. Partnerships are one means for public libraries to meet the heightened demand for their services without a corresponding increase in staff and resources.

In particular, partnerships are becoming increasingly prevalent within the e-government realm. The latest survey data reveals that 30.9 percent (up from 24.7 percent reported in 2010–2011 and 20.5 percent reported in 2009–2010) of reporting libraries indicate that they partnered with government agencies, nonprofit organizations, and others to provide e-government services. As discussed above, government agencies at the state and local levels have gradually been shifting responsibility for various services to public libraries over the past decade, without providing any funding to offset the costs associated with libraries taking on these additional responsibilities. Furthermore, in many cases, collaborations with government agencies and community organizations present public libraries with the opportunity to provide services that would be difficult, if not impossible, to provide on their own.

Detailed descriptions of several existing partnerships between public libraries, government agencies, and nonprofit organizations are discussed below to highlight the unique ways in which each strives to meet particular community needs. Three partnerships focus on providing services to immigrants, and two focus on providing social services.

Immigration-related services, in particular, have provided a fertile ground for partnerships as the United States Citizenship and Immigration Service (USCIS) has continued to shift a growing number of its core services online. Because many immigrants lack the means to access, understand, and use e-government, however, the ability of libraries to function as intermediaries has been particularly important in this area.

In 2000, the **Hartford Public Library (HPL) in Connecticut** created The American Place (TAP), a program with the principal goals of helping an increasingly diverse group of immigrants secure citizenship and achieve language literacy (Naficy, 2009). By forming innovative partnerships that utilize local resources and securing grant funding, HPL has taken steps to create a community-wide approach that involves USCIS, the local school district, and nonprofit agencies to reach the target populations. For example, in 2010, HPL secured grant funding to train volunteers from the Hartford Public Schools and community organizations in the use of instructional technologies so that they could lead citizenship education classes and guide patrons through computer-based self-study courses. In addition, TAP works with the federal government to provide passport services and voter registration for newly naturalized citizens.

TAP seeks to connect with people online, as well as in person. Recognizing that navigating the USCIS website is a major challenge for many immigrants, TAP "streamlines information" to help guide library staff, immigrant patrons, and local organizations that assist this particular population (Naficy, 2009, p. 166). TAP's website divides information into various categories relevant to the immigrant experience, including a "Welcome to Hartford" section that features important community information links, such as housing information and the city's website.

Austin Public Library (APL) in Texas created the New Immigrants Program (NIP) in 2000 as a result of recommendations made in 1998 by a task force charged with investigating the effects of then-recent changes to immigration laws on local residents. The APL initially opened English and citizenship centers in three APL branch locations. Within several years, however, the NIP expanded to eight locations, the study centers were renamed New Immigrant Centers (NICs) to better reflect the program's expanded mission, and the city increased the number of bilingual library employees in response to the changing demographics of surrounding communities (Miranda-Murillo, 2006).

In addition to housing study centers that offer computer and Internet access, the NICs host English conversation programs and English as a second language (ESL) classes. Since the inception of the program, APL has partnered with both Austin Community College and the Austin Independent School District to offer ESL classes. TAP also maintains an online presence through a website that provides Internet-based tools to help immigrants with their English-language skills, as well as links to USCIS information and international news.

Established in 1977, the New Americans Project (NAP) run by the **Queens Borough Public Library (QBPL) in New York** was a pioneering effort to provide better services to immigrants through ESL classes, cultural arts programs, coping skills programs, and collection development in a variety of other languages (Carnesi & Fiol, 2000). Due to the linguistic diversity of its staff (Winkel, 2007), QBPL is able to provide programming in a wide variety of languages and on a wide range of topics, often in conjunction with one of the many community organizations that are part of its extensive network of partners. In addition to reaching out to immigrants through programming, QBPL has also compiled a number of citizenship and immigration resources on its website, including referral lists for both citizenship and ESL classes offered by various community organizations (e.g., the Turkish Cultural Center, Catholic Charities), as well as the New York City Department of Education. Also available through the QBPL is a community resources database of agencies offering low-cost or free social and human services, searchable by services offered, locations, target groups, languages, and ethnic groups.

A partnership with the Mayor's Office of Immigrant Affairs, focused on assisting immigrants with the application process for the Diversity Visa Lottery, is a prime example of successful e-government collaboration. Shortly after the U.S. Department of State mandated that the application process be completed online, a partnership between QBPL and the Office of Immigrant Affairs was conceived following city officials' recognition that the electronic application system "created another hurdle for some low-income immigrants who lack computer access" (Yaniv, 2005). Detailed guidance prepared by the Office of Immigrant Affairs is published on QBPL's website, thereby ensuring that immigrants are receiving accurate information from the actual provider of the e-government service. In addition to encouraging applicants to use the library's computers to complete the application, QBPL has also set up designated times at different branches during which immigrants can receive assistance with scanning photographs to be submitted with their applications.

Innovative partnerships are also being cultivated to provide social services that meet specific community needs. "Baltimarket" is a collaboration among the **Baltimore City Enoch Pratt Free Library System**, the Baltimore City Health Department, the Maryland Institute College of Art, and Santoni's Super Market, the primary goal of which is to provide Baltimore residents currently living in underserved "food deserts" access to fresh and healthy foods. Through Baltimarket, residents can order groceries online at their local library branch and then collect their food on a designated pickup day. Each partner has a clearly defined role: the libraries provide the space and computers to facilitate the online ordering, the grocery store delivers the groceries to the libraries, and the local government oversees the program and ensures that communication flows among the various partners.

What differentiates this online grocery order system from those run by major grocery chains are the accommodations made for those who are on the wrong side of the digital divide. The availability of computers—as well as people to provide one-to-one assistance in using the online grocery order system—at the program sites makes the program more accessible to those who are unable to or are uncomfortable with using an online ordering system at home.

In July 2009, the **Alachua County Library District in Florida**, working with the local office of the state's Department of Children and Families, the Partnership for Strong Families, and Casey Family Programs, opened a new facility (the Library Partnership) designed to be a one-stop resource for the surrounding community (Blumenstein, 2009). In addition to 4,500 square feet devoted to the library, this facility also houses approximately forty nonprofit organizations and local government agencies that provide social services focused on child welfare. Partners include FloridaWorks (the regional workforce board), the Alachua County Housing Authority, the United Way, and Head Start.

Building upon the library's long-standing commitment to the development of e-government training services and resources, staff members at the Library Partnership help individuals access the online forms and applications now mandated by many social service agencies in Florida. Because of the way in which child welfare issues are intertwined with other important social issues—including health, employment, education, and literacy—this partnership views robust e-government service provision as one component of a broader collaborative effort to better address the needs of children and their families. The Library Partnership's success is leading to the construction of another library partnership site, with a focus on poverty. Budget cutbacks for social services are straining the ability of partnership agencies to staff both the Library Partnership and the new location; however, partners are willing to participate on a more limited basis.

What each of these partnerships demonstrates is that, notwithstanding criticism that public libraries are becoming increasingly irrelevant, their role in communities across the country is not diminishing, merely evolving. Their value now lies less with the printed information that is available within the four walls of the library and more with the myriad services that they provide in an effort to connect members of the public with information that is central to their day-to-day lives. As Watson (2010) observed, "for [l]ibraries . . . the vision and purpose must switch from resource provision to being about people and making a real contribution to the learning landscape" (p. 51). While partnerships are often born out of economic necessity, they are demonstrating a clear potential to transform the means through which libraries and other organizations provide vital services. The realization of this potential, rather than cost savings, may ultimately be the greatest contribution of these partnerships.

IMPACTS OF EXPANDING SERVICE ROLES

With a better understanding of both what libraries are currently doing and how they are doing it, the book will turn now to the ways in which these changes have impacted the use and the perceptions of the public library. Interestingly enough, at the same time that public libraries have become a key provider of Internet access and training within their communities, they have been confronted with repeated charges of their growing irrelevance in this country. Data about library usage, however, tells a remarkably different story. Many different data points demonstrating library usage increases were discussed in the preceding chapter, but a few are worth reiterating here:

- Between 2006 and 2008, the number of Americans with library cards increased by 5 percent, in-person library visits increased by 10 percent, and library website visits increased by 17 percent (Davis, 2009, 2011).
- In the current extended economic downturn, the use of public libraries and library computers for job-seeking activities, social services, e-mail access, entertainment, and other purposes has increased substantially. In 2009, more than 14 million people were considered regular users of library computers just for the Internet access (C. Hill, 2009a).
- Since the beginning of the economic downturn, most libraries have seen around a 25 percent increase in overall usage, with some actually being forced to handle up to a 500 percent increase in usage (Sigler et al., 2011).

The huge increases in public library usage have gotten the attention of many print, radio, and television media outlets; in one of the early years of the Great Recession, media outlets around the country began to tell the story of the yeoman efforts of libraries to meet spiraling community needs (e.g., Carlton, 2009; CNN, 2009; Gwinn, 2009; Jackson, 2009; Van Sant, 2009).

A key reason for these significant increases in the usage of libraries is the fact that they attempt to connect patrons to all levels of information access. The computers and related Internet technologies ensure physical access to those who have insufficient or no other means of access. The training and assistance promotes intellectual access for patrons with limited or no digital literacy. The range of social services, partnerships, education programs, and outreach activities in which libraries now engage serves to foster social access to information by integrating it into the larger community context.

In addition to positive trends in the overall usage of libraries, there is also ample evidence that the public library remains relevant to a wide range of individuals, cutting across a variety of demographics (e.g., age, income, race, education level). A handful of statistics from the Opportunity for All report will suffice to demonstrate this point:

- **Age:** Youth (between fourteen and twenty-four years old) make up a quarter of all patrons, but the second- and third-largest groupings of patrons, respectively, are people in their middle years (forty-five to fifty-four) and seniors older than sixty-five.
- **Income:** "Overall, 44 percent of people in households living below the federal poverty line ($22,000 a year for a family of four) used public library computers and Internet access" (p. 2).
- **Race:** Public-access Internet usage at libraries is highest among people of mixed race and Native Hawaiians/Pacific Islanders.
- **Education Level:** Individuals with education levels below a high school degree, as well as those with some college or a two-year degree, are more likely than high school graduates to take a library computer class (Becker et al., 2010).

These statistics highlight how the Internet-enabled services now provided by libraries are sought not merely by one small segment of society but by a broad spectrum of individuals with different needs and interests.

Both the increased usage experienced by many libraries in recent years and the benefits reaped by communities when libraries form partnerships with government agencies and nonprofit organizations to offer improved and often innovative services reveal positive developments occurring in libraries across the country that could serve as vehicles for advocacy. Through partnerships, for example, libraries are making use of existing in-house resources—notably, Internet access, technology training, and knowledgeable staff—to play a vital role in the provision of e-government services to members of the public. The narrative of how libraries provide these in-demand services could help to form the basis for libraries' appeals for increased funding:

> Through education, access, equity, inclusion, engagement, and simply by existing, public libraries are strengthening the communities in which we live. Unfortunately, many of our users and nonusers alike, for the most part, still think of public libraries primarily as book reposi-tories. Understanding our role in community building and being able to articulate this role is essential to the work we do. (Scott, 2011)

As will be discussed in subsequent chapters, however, libraries continue to struggle with demonstrating their value to policy makers, as well as to the public at large.

These struggles with demonstrating their value in political and policy contexts can result in significant missed opportunities to increase support for libraries. One prominent missed opportunity can be found in the incredibly successful efforts of public libraries along the Gulf Coast and throughout the Southeast to assist their communities during and after the particularly devastating 2004 and 2005 hurricane seasons—Katrina, Wil-ma, Ivan, Dennis, and Rita, among others. Public libraries with their Internet-enabled technologies and assistance played key roles in helping evacuees and those in devastated areas to

- find missing and displaced family members, friends, and pets;
- download and fill out Federal Emergency Management Agency (FEMA) forms and insurance claims;
- find information about the conditions in and view photos and maps of their communities; and
- check the state of their individual homes and places of work (Bertot et al., 2006a, 2006b).

For example, one small community reported that the library's computers were used to help evacuees from New Orleans complete over 45,000 FEMA and insurance claims in the month after Katrina made landfall. In many communities, the libraries were praised as "a godsend" and other terms that drove home the magnitude of their positive impacts in prepar-ation, response, and recovery from the catastrophic storms (Bertot et al., 2006b). Additionally, public libraries also performed enormous services for the affected communities as a whole by

- helping them prepare through the creation and distribution of emergency preparedness guides, disaster preparedness workshops, and coordinating volunteer programs;
- providing emergency information reference services during and after the hurricanes;
- giving shelter during and after the hurricanes;

- recharging electronic devices and keeping prescription medicines refrigerated;
- providing food, medical supplies, roof tarps, and many other vital supplies; and
- working with relief organizations and government agencies—including FEMA and the National Guard—to get aid to the places where it was needed (Jaeger, Langa, et al., 2006).

The myriad ways that public libraries helped their communities throughout the 2004 and 2005 hurricane seasons helped to cement the notion in the minds of the public—even nonpatrons of the library—that libraries are central to their communities and central to the provision of Internet access (Jaeger & Fleischmann, 2007).

The responses of libraries in helping their communities during these disasters also helped shape the development of electronic tools for communities to respond to emergencies (Jaeger, Fleischmann, Preece, Shneiderman, Wu, & Qu, 2007; Jaeger, Shneiderman, Fleischmann, Preece, Qu, & Wu, 2007). The roles of libraries have continued to expand to helping communities cope in similar ways with many other kinds and sizes of disasters in subsequent years, from tornado outbreaks and flooding to wildfires, droughts, and even the East Coast *derecho* of 2012 (Cook, 2012). While many of these efforts have not received much national attention, the work of public libraries in helping the communities of coastal New Jersey, New York, Connecticut, and other areas that were devastated by Superstorm Sandy in fall 2012 did garner considerable attention in the media.

Unfortunately, the profession and its professional organizations failed to use these successes as the basis for arguing for greater government support in policy and funding. In fact, the inertia of librarians in conveying their successes in these areas allowed an embarrassed FEMA to try to cover for some of its epic failures in responding to Katrina by claiming that, contrary to press reports, libraries played no useful role in response to the hurricanes (Bier, 2006; Chertoff, 2005; White House, 2006). By not engaging and contradicting this campaign by FEMA to use falsehoods to improve its standing in the eyes of Congress, public libraries managed to snatch defeat from the jaws of victory, losing the chance to demonstrate unequivocally their importance in contemporary society. Instead, members of Congress walked away from the events of those two years none the wiser about the extraordinary services of libraries to their communities in distress.

The failure to tell this story of libraries and communities in the political and policy context is far from an exception. It has been replicated by the failure to demonstrate the roles of libraries in delivering e-government and in providing services throughout the Great Recession and in creating innovative partnerships to meet unique community needs and in so much else. The counterproductive and irrational fear of engaging in political discourse has led libraries to even fear telling the story of their successes in the political arena, with profound consequences. Libraries, however, must overcome this paralysis-inducing fear—their ability to demonstrate their value and engage directly in policy and political processes will undoubtedly have a significant impact on their future support.

SIX

Engagement and Valuation of the Public Good

The ideologies of neoconservative politics and neoliberal economics place institutions of the public good such as public libraries in the position of needing to directly and actively engage the political and policy-making processes and advocate by expressing their value in language that makes sense to political actors. Libraries, unfortunately, have not found a successful way to accomplish these needs, leading to many negative repercussions in terms of financial support and decisions of policy and politics. Alongside the political and policy consequences of these insufficient efforts at engagement in the policy-making process, the primary response of libraries to the predominant political and economic ideologies has been assertions of value. As public services are expected to prove their value as a prerequisite to receiving funding in the current political climate, public libraries have faced the difficult challenge of quantifying the value of education and community support. Most libraries and national organizations have unhelpfully fallen back to assertions—rather than data-driven demonstrations—of library value.

Based on public opinion, public libraries seem like they should be well positioned to receive all of the policy, political, and financial support that they need. A 2006 national survey found that 71 percent of citizens say public libraries spend their money well, and 52 percent of citizens favor tax increases if their local libraries need additional support (Wooden, 2006). Seven years later, another national survey found even greater support for public libraries. Among Americans aged sixteen and older, 91 percent believe that public libraries are important to their communities, and 76 percent say public libraries are important to their families (Zickuhr, Rainie, & Purcell, 2013). In the past year, 59 percent of respondents to the 2013 survey had visited a public library in person and/or online. In sharp contrast, the same survey found that only 26 percent of respondents thought positively of government as a whole.

Members of the public overwhelmingly state that libraries are important to their communities and families and that libraries should receive the funding they need, even if through tax increases. If these views are not adequately conveyed to public officials, or if public officials do not share these beliefs, the public support for libraries will not translate into support in politics, policy, or funding. And, unfortunately, the lack of sufficient support has become commonplace. A 2013 survey found that 48 percent of librarians feel their local government is committed to the value of the library in the community, 44 percent feel that the local government is neutral to the public library, and 8 percent feel the local government is unsupportive and does not value the library as part of the community (Schwartz, 2013). These numbers indicate that a majority of local governments (52 percent) are seen as less than supportive of public libraries, while the 48 percent that are perceived as recognizing the value of the library to the community still may not adequately support it. "Public libraries are beloved institutions, but they can't survive on accolades alone" (Wooden, 2006, p. 4).

It is a very legitimate question as to why consistently high levels of support for libraries do not translate into libraries receiving funding at the levels they seek, garnering respect in political discourse, or benefitting from supportive policy decisions. The answer likely lies within the realm of library advocacy. "Our advocacy efforts must convince officials that libraries are essential and critical community services. Otherwise, like other services perceived as worthwhile, library budgets will suffer greater cuts than services seen as critical" (Dougherty, 2011, p. 46). This sentiment is correct, but hardly new; the difficulties faced by public libraries in navigating governmental structures to receive adequate support have been recognized for nearly a century (Hinton, 1938). Many of the books that have been written on lobbying for support for public libraries in local, state, and national politics have taken the same message through the years (e.g., Abbott-Hoduski, 2003; Halsey, 2003; Josey, 1980; Josey & Shearer, 1990; Turner, 1997). The key issue is why library advocacy efforts continue to fall short.

THINKING LOUDLY

In chapter 1, in an effort to describe the public library's place in the contemporary political world, we referenced the following quote by Archilocus: "The fox knows many things, but the hedgehog knows one big thing." The majority of the political, policy, advocacy, and funding problems faced by public libraries—foxes in a political and policy-making world dictated by hedgehogs—are tied to this situation. Public libraries are currently struggling to exist in a political climate defined by hyperpartisanship and entrenched ideology that is quite hospitable to a hedgehog, but not to a fox who thinks in variables and shadings.

Studies of politicians, newscasters, media commentators, and even public intellectuals have demonstrated both that they are overwhelmingly hedgehogs and are rewarded for being so with greater amounts of attention and airtime (Silver, 2012a; Tetlock, 2006). A defining element of a hedgehog is the ability to take any new information and find a way to make it support the ideology that they espouse. When hyperpartisans with opposing views are given the same information, both sides will make the new information fit their respective ideologies (Silver, 2012a).

With a badly divided electorate, politicians and policy makers are rewarded with support by certain segments of the population for being hedgehogs. Entire mainstream "news" channels and sites are devoted to covering the events of the day from a particular hyperpartisan viewpoint, providing platforms for the voices of the hedgehogs of different political persuasions. As a result, public discourse has become dominated by hedgehogs, even if they are hedgehogs of competing political ideologies.

The public library, in contrast, is the most fox-like institution imaginable. As earlier historical chapters on libraries demonstrated, the public library has done nothing but change to meet community needs as they arise, continually redefining what they do for their patrons. They collect a wide assortment of multidisciplinary information sources and materials to meet a broad range of information needs, repeatedly taking stands in support of freedom of expression and freedom of access to diverse perspectives and opinions. And the library discourse is absolutely choked with self-reflection and self-questioning. The combination of adaptability and self-reflection, though, can easily be perceived as weakness by those who function with absolute and unwavering certainty.

Thus the public library, by its extremely fox-like nature, runs contrary to the hedgehog-like nature of the vast majority of politicians and political commentators and other key public voices about the political and policy-making processes. Foxes inherently challenge public leaders regardless of political perspectives, as public leaders tend to be hedgehogs with their focus on unifying theories and grand explanations (Cuban, 1995). This tension is in addition to the animosity toward public libraries of politicians and policy makers that adhere to neoconservative political and neoliberal economic ideologies.

The determination resulting from the combination of these ideologies and a discourse favoring hedgehogs can be seen in a 2013 article in *Forbes* magazine. As was examined in chapter 4, *Forbes* caused quite a stir in 2012 for naming the MLS to be the worst master's degree (Smith, 2012), and they were criticized for using a highly flawed methodology as the basis of this determination (Bertot, Jaeger, & Sarin, 2012). A year later, *Forbes* used exactly the same methodology and made the same conclusion about the MLS. "The low pay rank and estimated growth rank make library and information science the worst master's degree for jobs right now" (Smith, 2013, n.p.). However, in true hedgehog fashion, *Forbes* took the negative response to their previous year's article as supporting their correctness. Noting that the job prospects for anyone who wishes to work in a library are "fairly limited," the article instead strongly recommends using an MLS to work in a corporation on big data, a career choice they deem "quite respectable" (Smith, 2013, n.p.). The distinction also shows the neoconservative political and neoliberal economic biases against public libraries—working in libraries is a terrible choice, but you can redeem yourself by working for a corporation. Sadly, these attitudes and ideologies are central aspects of the political and intellectual climate in which public libraries must engage in advocacy.

WHERE DOES THE PUBLIC GOOD GO?

As a starting point for examining the relationship between public libraries and advocacy, the nature of the public library as an institution of the public good merits consideration. Public goods include clean air and water, police and fire departments, health care, national defense, and public education and public libraries, among much else. They are typically considered in economic terms, yet they are the foundations of a democratic and healthy society. A public good has two essential attributes: it is open to all (nonexcludability), and the use of it by one person does not limit the use by another person (nonrivalry).

To economists, public goods use basic inputs of public capital and public labor to provide services (hours open, services available, resources, and materials) that are then measured in terms of observable outputs, such as crimes solved, emergency patients saved, student achievement tests scores, and library circulation data. The output measures used are not accurate portraits of the efficiency or productivity of services, though, as the measured outputs are heavily dependent on the engagement and efforts of members of the public (De Witte & Geys, 2011, 2013). Teachers, for example, can do an excellent job of preparing their students for a standardized test but cannot control whether the students study or get a good night of sleep before taking the test.

Close cousins to public goods are common-pool resources, which are nonexcludable but limited (Apesteguia & Maier-Rigaud, 2006). Picking fruit from trees in a public park is an example of a common-pool resource. The fruits are there for everyone to take, but once the last piece of fruit is picked, it is not available until the next spring. Unlike common-pool resources, the materials and training in the library are not an exhaustible resource, unless the library is defunded to the extent that it is unable to provide adequate resources.

Public libraries can be seen as a public good in several distinct and equally significant ways. First, "they perform critical functions that benefit the entire society" (Ramey, 2013, n.p.). Political philosophies related to republican government have historically presumed an educated populace, which is entirely dependent on members of the public having the means to educate themselves (Sandel, 1996). In many nations, public libraries are the one entity that exists to fill this need. On an individual basis, patrons have many chances to improve their lives through opportunities made available by the library. Moreover, communities benefit from these opportunities for individual patrons as well as from the library's community-building facilities, resources, and services. Individuals who never interact with the library therefore still reap the benefit of living in a better-educated and better-connected community. Second, "they are a public good in the classic economic sense" (Ramey, 2013, n.p.). Simply put, they are open to all members of the community, they are primarily paid for through local public funds, and the use of the library by some members of the community does not prevent other patrons from benefitting from it as well. Third, public libraries are tied to the ideals of the public good (Ramey, 2013, n.p.). Public libraries are inextricably linked to the fundamentals of democracy, including community, public education, meritocracy, civil rights, and civic engagement, among others. "Public libraries are always going to be about people—the connection of people to resources, the connection of people to technology, the connection of people to people" (Kent, 1996, p. 214).

As detailed in preceding chapters, the neoconservative political ideology and the neoliberal economic ideology have combined to create a distrust of institutions of the public good among many politicians and policy makers. The long-standing conception of the public library as a pure public good, particularly a public good whose benefits are extraordinarily hard to quantify in economic terms, is not enough to gain traction in the political and economic climate in the United States.

CONFUSION HAS ITS COST

In many ways, shaping an effective national advocacy strategy for public libraries can seem unachievable. As there are so many public libraries in the United States and their circumstances are so divergent, no general advocacy strategy can capture all of their diverse situations and needs (Lyons, 2013). Public libraries also have very significant variations in funding, number of full-time staff members, percentage of staff members with an MLS, quality of Internet access, and other factors that heavily influence the ability to provide services to the community (Sin, 2011). However, there is a clear way to craft a message about support that works for all public libraries. The quantity of library services—materials, resources, programs, and outreach available—has a positive impact on the frequency of usage of the library by community members and the perception of the importance of the library (Sin, 2012). Thus, public libraries are widely different in composition and needs, but united by the fact that greater funding and political support equates to better service to their communities.

Local friends of the library groups, state library organizations, professional groups, and national library organizations all make efforts to advocate for public libraries, and many of these efforts have been ongoing for a long time. As noted earlier, ALA founded its Washington Office to lobby on behalf of libraries many decades ago. Unfortunately, several major challenges to library advocacy have stymied the library profession:

- Library advocacy often uses comparisons that have nothing to do with the role of the library in the community, such as the oft-repeated statistic that there are more public libraries than McDonald's restaurants and five times as many public libraries as Wal-Marts (Lyons, 2009). While these types of statistics can get attention, they reveal nothing about the importance of the library to the patron or the community.
- Many librarians do not feel that advocacy is part of or relevant to their job, and many are afraid of facing negative employment repercussions for engaging in advocacy for libraries (Jaeger, Gorham, Sarin, & Bertot, in press).
- The lack of marketing training or a culture of lobbying limits the ability and willingness of libraries to market their services, which is increasingly an expectation for public service entities (Parker, Kaufman-Scarborough, & Parker, 2007).
- Only a small number of MLS programs even offer students the opportunity to take courses on advocacy, lobbying, or marketing as electives (Hussey & Velasquez, 2011).
- We do not learn well from past experiences. The recession of 1990–1992 had economic impacts on public libraries similar to those of the Great Recession—leading the ALA to have to caravan across the country to raise local media attention and a national rally in Washington, D.C., to raise national media attention in the summer of 1991—but librarians have not been quick to learn from these past advocacy efforts (Dougherty, 2011).
- The issue of self-imposed voicelessness discussed earlier is a significant problem. "We do not sing our praises loudly enough. We do not tell our stories compellingly enough. We do not take credit for our achievements, and we certainly do not assert our position as the very public heart and soul of the information age" (Kent, 1996, p. 212).

- As detailed above, the stance of neutrality is inherently designed to undermine the ability of libraries to advocate for themselves in any meaningful way (Jaeger, Gorham, Sarin, & Bertot, in press).
- Many library advocacy efforts and slogans have been safe and non-controversial (e.g., "Read"), yet effective advocacy requires "genuine courage, not only because we may be criticized as overreaching, but also because we ultimately don't control the outcome" (Hummel, 2012, p. 5).
- These same safe advocacy efforts and slogans do not adequately convey what a library does. Having invested decades of effort into campaigns based around reading, librarians have been very successful in creating an association between libraries and one specific role they play, rather than crafting a campaign that better communicates the huge array of community contributions made by public libraries.

The politicians who have not been kind to libraries over the past several decades have done so for more than ideological reasons. In surveys of politicians about public libraries, a majority believe that libraries themselves hurt their own support by inadequate marketing, a lack of advocacy, differences in operational structure, and isolation from the rest of government (Wooden, 2006). Many of these issues are reflected in the list above.

In all fairness, successful library advocacy hinges on several elements beyond the control of libraries. Libraries typically do not serve populations that have a dominant voice in politics. Public libraries are significantly important to the poor, immigrants, urban residents, the homeless, children, the unemployed, people with disabilities, and those with lower levels of education, among others, none of whom are a particularly well-represented voice in political decisions. The ability of each of these groups to lobby on their own behalf is hampered by a lack of both disposable income and political skills (Baumgartner et al., 2009). Moreover, the likelihood that they will ever be the intended beneficiary of a policy change advocated by lobbyists is small because the interests of these low-profile groups generally are not part of the equation when lobbyists are determining what issues to take up and how to frame these issues. Their voices are almost always absent in "the corridors of power as reflected on K Street" (Baumgartner et al., 2009, p. 28). By being champions of the powerless, the public library not only serves groups who are generally ignored in politics and policy making but also associates itself with many groups that the rest of society wishes to forget even exist.

Further, the ability to successfully advocate for libraries hinges on the transparency of government budget information and processes to stakeholders (Hussey & Velasquez, 2011). If financial and policy decisions are made in ways such that libraries and their supporters have no warning that the decisions are being made or information about how the decisions are being made, advocacy will be nearly impossible. In addition to being politically disinclined to feel favorably about institutions of the public good, policy makers and politicians making decisions that impact libraries also generally know little about what libraries actually do. For example, politicians who favor reducing library funding or closing library branches are typically unaware of the socioeconomic contributions of libraries (Svendsen, 2013).

The area of e-government provides a vivid example of the depth of this unawareness. Since the advent of e-government, public libraries have provided the infrastructure and training for access to the rest of government (Milam, 2001). As more and more things have been moved online, government has provided money for infrastructure but has not given attention to public information distribution and management, duties which libraries have assumed (Shuler, 2002). Politicians and government agencies love using e-government and love the savings it provides to government, yet primarily remain blissfully unaware of the burden it has created for libraries. As a result, these responsibilities have rolled down to the lowest political level—local public libraries—with no attendant support from any level of government (Jaeger & Bertot, 2011).

The FCC's 2010 National Broadband Plan reveals the impact of such unawareness on specific policy making. It discussed expanding broadband access at a range of institutions that they labeled "public computing centers": "health clinics, community colleges, schools, community centers, libraries, museums, and other public access points" (p. 10). Yet providing public access has always been a responsibility placed on libraries and schools, with public libraries providing the only free public computer and Internet access in more than two-thirds of communities in the United States (Bertot, Gorham, Jaeger, & Taylor, 2012; Strover, Chapman, & Waters, 2004). The idea of public computing centers directly parallels a failed program of the Clinton years—community technology centers (CTCs) were places of computer access without the support or training that are provided by libraries, and, not surprisingly, the program failed due to lack of usage of the computers (Strover, Chapman, & Waters, 2004). An absurd policy situation like this interrelationship between public libraries and e-government can only occur because of a complete disjunction between the way political and policy decision makers think about libraries—or, more aptly, do not think about libraries—and what libraries are expected to do as a result of community expectations and the results of politics and policy.

The public library "is commonly seen as a physical entity, rather than a force in the world" and thought of in terms of collections rather than "the actions, interactions, and transformations that its existence makes possible, every day, for people from all walks of life" (Hummel, 2012, p. 4). This physical focus weighs heavily on funding considerations. In discourse about cutting budgets, the "library" part of public libraries is usually emphasized by those favoring budget cuts—giving prominence to the role of Google and other Internet products in making the library irrelevant—but the public library is an irreplaceable community institution because of the "public" part of its name (Kent, 1996). Worse is the fact that advocates for public library support also typically emphasize the "library" over the "public," even though they are well aware of the enormous range of major contributions that public libraries make to their communities.

A great but extremely necessary challenge for public libraries is to engage political and policy-making processes with advocacy strategies that demonstrate the value of libraries and the reasons they should be supported in language that makes sense in the current political climate. Just as public libraries view seeking ways to engage community members as central to their mission (Kranich, 2010), they also need to learn to view engaging the political process as equally central to their mission. Without the latter, the former will grow more and more difficult.

ARTICULATING VALUE, DEMONSTRATING VALUE

As a result of the neoconservative political climate and the neoliberal economic climate, effective advocacy hinges on the demonstration of value. Libraries have to look for different ways to measure their value to society and clearly express that value. Bringing together the library's historical ideals of providing knowledge and information for all citizens with the current practical demands and needs of those in their communities, libraries provide the much-needed resources and support many people seek. Increasingly, libraries offer their communities otherwise unavailable combinations of resources, services, space, outreach, and expertise to resolve and meet community challenges in the areas of education, government engagement, employment, and other articulated community needs.

In a policy environment that emphasizes business metrics for value like return on investment (ROI) and that seeks quantifiable social goods to prove economic contribution, the public library faces enormous challenges in articulating and demonstrating the value of all that they do in measures and language that resonate with the politicians and policy makers who determine the levels of support that libraries receive in funding and policy decisions. Many of the activities of the public library are expressly intended to have a social rather than economic benefit; community space, for example, is meant to build a sense of community. Finding ways to leverage an economic value from a service, resource, or program intended to build a sense of community is a considerable challenge. Yet doing so is critical to the ability of libraries to meet the demands of policy makers seeking economic contributions from all social services. This challenge is exacerbated by the fact that most politicians approach value in terms of a business perspective that, as detailed above, does not fit comfortably with the history, goals, or activities of the public library. Public libraries have much value if we demonstrate it through available data, and there are some obvious places to start.

To be able to measure and demonstrate value, it is first necessary to determine what we mean by the value contributed by public libraries. *Value* can be defined in many ways, though most associations of value—including the expectations of value for adherents to neoconservative political and neoliberal economic ideologies—refer to it in a monetary or economic sense. The *Oxford English Dictionary*'s definitions of *value* are evaluative, emphasizing the materials, benefits, sum, and importance of an object, person, or thing from the perspective of the person making the judgment (*Oxford English Dictionary*, 2013a). Therefore, "value" in and of itself is a subjective term that changes based on the thought processes of those who make the determination of its definition. Value reflects on the perceived innate quality of something, whether that thing is a physical item or an abstract idea.

When considering the meaning of the word *value* as it is used in the field of library science, there are many varying perspectives on how libraries show their value to society. The discussions within librarianship do not exist in the abstract, however, and are heavily influenced by other perspectives on value and the expectations for value from those making decisions about policy and funding. Table 6.1 provides an overview of this range of diverse, and frequently divergent, perspectives.

Part of the challenge of determining the way in which to articulate library value is tied to the nature of what libraries do. Public libraries are educational institutions, and much of what educational institutions do is extraordinarily hard to quantify as a number. Additionally, funding for public libraries, like that for public schools, is primarily allocated by a local municipal body from tax monies. As such, libraries and schools might be expected to have similar definitions of value. Unfortunately, metrics from other educational institutions do not offer much help in producing a means to articulate and demonstrate library value.

From an educational perspective, value is most often calculated for specialized forms of education, such as vocational education or bilingual education or supplemental education, such as prekindergarten or postsecondary education (Labaree, 1997). Emphasis is placed on the evaluation and determination of value of various individual components of education. The movement of standardized tests to measure basic competencies that underlie No Child Left Behind, Common Core, and countless state-level educational competency examinations reflects this approach. The value of the typical K–12 public education is assessed through teacher evaluations, standardized tests, and similar metrics, but not often de-

Table 6.1. Selected Articulations of Value by Perspective

Field	Value
Library Science	Products are consumed by clients/customers
	What libraries do
	Benefits of use of library materials
	Return on investment (ROI)
	Librarians' Axiom
Education	Focus on components and types of education
	Teacher evaluations
	Standardized tests
Economic	Monetary worth
	Amount for exchange
Business	Value creation
	Return on investment (ROI)
	Public goods

Source: Jaeger, Bertot, Kodama, Katz, & DeCoster (2011).

termined or promoted as a whole entity (Rothstein & Jacobsen, 2006). Such assessments have placed sizeable constraints on what teachers have to do in the classroom, but they have created specific standards by which all teachers and students can be measured quantitatively.

Schools, like libraries and other public-sector or nonprofit organizations, have perhaps been slow to adopt the terminology of business in their self-evaluation or promotion. Yet, by using metrics based on numbers and assessments that appear businesslike, schools have fared better than libraries in arguing for financial support from adherents of neoconservative political and neoliberal economic ideologies. Libraries, however, are not able to perform assessment tests on patrons to determine how much they learned from the library or how well they fit predetermined metrics for achievement. As educational approaches to value are not of enormous help to libraries, another option is to try to learn from business and economic perspectives, which are most closely tied to value in a financial sense.

Library value is, in fact, often seen through the lens of a business model (Sykes, 2003; Van Moorsel, 2005). This approach to library value is evidenced by the widespread embrace of viewing patrons as "clients" or "customers" and treating the library as a business entity (Van Moorsel, 2005). The library is seen as a place where products (such as books and computers) and services (such as workshops and classes) are consumed by the library patron/client. In this approach, value is measured by the amount of use/nonuse of these products and services. "The value of a product/service offering is determined by client use. Unused, a product/ service has no value" (Van Moorsel, 2005, p. 29). All parties involved, the library patron and the library itself in this case, would need to have the same definition and conception of economic "value" in order for the library to evidence its worth to the broader society.

Reviewing the library science literature for definitions of value brings to attention the importance of the patron and the patron's needs when it comes to finding information. What the patron deems a valuable service or commodity needs to be of utmost importance to a librarian. When looking at libraries from a business angle, the job of the library and librarian is to satisfy the patrons, and give them what they desire when they walk into a library, whether that is a novel, computer access, government information, a class, or some other resource or service. In terms of value, then, the library can argue that its value lies in its impacts on "the lives of its customers" (Matthews, 2007, p. 136).

Not surprisingly, the idea of treating patrons as customers, and referring to them as such, is far from a universally popular notion among librarians (Auld, 2004; Budd, 1997). In 1998, *American Libraries* magazine published an article in which the author argued for the advantages of running public libraries as if they were bookstores (Coffman & Varek, 1998). While libraries have subsequently embraced many of the ideas in the article, the national bookstore chains to which the author pointed as service models to emulate have mostly gone out of business, indicating that such bookstore chains are probably a terrible model to emulate. For example, in 2003, the London library system opened what they labeled "Idea Stores"—heavily branded libraries modeled on retail principles that have customer service experts but, oddly, no trained librarians on staff (Ezard, 2003).

Other recent suggestions for measuring library value have hewed much closer to traditional approaches within the library literature. Such suggested approaches include qualitative metrics for documenting the ways in which libraries are perceived to build community trust (Brown, 2001), contribute to quality of life (McCook & Brand, 2001), help patrons (Durrance & Fisher, 2005), change lives (C. Hill, 2009b), and create social capital (Johnson, 2010). While all of these approaches may document the actual value of libraries, they will likely not gain traction in the current data-driven political environment, as they all rely upon qualitative explanations of the importance of libraries. Such explanations of value will fail to resonate in the age of austerity, as they will be seen as too similar to assertions, rather than demonstrations, of value.

SEARCHING FOR LIBRARY VALUE

The *Oxford English Dictionary* offers a second definition of *value* as "the material or monetary worth of a thing; the amount at which it may be estimated in terms of some medium of exchange or other standard of a similar nature" (*Oxford English Dictionary*, 2013b). Since *thing* is a vague term, it is easy to bridge the concept of the monetary worth of intangible items such as information and data, factors which have always been viewed as essential to economic success, to their evolution as commodities in and of themselves.

The monetization of intangible concepts such as information and knowledge has created complications from business and economics perspectives. Time-tested formulas do not exist by which the monetary value of these concepts can be measured, though certainly information does have a value, and that value can vary by timeliness, quality, individual and/or societal need, and a range of other factors (Kingma, 2001). If said information, knowledge, and/or data results in the creation of a commodity, then perhaps a monetary figure can be proposed. But when information itself becomes the commodity, it is extremely difficult to impose an accepted, validated, and reliable fiscal value. This is an area in which libraries in particular struggle, as providing access to information is, at the very least, one of their core functions.

In a climate that emphasizes the value of social institutions in terms of financial measures, the majority of concepts of value suggested in the library literature do not successfully translate the activities, services, and resources of a public library and their contributions to patrons, communities, and society into dollar figures. Application of the concept of ROI in libraries highlights this disjuncture. The concept of ROI is a common and frequently used metric for businesses to calculate the all-in costs, from development to production to marketing to sales, of products. ROI is calculated after the sale of a product or service, deducting the total amount of effort and resources used in research, design, development, implementation, evaluation, and marketing. This way of thinking about value thereby steers the definition of value toward an economic viewpoint of the word. From this approach, information specialists and librarians cannot maintain their value based on what they *can* or are able to do, but on what they *actually* do (Sykes, 2003). Results then are a significant aspect to defining the value of an information professional or librarian. How information professionals contribute to the larger community, whether that community is an organization, business, or city, is what gives them their value. This approach can be seen in studies that compare the costs of the collection and library operation to estimations of the benefits of the use of the library and its materials (Matthews, 2007).

The typical formula for determining ROI can be summarized as "'Price' minus 'Cost' divided by 'Sales'" (O'Neil & Hansen, 2001, pp.

708–710). A positive ROI proves that the initial cost outlay for a product was a worthwhile investment. The ALA's *Advocating in a Tough Economy Toolkit* (2009) argues for the use of these types of ROI tools. Following this business model, several libraries, as well as the ALA, have created ROI calculators to emphasize the cost-saving nature of their information products:

- The peer-based ROI calculator created by the Library Research Service for Colorado's public libraries (http://www.lrs.org/public/roi/calculator.php). Using four basic categories, Colorado public libraries can select from a similar library system to calculate the monetary benefit to their communities.
- Using a total of twelve categories based on the one created by the Maine State Library (http://www.maine.gov/msl/services/calculator.htm), the Library Research Service has also created a slightly more complicated ROI calculator for taxpayers to estimate the return on tax dollars offered by libraries (http://www.lrs.org/public/roi/usercalculator.php).
- The ALA's Library Value Calculator (http://www.ala.org/ala/issuesadvocacy/advocacy/advocacyuniversity/toolkit/makingthecase/library_calculator.cfm) was created by the Massachusetts Library Association and uses eighteen categories to calculate taxpayers' returns.

While certainly providing a clear visual to theoretically calculate tax investment compared to returns for communities, complications arise when reviewing the valuation systems used for the categories.

Using these three major examples of ROI calculators to prove the fiscal worth of libraries, single-source prices appear to be a common method of measuring value, such as Amazon for book costs and Barnes and Noble for e-book download costs (http://www.swissarmylibrarian.net/librarycalculator/valuecalc_costs.html). The sources used are a good starting point by which to gauge costs; the aforementioned ROI calculators, however, do not actually average costs, since *average*, by definition, indicates a measurement of more than one source. Additionally, none of the calculators adjust for diminishing value, depreciation, inflation, or other cost fluctuations. Cost valuations remain static, which, while certainly assisting with advocating for the community value of libraries, is not necessarily a true measure of ROI. The utility of all the calculators is ultimately undone by the fact that the mechanistic counting and measuring of library activities as widgets fails to demonstrate the importance of library information, services, programs, and outreach provided to communities.

In part, this is an issue that public libraries and the LIS research community invited, through efforts such as *Output Measures for Public Libraries* (Zweizig and Rodger, 1982) and subsequent assessment approaches built upon output measures that emphasize the quantity of a library's resources and the extent to which patrons consume these resources, rather than the value of the products produced and/or added by the library. Indeed, these initial efforts were instrumental to the development of the national Public Library Statistics collection effort currently managed by the IMLS (IMLS, 2011b). As such, the predominant library assessment framework that evolved and to some extent still exists today measures how often materials (print, digital, and other) circulate and how often resources (e.g., public-access computers) are used—with the assumption that more use is of greater value than less use. These mechanical measures, however, reveal absolutely nothing about the impacts of the usage on the patrons or the community or the uniqueness of what libraries provide as a social institution rather than a repository of materials.

These measures seem even more out of step with value demonstration in the age of austerity based on the fact that austerity may very well serve as a backdrop for the reinvention of communities. Funding education is one major issue facing communities in an environment of austerity, with some communities grappling with numerous challenges in the areas of literacy and dropout rates (National Center for Education Statistics, 2009). Other community issues exist as well, in areas such as health and wellness, employment, and economic development (Seattle Foundation, 2009). In today's constrained financial environment, the issue is less how to meet each of these challenges through traditional approaches and more about rethinking and mobilizing local assets such as public libraries, schools, and other community organizations to meet these challenges. This movement, dubbed "smart cities," involves innovative combinations of open government, engagement efforts, crowd-sourcing, and other techniques to benefit communities. In this context, there is a need to view the role of the public library as an engaged participant—with articulated goals and measurable objectives—to demonstrate its value. One scholar of urban planning has dubbed public libraries "the economic engines" of urban areas that draw people downtown and "generate increased business for local merchants" (Senville, 2009, p. 18), making public libraries central to the concept of a smart city.

One option for public libraries therefore is to focus on emphasizing value creation—"to achieve competitive advantages, a firm must create more value than its competitors in the industry" (Lin & Lin, 2006, p. 93). While it may be a ubiquitous perception that libraries have vast competition in the area of information dissemination, no other organizations provide such an all-encompassing wealth of information and education to use the information as the public library. Search engines and other Internet resources lack the ability to provide education, literacy training, or guidance in using or selecting information sources (Waller, 2009). Because libraries' revenue streams are derived from funding by their local communities, however, there is not an empirical way to prove their financial worth in the same way in which business analysts can gauge, for example, the value of Google.

While it is possible to draw similarities between libraries and an information-oriented company such as Google, libraries offer a physical location not only in which people can be assisted in their information searches, but in which people with limited or no knowledge in a subject can access a resource or call upon the expertise and knowledge of an information specialist who can help them develop the skills and literacies needed to accomplish their information-related goals. The ubiquity of Google as a locator of information, in contrast, presupposes a level of technological knowledge and information literacy, not to mention access to the technologies through which one can access the site.

Since public libraries can be viewed as organizations providing a product (access to information) to patrons/consumers (the public), and since patrons/consumers already have preconceptions about libraries (whether good, bad, or neutral), it follows that libraries, much like any other organization providing a product, should take a proactive stance on how they brand and market themselves. "When the local library comes to mind, there should be a key message or picture of the library that residents recall" (McClure, Feldman, & Ryan, 2006, pp. 152–153).

Such steps would require overcoming some librarians' inherent resistance to marketing the library (Jaeger, Bertot, Kodama, Katz, & DeCoster, 2011; Jaeger, Gorham, Sarin, & Bertot, in press; Parker, Kaufman-Scarborough, & Parker, 2007). By creating business plans that include branding and value creation, libraries can enhance their existing and established product lines and thereby highlight their fiscal and other contributions to the public. "Brands, after all, are nothing but the information—real or imagined, intellectual or emotional—that consumers have in their heads about a product" (Evans & Wurster, 1997, pp. 72–73). Thus, branding and marketing efforts have the potential to help public libraries to define and create value (perceived or real) in the marketplace that can then be employed as a basis of demonstrating value to politicians and policy makers.

Simultaneously, however, the library profession needs to enhance its use of empirical assessments and measure the contributions of public libraries to community challenges such as education, employment and economic development, and health and wellness. For far too long, public libraries have relied on input (resource investment) and output measures (resources available and used) to demonstrate value (Jaeger, Bertot, Kodama, Katz, & DeCoster, 2011). These only go so far, but more importantly, we are seeing a downward trend in key output statistics (Swan et al., 2013). As a narrative, public libraries traditionally have equated increased usage with value—but what happens when usage goes down, as we are seeing in key areas such as library visits? Does this mean decreased value? Output measures are limited and do not answer the critical questions about the impact of library service usage on literacy, community health, building a twenty-first-century workforce, and many other important contributions to communities.

Even with these attempts and their limitations, libraries still come up against the same problems as economists when attempting to quantify an intangible asset such as information. "Economists define information as a phenomenon to reduce uncertainty and it is usually studied in terms of exchange values" (Repo, 1989, p. 68). Information as a public good, though, has received some attention within the greater study of economics:

> [Public goods] . . . are not divisible into units that can be sold separately. Consumption by one person does not reduce the amount available to others. . . . Common examples of public goods are streets and roads, national security, and public libraries. Though it is hard to define exactly where the borderline between public and private goods lies, it is obvious that many available information products and services have some characteristics of public goods. (Repo, 1989, p. 72)

Because politicians and policy makers are comfortable and familiar with ROI calculators and other business-based metrics, using these tools to quantify the value of public libraries may be a useful method. But to truly calculate community value, public libraries need to employ measurements of services provided by libraries, including information and knowledge sharing, technology, literacy training, homework help, meeting spaces, and employment resources, to name a few, that are of a fiscally indefinable nature.

One area that clearly offers great potential to measure and express the economic value of public libraries is in the Internet-based services and resources that assist in education, technological literacy, job seeking, applications for social services, and other measurable contributions to the economy. If libraries can express the numbers of jobs and social services applied for and received, for example, they can show real economic value: adding employees to the economy, simultaneously decreasing the need for unemployment benefits and increasing the number of taxpayers, while also reducing the need for specific government agencies outside of libraries to assist people applying for social services. A 2010 study estimated that 30 million people had used library computers and Internet access to search for employment, with an astounding 3.7 million people actually being hired for a position they applied for through the library computers (Becker et al., 2010). The enormous contributions of the public library in the ongoing economic downturn need to be recorded and demonstrated to those making funding decisions. Demonstrating these types of numbers may enable libraries to speak in the language of policy makers, who currently exist in an environment that requires even traffic lights to have a demonstrable economic contribution.

That the potential of Internet-based services and resources is the key to demonstrating library value to policy makers is particularly ironic in light of the resistance to the Internet in libraries strongly expressed within some quarters of librarianship itself. But the changing nature of public libraries through time means that they have been able to adapt to changing social needs and economic circumstances. The Internet is evidence of this ability to evolve. While the definitions of the institution we call the public library may shift and change depending on the social and economic climate of a particular era, their importance to patrons and communities is evident and unmistakable.

The Internet-enabled roles of public libraries offer a clear example of how libraries can articulate and demonstrate value in the economic language that is essential to communicate with politicians and policy makers. Providing data-driven demonstrations of library value ultimately will not overcome all of the resistance to public libraries that has been created by neoconservative political and neoliberal economic ideologies. However, even if libraries cannot be kept out of harm's swift way, politically engaged and data-driven advocacy will at least make it more difficult for politicians and policy makers to render with impunity decisions that are detrimental to libraries.

SEVEN

Demonstrating Library Value and Advocating for Support

As the previous chapters have demonstrated, there is no shortage of opportunities for public library practitioners, educators, researchers, students, and patrons to engage policy-making, political, and funding processes to advocate for outcomes that support public libraries. Many recipes have been offered for engaging in policy or politics or funding, but they tend to oddly treat these elements as unrelated, and few of the approaches offered tie the advocacy to actual data to support the positions being advocated. This lack of coordination is also reflected in the entities seeking to influence policy-making, political, and funding processes on behalf of libraries. For example, the ALA has a Washington Office of Government Relations, a Committee on Legislation, an Office for Library Advocacy, and a Federal Library Legislative and Advocacy Network, among other parts of its national organization working to influence policy and politics. Having so many voices does not result in a coherent or coordinated approach.

To better advocate for public libraries and the best interests of library professionals and patrons, library advocacy needs to be coordinated and coherent at several levels:

- the message should be conveyed consistently by voices within the library profession and library supporters;
- outreach to decision makers and community members needs to be simultaneous and related;
- the message should be presented in terms that make sense to members of the community and to decision makers;
- the message needs to be based on data that will be understood by decision makers; and

- policy, politics, and funding need to be seen as an interrelated set of issues.

Achieving these goals is much more complicated than it sounds, which likely explains why public libraries continue to struggle to positively impact decisions in policy, politics, and funding.

The ALA's *Library Advocate's Handbook* (2003) outlines advocacy as a process of defining goals and objectives, assessing the context, identifying tasks, communicating a message, crafting a work plan, and evaluating the outcome. While these approaches are sensible in the abstract, the largest problems libraries face in political and policy processes are not related to their failure to be systematic about engagement. The problems relate to engaging in a way that does not present the full picture of public libraries—politics, policy, advocacy, history, and services as a united whole—in society. The ultimate goal of demonstrating library value and advocating for the support of libraries is to change the current political and policy discourse into an environment far more supportive of public libraries and their contributions.

BEYOND THE LIGHTHOUSE

Advocacy for public libraries based on active engagement with policy-making processes and employing data-driven demonstrations of value in the language of political discourse will help to improve the standing of libraries under policy and funding decisions. However, these efforts must also be accompanied by a broader engagement to help members of the public at large better understand all of the contributions of the public library.

The study that found 91 percent of members of the public believing that public libraries are important to their communities also found, alarmingly, that only 22 percent of respondents were familiar with most or all of the services offered by their public library (Zickuhr, Rainie, & Purcell, 2013). The public library clearly needs to apply advocacy and marketing initiatives that will reach both nonpatrons of the public library (so that they will at least understand its contributions) and patrons of the library (so that they will be able to avail themselves of all aspects of the public library). This engagement also needs to include efforts to shift how the public library is conceived within the range of public goods—the concept as it is generally understood does a great disservice to the breadth of contributions of the public library.

When someone is trying to explain the idea of the public good, the odds are rather high that a lighthouse will be used as the example, particularly in textbooks. Lighthouses carry enormous societal benefits for all members of the public—primarily, allowing for the safe delivery of food and other essential goods and passengers over water—while also incentivizing the operation of ships by protecting the investment of shipowners. Without lighthouses, there would be less shipping or no shipping at all, significantly raising the prices on many goods or making them unavailable altogether. With reduced shipping, cities that have ports may struggle to support their own economies. Yet building a lighthouse is expensive, far too expensive for most individuals and companies that own ships.

Governments build lighthouses, then, because they benefit the public and the economy in many important ways. They are a clear example of the public good. However, they are only one kind of public good, and thinking of all public goods as the equivalent of lighthouses serves to limit the ability of some public goods to serve the public to their fullest potential. The cost of building and operating a lighthouse is the same on any given day if one ship or if one hundred ships pass by the lighthouse. The amount of the input provides the same result no matter how many times the lighthouse is used. And greatly expanding the budget of a lighthouse will not significantly change what the lighthouse contributes to the community. It is a public good, but the extent of the public good is finite.

Public libraries help the community in many different ways and provide many resources and services that would not otherwise exist in a community. In contrast to lighthouses, they are a very different kind of public good. The contribution of public libraries to the public good is not static. The more plentiful and stable public library funding is, the more people it can help; the greater number of services, resources, and materials it can provide; the more community partnerships it can create; and the bigger impact it can have on its community. The size of the public good generated by the public library grows with the amount of support given to the library. Due to their resources and the skills of staff members, public libraries can become centers for social services, emergency response and recovery, e-government, digital literacy and inclusion, job training, and innumerable other contributions to the health of the community, so long as they are provided sufficient support. The public library is, in short, a public good that can adapt and expand through proportional increases in funding. The inherently fox-like nature of the public library makes it a very unique public good.

To adequately convey the impact of public libraries, we need a term that better captures the nature of public libraries as a public good. They are more than just a public good; they are a *community good*. The more the public library is supported, the more value to the community it generates and the more members of the community it helps. This is a very rare attribute among public goods, as most public goods—from parks to traffic lights—have a discernable upper limit on how much they can support the community. Just as economists distinguish between public goods and common-pool resources, the nature of the public library as a unique kind of public good—a community good—must be made clear through our advocacy efforts.

Explaining the nature of public libraries as a community good is an essential part of better advocating for public libraries, but it is merely a part of the argument. The picture that libraries have of themselves, and thus the picture they present externally in advocacy, is not a mosaic but merely a series of fragments. The fact that this book is the first attempt to bring the politics, policy, advocacy, history, and services related to public libraries together demonstrates a failure to create integrated portraits of what libraries do for their communities and how those contributions can be articulated to drive support of libraries. The public library as a community good may be the linchpin of the argument, but advocacy must present the nature and contributions of the public library as an integrated whole.

REASSERTING THE PUBLIC GOOD, ASSERTING THE COMMUNITY GOOD

Crafting a more detailed and more nuanced description of the library's contributions as a public good and deploying this description is the foundation of increasing the effectiveness of advocating for policies and funding decisions that will help public libraries succeed. Politicians and policy makers do not typically focus on how their decisions impact everyday people's lives in the long term; they must be educated about issues "to be cognizant of the real-life consequences of their policy choices" (Greenberg & Dratel, 2005, xxiii). The fact that policy makers and politicians frequently fail to comprehend the ramifications of their decisions for libraries is due in no small part to the way libraries present themselves. Public library advocacy has to do a far better job of explaining how funding and policy choices impact public libraries and their ability to effectively serve as a community good.

If politicians and policy makers understood that their choices expand or limit the ability of public libraries to serve the community good, different policy and political choices might be made. Based on the materials discussed throughout this book, a thorough approach to trying to continually and productively engage political, policy-making, and funding processes on behalf of public libraries might begin with the following:

1. Creating and using meaningful data to articulate the community good. Instead of relying on assertions of value, libraries must learn to demonstrate their value in terms that make sense to decision makers (Jaeger, Bertot, Kodama, Katz, & DeCoster, 2011). A combination of means can be used to demonstrate value, including an analysis of the economic benefits of use of library materials, ROI, the Librarian's Axiom, measures of products consumed by pa-

trons, and the larger social benefits of funding libraries as a way to support local communities, among many others. The activities and impacts of the public library need to be conveyed through the data and language that are the coin of the realm in the kingdom of austerity (Jaeger, Gorham, Sarin, & Bertot, in press).

2. Raising a voice. Public libraries have to learn to speak for themselves in a strong and coordinated voice. Public libraries will be more likely to make an impact by simultaneously communicating the value and contributions of the library through marketing (e.g., selling to the community) and advocating for policies that positively impact libraries (e.g., lobbying in the policy process) (Nelson, 2006).

3. Empowering all members of the library staff to advocate. In training public librarians in advocacy, one author of this book has repeatedly been told that front-end librarians do not see advocacy as part of their position, though many feel quite the opposite. One public librarian recently stated in one of these training sessions, "Advocacy isn't part of my job. It's part of my library director's job but not mine. In fact, if I did try and advocate, I'm pretty sure my director would be angry with me for stepping on his/her toes" (Jaeger, Gorham, Sarin, & Bertot, in press, n.p.). Empowering all members of the library staff to be advocates for the interests of the library will greatly increase the number of educated voices of support.

4. Spurring other voices to speak for the library. Effective library advocates can be trustees, friends of the library, patrons, library partners, community members, community leaders, educators, and retired library staff (Imhoff, 2006).

5. Using many avenues to engage in the discourse. Successful advocacy campaigns can include support of high-level community members, organized committees, speaker bureaus for community events, polling, public relations, focusing on the groups most likely to be supportive and engaged, guest editorials in local media, statements of support from local politicians, information tables in libraries, advertisements, and endorsements from colleges and universities, homeowner and condominium associations, celebrities, unions, and Chambers of Commerce (Imhoff, 2006).

6. Using new technologies and tools to advocate. When New York City was considering cutting library funding so significantly that it would necessitate the closure of forty-five public library branches, Christian Zabriskie, the founder of Urban Librarians Unite and a New York City librarian, wrote an articulate and affecting explanation of the potential toll on individuals and communities of such closures for the *Huffington Post* (Zabriskie, 2013). By using such a channel to disseminate his message, it was quickly picked up in

social media and even shared by some celebrities encouraging their followers to advocate for library support.

7. Becoming educated and remaining engaged. For a number of reasons discussed earlier, the majority of public librarians have historically disconnected themselves from political and policy processes, instead clinging to a carapace of neutrality (Jaeger, Gorham, Sarin, & Bertot, in press). This approach is the diametric opposite of what is currently needed. If everyone is using omnipresent media to argue their point of view, public libraries need to be informed and vocal to have any chance of being heard.

8. Looking for ramifications that may not be intended. Many of the consequences of political and policy decisions for public libraries are not the intent of those making the decisions, for whom libraries are rarely a consideration. As a result, many laws—like copyright laws and national security guidelines—have unintended major impacts on public libraries (Jaeger, Bertot, & Gorham, 2013). A key aspect of being educated and engaged with policy, political, and funding processes means forbearance against decisions that will have significant unintended consequences for libraries.

9. Perceiving politics, policy, funding, advocacy, history, and services as an interrelated system. Too often, the impacts on public libraries are viewed as discrete factors (e.g., "technology usage is up") or as limited correlations (e.g., "technology usage is up because the economy is bad"). While the basic correlation may be true, the big picture involves the interrelationships between many factors. Without seeing those factors as a complicated system, and advocating accordingly, the risk of arguing for the wrong outcome rises considerably.

10. Speaking to decision makers and members of the community in terms that assume some intelligence, at least on the part of public library professionals. Glittery distractions like how many more libraries there are than McDonald's restaurants or Wal-Mart stores or Jiffy Lube centers do little to convince people that public libraries have real value or what that value might be.

11. Being honest about the implications of funding decisions. Libraries must "make the library's expenditures understandable to as many constituents as possible" (Holt, 2013, p. 68). Public libraries must convey that they are effectively using money to do what the community needs, but they also must show that insufficient funding results in negative shifts in services and resources.

12. Crafting messages that show what the library means to individuals and to the community. Most people, even those who regularly use the library, do not know the full range of its services and contributions to communities (Zickuhr, Rainie, & Purcell, 2013). Con-

veying everything that the library does and why it matters is a central component of improving advocacy.

13. Crafting messages that vary by interests of different decision makers and stakeholder groups. The wide range of contributions of a public library to individuals and to communities ensures an equally wide range of potential messages. Complementary messages tailored to the primary focus of different groups can cultivate support from a number of different groups who might not be swayed by a single monolithic message.

14. Making the case for the public library as a unique part of a broader social system. The library is an entirely unique public good—a community good—the chameleon able to change itself to meet new or pressing community needs as they arise. This wholly unique nature needs to be central to library advocacy. Public libraries are truly irreplaceable, and there is no shame in reminding policy makers, politicians, and community members of this fact.

These steps are offered as a logical place for starting the dialogue, as the advocacy and value demonstration challenges facing public libraries are currently so large that the correct answers will only become obvious through much trial and error.

For example, the issue of how to best frame and demonstrate the value of public libraries in political, policy, and funding discourse depends on the answers to several major questions:

- How can libraries use the language of the new public philosophy to convey our contributions so that politicians and policy makers will understand the message?
- How do statements of neutrality affect our value in the minds of politicians and policy makers?
- How can MLS programs, professional organizations, and continuing education programs be designed to incorporate principles of advocacy into the training of all library professionals?
- What research topics can library scholars pursue to provide data that will best help libraries demonstrate their value?
- How can libraries influence the perceptions of value that shape funding decisions?
- How can the philosophical ties between libraries and democracy be more meaningfully conveyed to show a tangible impact?
- How can libraries counter the narratives created by neoliberal economic and neoconservative political ideologies?

These will not be simple questions to answer, but the key thing is to start engaging and advocating in a much more coherent and committed manner than has been attempted thus far. Fear of mistakes cannot be a barrier, though, as trying and learning from mistakes will have fewer negative ramifications than not trying at all.

WE'RE ALL ALONE?

The areas of focus and questions for further consideration above are offered as key parts of an approach for public libraries and their supporters to effectively engage political, policy-making, and funding processes. But planning and strategizing alone will not guarantee success in sustaining support of public libraries in the contexts of policy, politics, or funding. Libraries have to make clear their contributions and relevance in an environment that can be rather hostile to the library and its goals.

Changing perceptions of technology have led to apathy toward libraries among those who do not use them. Many media commentators who are ready to bury the public library admit to never using them or having any idea what goes on inside them now (Rosenblum, 2013). They primarily come from the affluent and educated classes who do not understand the community good provided by the public library (Zabriskie, 2013). In fact, refuting these pervasive but uninformed critiques can seem like a job in itself (Meade, 2013). Nevertheless, the affluent who have moved more and more of their social, educational, and commercial activities online are a large and vocal force. Most of the private-sector entities that filled similar community space and community learning roles as public libraries— bookstores, music stores, video stores—have disappeared in the past decade (DePillis, 2013).

The first twenty years of the Internet age have shown that many social institutions may be less permanent than previously thought. Public libraries would be wise to remember that another part of the country known as an "arsenal of democracy"—the derelict but once-vibrant industrial region of the United States now called the Rust Belt—was until recent decades considered one of the defining elements of the country and one of the keys to future success for the nation (McClelland, 2013). The historical importance of public libraries and the public goodwill for them will not be enough to ensure positive political, policy, and funding outcomes.

The past twenty years have also seen some fairly titanic shifts in national political structures that make changing the national political discourse even more challenging. Along with the previously discussed rise of neoliberal economic and neoconservative political ideologies as the core of national governance, changes in the structure of elections to national office have resulted in a much less dynamic conversation at the national level.

In 1992, there were 103 members of the House of Representatives from swing districts, in which either party had a realistic chance to win in any given election; now there are only 35 swing districts left (Silver, 2012b). In contrast, 242 districts are hyperpartisan, consistently delivering landslides for one party. Resulting largely from the redistricting of seats in the House of Representatives to make them "safe" for the party doing the redistricting, this means that the vast majority of members of the House only face a viable challenge to their seat in the primaries. The focus on the primary serves to fuel partisanship by making the races about pleasing the base of the majority party rather than courting mainstream voters in a general election.

Major increases in fundraising and campaign spending, particularly on negative ads, have served to suppress interest in politics by middle-of-the-road voters (Pearlstein, 2012). Ads that are negative and ideological alter the composition of voters on election days by simultaneously energizing the hyperpartisan base and alienating moderate voters, furthering the partisanship of the people who get elected. With growing disregard for moderate voters, elections have become a tragedy of the commons, with the self-interest of politicians serving to embrace the partisanship that inhibits the functioning of the political system. The ability to solve societal issues relies on the cooperation of actors with different perspectives, based on the ability to hold others accountable and keep them involved (Young, 2006). Not surprisingly, making elections more partisan and less appealing to mainstream voters does little to promote cooperation between different stakeholders.

The hyperpartisan atmosphere in Washington has polarized the members of Congress on both sides of the political aisle, with institutions and programs that formerly received consensus support becoming the subject of obstructions, filibusters, and antipathy due to ideology (Mann & Ornstein, 2012). New policies are likely to be rejected, and the parties can be seen as actively trying to sabotage existing laws simply to score political points (Sargent, 2013). "Partisans who expect every idea to fit on a bumper sticker will proceed through the various stages of grief before accepting that they have oversimplified reality" (Silver, 2012a, p. 452). Even social institutions that formerly enjoyed near-complete consensus, such as public libraries, have turned into partisan issues in this environment.

The resistance to change in Congress is also tied to the age of members and the lengths of their stays in office. Keeping the same people in power is not likely to produce different results. In 2011, the average Republican in Congress was 56 years old, and the average Democratic member of Congress was 60.8 years old, up about five years from a decade previous. In 2013, then-eighty-seven-year-old congressman John Dingell had spent more than two-thirds of his life in Congress. Redistricting has served to not only make districts more partisan and end the term limits movement; it has also made getting reelected easier, extending the number of times most members of Congress serve, so people in Congress serve much longer and become more entrenched while they are there (Cillizza, 2013a).

The entrenched and partisan nature of Congress has also negatively impacted its ability to pass any laws. The 112th Congress passed fewer laws than any preceding Congress since records have been kept (Cillizza, 2013b). This historic level of nonproductivity occurred in spite of the 112th Congress recording the fifth-highest recorded total of votes. Most of these votes were taken for partisan reasons and were doomed to fail, such as the more than 60 votes taken to repeal the Affordable Care Act during the 112th Congress (Milbank, 2013). In late 2013, a veteran Washington reporter published a book detailing the ways in which the enormous influence of special interests, political action groups, and the promises of lucrative consulting jobs after retirement from government service now conspire to sustain a permanent moneyed, governing class that provides limited incentive for Congress to pass any legislation (Leibovich, 2013).

Entering such a partisan and entrenched environment can be very risky for any community-minded group. For example, climate scientists, by trying to directly engage in political battles to advocate for policies and funding decisions that will help reduce global warming, have hurt their position by poorly engaging in politics and policy making. The number of Americans who believe in climate change is actually decreasing, in spite of the none-too-subtle increases in temperature and extreme weather events. Because they have not engaged the policy process as a politician would, climate scientists have made a case to the public that did not resonate (Silver, 2012a). As scientific evidence generally cannot be expressed in terms of black and white or with 100 percent precision, the hyperpartisan atmosphere serves to make scientific evidence seem uncertain and confused. Conservative politicians and political groups have been able to conflate the exploratory nature of scientific research with real, ongoing changes in the environment to convince many members of the public that global warming is merely the aimless blade of science seeking more research funding.

RESPONSIBILITY ROLLS DOWN

As the example of global warming demonstrates, better engagement in the world of politics and policy making will not be easy and will not be without risk. It is not a choice of whether or not to engage political and policy-making processes, however. Doing nothing different is the worst possible option. Other agencies of government have learned that passive public libraries are a place to which they can devolve many responsibilities and obligations (Jaeger & Bertot, 2011). More perniciously, the events of recent years have shown that inaction and limited engagement leads to politics that degrade libraries, policies that simultaneously constrain library activities and call upon them to take on additional responsibilities, and funding decisions that bleed libraries dry.

Libraries and their supporters must not only engage political, policy-making, and funding processes; they must do so in ways that are not based on the notion of being all things to all people. While the unique nature of the public library as a community good allows it to serve its community in a wide-ranging and adaptable manner, trying to be all things to all people is as much of a problem as a lack of funds. Justifying continued support by taking on every task sent the way of public libraries by other government agencies will only lead to paralysis and inability to provide any services effectively.

Looking for support by assisting larger policy initiatives sounds good initially, but this approach can be problematic for libraries as they struggle to meet mounting responsibilities and get involved in political fights for which they have not prepared themselves. Many libraries already find themselves in this predicament. Since 2000, public libraries have taken on significant new roles in providing e-government, social services, tax filing, immigration processes, disaster response and recovery, and many other areas, usually without gaining any additional support for taking on these duties. The risks with this strategy—and the accompanying lack of rewards—were evidenced in the summer of 2013.

Under the Affordable Care Act, about 7 million people are expected to sign up online for health insurance, and a great many of them will depend on public library resources and services to do so (Eberhart, 2013). With 15 percent of American adults being nonusers of the Internet (Zickuhr, 2013), much of the work with health-care enrollment will begin at teaching basic digital literacy. Many of these will be additional patrons beyond the 28 million public library patrons who currently use library computers to search for health and wellness information on a regular basis (Pera, 2013). The U.S. Department of Health and Human Services is expecting considerable support from public libraries in both informing people about options and helping them enroll, without providing any support to help libraries meet these expectations. As IMLS Director Susan Hildreth noted, "there are no federal funds to support this program" (Eberhart, 2013, n.p.).

President Obama recorded a special video message thanking librarians for helping with the implementation of the Affordable Care Act, but only allowed the ALA to show the video once at its annual convention. Members of the public were not allowed to see the video (Morrongiello, 2013). In summary, the national leaders representing public libraries in the ALA and IMLS acquiesced to an enormous new burden to inform and help enroll millions of uninsured people in a new online government program without receiving additional funding and with the only recognition of their assistance being a recorded message that could be played once, entirely away from the eyes of the public.

Not only is the situation absurd; it also has the potential to cause enormous problems for librarians working in public libraries in states that are refusing to comply with the law. Along with the aforementioned incessant attempts by Republicans in Congress to repeal the law, some Republican-led state governments are trying to undermine the law by preventing it from being implemented in their states (Somashekhar, 2013). These efforts range from limiting consumer protections to preventing federal workers from promoting enrollment. In Missouri, however, the voters approved a ballot initiative that bans state and local government officials from helping to implement the law. This places the public librarians of the state between a state regulation barring them from helping patrons sign up for insurance under the Affordable Care Act and a national initiative from ALA and IMLS saying they are professionally obligated to help patrons with the same. More politically engaged organizations would have anticipated such potential difficulties in this political climate and planned around them.

Similarly, if the issues that the library tries to engage are not well chosen, the results will be detrimental. As previously discussed, the CIPA lawsuit is such an example. The decision to challenge the popular law on its face, as opposed to waiting for its implementation, allowed libraries to be portrayed as defending content to which much of the public objected, rather than protecting patrons from the expansiveness of a law affecting access to important information by actual patrons. Taking on pet issues of the library community that are not of great significance to the public at large or that are not yet ready for public debate or that are simply too unpopular to succeed will result in an erosion of public support, along the lines of the climate scientists ineffectively working to change policy in order to halt global warming.

Libraries cannot take on every role thrown at them by other agencies, and they must choose the issues that they engage carefully. An important guiding principle for libraries engaging policy, political, and funding processes is that the issues that are engaged and the advocacy stances that are taken should tie directly to the communities that public libraries serve. Part of this strategic engagement also needs to account for the differences among libraries themselves. Different libraries have different amounts of space, staff, technology, and other resources that shape the practical ability to provide specific services. A large, urban public library system may have dozens of branches, thousands of computers, and hundreds of librarians with which to engage a new task. In contrast, rural public libraries—those serving communities of fewer than 25,000 people—have on average less than one (.75) librarian with a master's degree from an ALA-accredited institution; an average total of four staff, including both full- and part-time employees; a median annual income (from all sources) of $118,704.50; and typically one building/branch that is open an average of forty hours per week (IMLS, 2013). Clearly, the average urban library system is going to have a much better chance of dealing with an influx of patrons looking to sign up for health insurance online than the average rural public library.

If standing still is no longer an option, the choices of which direction to move in can seem overwhelming. Inertia is facilitated by the overwhelming number of historical cases where the failure to plan for the correct challenges had terrible outcomes. Just as one example, the catastrophic loss of lives, planes, and ships inflicted by the Japanese navy on the U.S. military at Pearl Harbor were made possible by the U.S. military planning for the wrong problem. The U.S. military feared not a military attack, but sabotage operations, so planes were kept wingtip to wingtip in open areas to make them easier to guard, and ships were moored close together for similar reasons (Wohlstetter, 1962). By placing all of their emphasis on the wrong threat, the U.S. military made their planes and ships much easier targets when the actual threat arrived.

Dwelling too much on examples such as these can promote inertia, a luxury that the public library simply does not have at this point. Public libraries have reached the point of absolutely needing to act. Fortunately, the way forward is clearer than it might seem. As a community good, the best chance that public libraries have for effectively engaging political, policy-making, and funding processes is successfully demonstrating positive outcomes in those same local communities that are so closely connected to their public libraries.

EIGHT

The Public Library in the Local Political Process

The decades in which the neoliberal economic ideology and the neocon-servative political ideology have defined national politics have not been particularly kind to local governments in many ways. Twenty years ago, predictions were made that local governments were "in for a decade of excruciating pain" (Osborne, 1993, p. 349), due to more responsibilities and expectations devolving to local government, a trend that continues to this day. These changes, however, have also led to local government becoming the level of government at which community challenges are met and where innovative approaches to community building are being generated. Just as public libraries have adapted in the changing political and economic climate, local governments have done the same.

Local governments have historically been seen as having either a public focus or a private focus in their operations, with public-focused local governments putting a greater emphasis on public planning, public infra-structure, and public service (Banfield & Wilson, 1963; Wolfinger & Field, 1966). While some city managers have applied private-sector principles to promote efficiency and treat citizens as customers of local government (Kearney, Feldman, & Scavo, 2000), a large number of local governments remain firmly public focused as they have taken on new responsibilities and expectations. Regardless of how it is framed, the embrace of manage-rial innovation within a local government has been shown to strongly determine whether that government will readily adopt new approaches and technologies to provide government services (Moon & Norris, 2005).

Innovation in local government is essential to the economic success of communities. "Cities are the new economic engines. They're also places where partisan politics must take a backseat to real postpartisan innova-tion and risk-taking" (Newsom & Dickey, 2013, p. 228). Simply to keep

residents, cities have to be more innovative than state or federal governments. If a city becomes noncompetitive, it is a lot easier for residents to
move to a new city than to a new country. The failure to be innovative
can kill a local economy, as evidenced by the massive multimillion bankruptcy filing of the city of Detroit in the summer of 2013 after so many
businesses and residents left the city. In fifty years, Detroit lost two-thirds
of its population, resulting in a city with 78,000 abandoned buildings
(38,000 of which are identified as public hazards) and 66,000 empty lots at
the time of its bankruptcy.

Successful local governments are also able to be more responsive to
community needs. The top-down, centralized, large-scale bureaucracy of
the federal government is not able to respond efficiently to a period of
rapid technological and social change due to the inherent structure of a
large, national government of a very large country (Osborne, 1993). Additionally, an innovative and responsive local government can make for a
much more vibrant and connected community. Community building, fa-
cilitation of participation, and development of partnerships are key roles
of vibrant local governments (Nalbandian, 1999). Such active government
promotes more active citizenship—better government performance at the
local level is facilitated by social trust and organized community engagement (Knack, 2002).

The hyperpartisanship and gridlock at the national level reinforce the
need for local governments to be active in trying to generate community-
level solutions to problems. Any local community waiting for the mounting problems and federal inaction to pass will be in trouble very quickly.
The "solutions to our country's problems are not coming from Washington D.C. They are coming from state and local governments all around
the country" (Osborne, 1993, p. 349). In many ways, the growing role of
local government in solving community problems is a return to the roots
of community problem solving in the United States.

ACT LOCALLY, BUILD NATIONALLY

In early rural American life, the barn-raising tradition arose out of necessity; small efforts and contributions from large numbers of people were
required to construct a building that would benefit the larger community
as a whole. Brought together by the harsh realities of frontier living,
settlers responded to the needs of their community. Whether motivated
by altruism, an expectation of a returned favor, or devotion to a shared
value system, the resulting collective action helped build strong social
ties as well as physical structures within communities. The modern
equivalents of raising barns—meeting diverse community needs from
keeping food pantries stocked to rebuilding after disasters to fixing
roads—now often involve combinations of local government organiza-

tions, nonprofits, and engaged community members working together (Hansen et al., 2014, in press).

Chapter 5 provided examples of innovative public library–based partnerships with other government agencies and nonprofits to provide services that would otherwise be unavailable in their communities, such as bringing access to fresh groceries into city food deserts. The examples in that chapter barely scratch the surface of the amazing services that public libraries are providing to their communities. Public libraries in the Pima County Public Library of Tucson, Arizona, have public health nurses in the libraries who provide free basic health care, answer health questions that patrons have, and help them navigate the social services structures (Kim, 2013). Public libraries in San Francisco have social workers to assist homeless patrons and recovering drug addicts. The innovative roles in responding to major hurricanes in the early 2000s have evolved into standard roles for public libraries to help their communities through more commonplace disasters, like recovery from tornadoes and wildfires (Bishop & Veil, 2013). All over the country, public libraries have developed programs, often as collaborative community partnerships, that meet community needs of all shapes and sizes that otherwise would likely be ignored (Taylor et al., in press).

Many public libraries also already have programs encouraging civic engagement. Many public libraries host regular events to spotlight civic issues in their communities. Such participatory forums on civic issues can increase information seeking, advocacy, and self-efficacy among members of the public (Schneck-Hamlin, Han, & Schneck-Hamlin, in press). Several national initiatives focus on the public library as a key means to increase civic participation, such as the ALA/Harwood Institute "Promise of Libraries Transforming Communities" initiative (http://discuss.ala.org/transformignlibraries/libraries-transforming-communities) and ALA's "Center for Civic Life" (http://discuss.ala.org/civicengagement). Part of these activities need to be attuning patrons to the need to advocate for decisions that support public libraries and other aspects of the community good.

Along with being uniquely responsive to local community needs, public libraries are primarily local-level entities in terms of funding. Figures 8.1 through 8.12 present comparisons of IMLS data from 2006 and 2011, revealing that the percentage of public library funding that comes from the local government continues to increase, regardless of the size of the population or legal service area of the library. "Legal service area" usually means (1) the geographic area for which a public library has been established to offer services, and (2) the area from which the library derives funding. For the purpose of this analysis, libraries were grouped into six categories based upon the size of the population served: (1) less than 10,000, (2) 10,000–24,999, (3) 25,000–99,999, (4) 100,000–499,999, (5) 500,000–999,999, and (6) greater than 1 million.

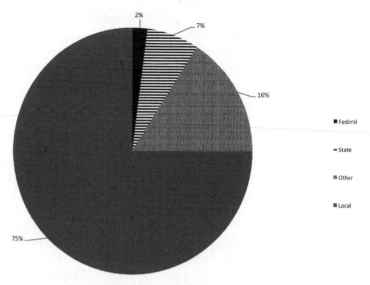

Figure 8.1.   Source of Public Library Funding (percent), Population Less Than 10,000 (2006) *Source:* IMLS, Public Libraries Survey, Fiscal Year 2006.

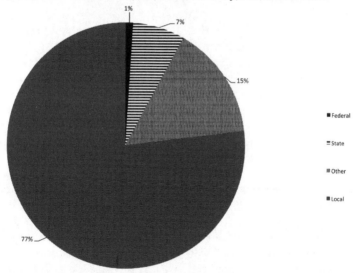

Figure 8.2.   Source of Public Library Funding (percent), Population Less Than 10,000 (2011) *Source:* IMLS, Public Libraries Survey, Fiscal Year 2011.

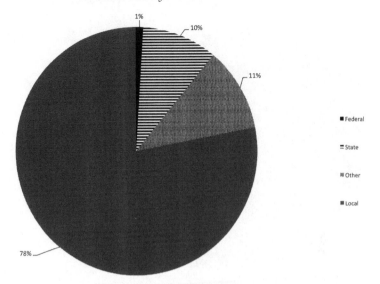

Figure 8.3.   Source of Public Library Funding (percent), Population 10,000–24,999 (2006) *Source:* IMLS, Public Libraries Survey, Fiscal Year 2006.

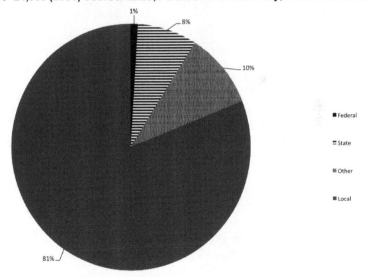

Figure 8.4.   Source of Public Library Funding (percent), Population 10,000–24,999 (2011) *Source:* IMLS, Public Libraries Survey, Fiscal Year 2011.

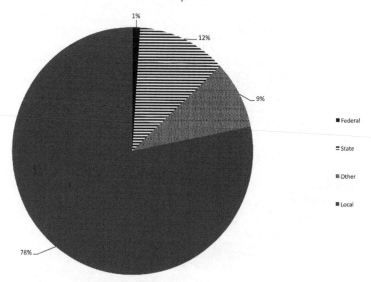

Figure 8.5.   Source of Public Library Funding (percent), Population 25,000–99,999 (2006) *Source:* **IMLS, Public Libraries Survey, Fiscal Year 2006.**

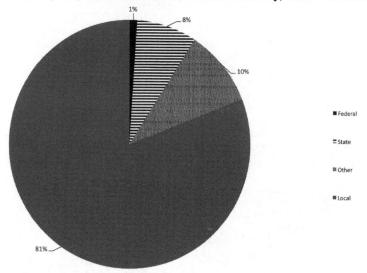

Figure 8.6.   Source of Public Library Funding (percent), Population 25,000–99,999 (2011) *Source:* **IMLS, Public Libraries Survey, Fiscal Year 2011.**

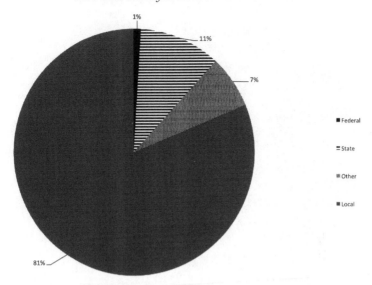

Figure 8.7.   Source of Public Library Funding (percent), Population 100,000–499,999 (2006) *Source:* IMLS, Public Libraries Survey, Fiscal Year 2006.

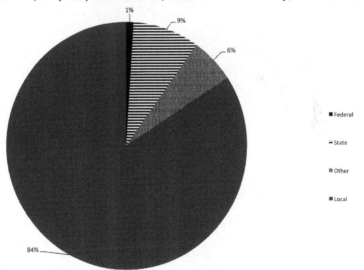

Figure 8.8.   Source of Public Library Funding (percent), Population 100,000–499,999 (2011) *Source:* IMLS, Public Libraries Survey, Fiscal Year 2011.

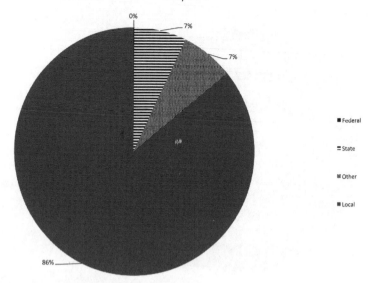

**Figure 8.9.   Source of Public Library Funding (percent), Population
500,000–999,999 (2006)** *Source:* IMLS, Public Libraries Survey, Fiscal Year 2006.

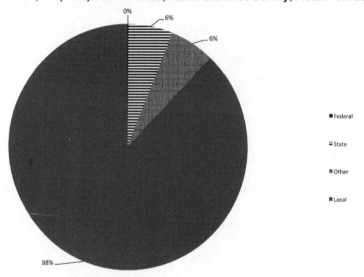

**ɡure 8.10.   Source of Public Library Funding (percent), Population
̣,000–999,999 (2011)** *Source:* IMLS, Public Libraries Survey, Fiscal Year 2011.

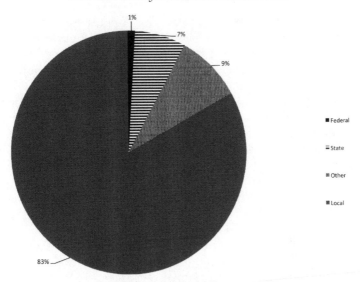

Figure 8.11. Source of Public Library Funding (percent), Population Greater Than 1 Million (2006) *Source:* IMLS, Public Libraries Survey, Fiscal Year 2006.

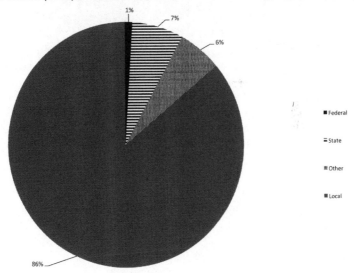

Figure 8.12. Source of Public Library Funding (percent), Population Greater Than 1 Million (2011) *Source:* IMLS, Public Libraries Survey, Fiscal Year 2011.

.de variations in whether this support is sufficient for each
rary (Alexander, 2008). As shown in figures 8.1 through
ainder of funding is primarily from other local community
g., donations, friends groups, grants), a small amount of state
and a minuscule amount of federal funding. Public library dis-
ith independent taxing authority do not have improved per capita
ig when compared to public libraries that are entirely reliant on the
government for funds. However, library districts with independent
ing authority have more reliable funding; as a result, library districts
ave both fewer decreases in funding and fewer years of sizeable increases (Anderson, 2003; Elliot, 2013).

When that local government funding is insufficient, and as state funding has decreased, libraries have to rely on donations, grants, friends
organizations, and other sources primarily from the local community.
The extent to which libraries have been able to cover the budgetary shortfalls created by reduced state funding varies. As reported in the *Library
Journal*'s 2012 survey, most respondents experienced a decrease in state
funding. Libraries in California were no different, reporting a 63.7 percent reduction in state funding. California libraries, however, also reported an increase of 4.8 percent in their total funding, indicating that
"other sources of funding" came to their rescue (Schwartz, 2013).

While many libraries have cafes and shops expressly to generate support for the library, some public libraries that receive insufficient funding
to support operations are now charging for specific services within the
library. These charges range from a fee for faxes, printing, notarizing,
scanning, photocopying, photo services, library cards for those who live
outside of the service area, meeting room usage, document searches,
interlibrary loan, and e-book checkouts, among many others (Alexander,
2013). Even when public libraries have to charge for certain services,
those charges are paid by people in the community.

The movement toward local governments being the center of community problem solving in the United States positions public libraries as
central to communities and community problem solving. A 2009 Seattle
Foundation study suggested that a healthy community depended on
meeting

- basic needs such as food, housing, a living wage, and equal treatment;
- health and wellness needs such as preventative care, consistent
  health care, long-term care, and prevention of domestic violence;
  education needs such as strong public education, early learning,
  and lifelong learning;
  economic needs such as job skills training, promoting small businesses, and supporting employers;
  arts and cultural needs such as arts education and arts funding;

- neighborhood and community needs such as social support, community engagement, and neighborhood living; and
- environmental needs such as conservation, environmental awareness, and balancing interests.

The public library is a vital part of meeting many such community needs; the typical public library plays a role in almost all of them. Even for less obvious ones, there are clear roles for libraries. For example, making artistic materials available in libraries and providing discussion forums about these materials "can positively impact library patrons' interest in becoming more critically engaged and foster a greater understanding of the issues raised" by the materials (Cocciolo, 2013, p. 1).

Public libraries are highly ingrained in their local communities, and local governments are the most innovative and responsive level of government in the United States. "The essence of successful library operations is building relationships" (Holt, 2013, p. 69), and the strongest connections that public libraries have are in their local communities. With their strong connections and parallel needs, local governments are clearly the best level of government for public libraries and their supporters to try to make substantive changes to the impacts of policy-making, politics, and funding decisions on public libraries.

Applying the strategies, objectives, and approaches detailed in chapter 7 to advocacy at the local level represents the best way for public libraries and their supporters to begin advocating for a future political, policy, and funding environment that is more supportive of public libraries. This approach of directly engaging policy and politics at the local level will give public libraries a better chance to demonstrate their value to their communities, local decision makers, and local funders. Local governments and voters will best understand the impacts of their own libraries, and local governments will be best positioned to support evolving library roles in the community through responsive and innovative governance. Focusing on local politics and policies will not address the problem of detrimental impacts of national-level decisions immediately, but it might work very well as a long-term strategy.

Historically, for librarians, "our interpretation of culture dictates our practice" (Bossaller & Raber, 2008, p. 18). If that still holds true, then a greater engagement in the culture of policy and politics will drive a practice better informed by and more attuned to the implications of policy and politics for the ability of the public library to serve the community. This heightened awareness seemingly would lead to a stronger sense of the changes to policy and politics that libraries need at the local, state, and national levels to provide improved service to their communities.

The game plan is based on starting at the local level and building upward. If public libraries all over the country begin to use data-driven value demonstration strategies to promote awareness and advocate for policies and political decisions that support the library in each community that has a library, the changes will likely gain momentum within states. If the majority of the local governments in a state have coordinated policies and politics related to local libraries, it seems quite feasible that these local stances would shape the stance of the state government. And, if all of the state governments have coordinated policies and politics related to public libraries, it seems possible that the policy-making and political debates at the national level might finally begin to account for public libraries in a sensible manner.

COMMUNITY GOOD AND COLLABORATIVE COMMUNITY SERVICES

Public libraries, as a collection of about 17,000 local institutions, have worked to establish a collective national identity and to advocate collectively at the national level, as evidenced by major organizations such as the ALA and the Public Library Association (PLA). Lumping together these adamantly local institutions, however, does not make for a coherent grouping in terms of political, policy, or economic positions. While they share broad similarities in intent and practice, they are actually a collection of more than 17,000 different community institutions.

The existence of these differences means that there is no "one size fits all" strategy for library advocacy. In recent years, larger library systems have fared comparatively worse in terms of funding.

> Budget struggles, whether at the federal, state, or local level, hit larger library systems the hardest, according to LJ's survey: those with service populations from 500,000 to 999,999 reported on average a 2.7 percent reduction in their budgets, and those with service populations above one million reported an average reduction of 1.8 percent. The 10,000–24,999 population range was the sweet spot, with libraries of that size reporting an average increase of 2.5 percent. (Kelley, 2012)

As further evidence of the hardship faced by larger library systems, figures 8.13 and 8.14 demonstrate the IMLS survey data showing that, between 2006 and 2011, the largest libraries saw the greatest reduction in full-time equivalent (FTE) staff.

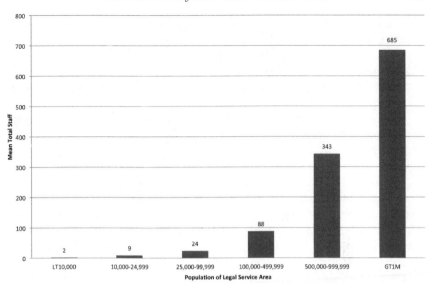

Figure 8.13.   FTE Staff (2006) *Source:* IMLS, Public Libraries Survey, Fiscal Year 2006.

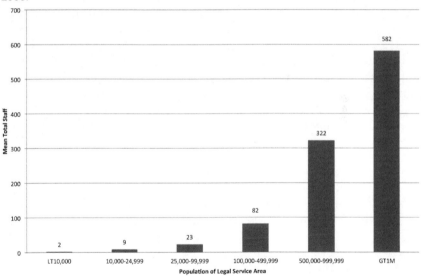

Figure 8.14.   FTE Staff (2011) *Source:* IMLS, Public Libraries Survey, Fiscal Year 2011.

Larger libraries, many of which are providing any number of the Internet-enabled service roles discussed throughout this book, have the capacity to collect the data necessary to support their claims that they are doing more with fewer resources. This is not to minimize the adverse impacts of budgetary cuts on smaller libraries, but the narrative is not the same.

Moreover, public libraries have always framed their activities in terms of the needs of the local community served by the library. Public libraries in wealthy communities have very different needs and services than those in high-poverty areas. Differences can be found in libraries of varying service populations, geography, political climate, infrastructure, and many other factors. Each public library has its own unique roles in its community. Individual libraries have long struggled to adequately convey their roles in society to even their local communities (Jaeger, Gorham, Sarin, & Bertot, in press). Devoting energy and resources to changing the political, policy, and economic context at the local level is both more practical based on the individuality of local public libraries and truer to their nature as community institutions.

To emphasize the potential of first focusing on fixing the policy and politics related to public libraries at the local level, it is worth returning once more to the new roles that public libraries have taken on as a result of serving as the social guarantor of Internet access and education. The partnerships that have developed reinforce both the nature of the public library as a community good and the ways in which new collaborative community services benefit the community and the local government.

As has been discussed in preceding chapters, during the past two decades, public libraries have assumed key roles in supporting social services, providing access to local e-government services, facilitating emergency response, job seeking, accessing health and wellness information, and supporting the local economy, among other essential roles (Bertot et al., 2006a, 2006b; Sigler et al., 2011; Taylor et al., in press). As part of their new Internet-enabled community services, public libraries have increasingly partnered with local governments and nonprofit entities to provide innovative services that neither could provide individually (Jaeger, Taylor, et al., 2012). Similarly, libraries are working with nonprofit organizations to serve a greater number of people, as well as to improve the services they are already providing to existing constituents (Hansen et al., 2014, in press).

Local governments historically have served as vital information sources for communities, and the local governments and residents in many communities now expect their public libraries to serve as the primary access point for

- local government information and services;
- communication with and a connection to local government;

- awareness of how their local government is working through greater transparency;
- trust in the local government;
- a sense of involvement and ownership in their government; and
- a way to participate in local government and the local community (Jaeger, 2009).

The capacities of local government, however, vary widely across the United States. Larger local governments are generally better equipped to pursue innovative Internet-based initiatives, often due to greater financial, technical, or personnel capacities available for e-government projects (Moon, 2002).

In the adoption of new technologies by local governments, there are concerns about how inclusive the technology is, as the "political and policy landscape [is] often made up of insiders and outsiders" (Axford & Huggins, 2003, p. 188). In many local communities, participation in Internet-enabled local government is limited often by difficulties in searching for and locating the desired information, as well as a lack of availability of computers, Internet access, and technological literacy for many individuals and segments of the population (Jaeger, Bertot, Thompson, Katz, & DeCoster, 2012). Such problems are exacerbated by a general lack of familiarity about the structure of government and the domain of different agencies, as well as attitudes toward technology and government adopted by many citizens (Burnett, Jaeger, & Thompson, 2008; Jaeger & Thompson, 2003, 2004). In most communities, however, the public library stands as an institution that allows community members to overcome these gaps in access.

In most communities, public libraries have taken on roles and responsibilities to address many of these challenges associated with technology education, access, and usage. Public libraries were originally drawn into the role of providers of e-government access, education, and training in the early 2000s by filling needs created when government agencies discontinued in-person services and began to require the completion of forms online, and subsequent emergencies then created new ways for libraries to assist their communities (Bertot et al., 2006a, 2006b). Since then, provision of e-government access, education, and training has become one of the central activities of public libraries (Jaeger & Bertot, 2011).

The development of a range of social networking tools in recent years has the potential to facilitate the collaborative ventures of local government agencies, public libraries, and nonprofit organizations. Nonprofits and government agencies at all levels are increasing their use of social technologies as a way to reach members of the public in new locations, extend government services, promote democratic participation and engagement, crowd-source solutions and innovations, and co-produce valuable community resources (Bertot, Jaeger, Munson, & Glaisyer, 2010; Jaeger, Paquette, & Simmons, 2010; Mergel, 2010; Pirolli, Preece, & Shneiderman, 2010).

The goal of collaborative community services provided by a combination of local government agencies, public libraries, and nonprofits and facilitated through websites and social media can be seen as part of a broader set of public engagement goals to promote what has been called "collaborative governance" or "participatory governance"—the inclusion of public agencies, nonprofit civic organizations, and individuals in addressing community issues (Ansell & Gash, 2007; Callahan, 2007; O'Leary, Gerard, & Bingham, 2006; Page, 2010). Such initiatives "blur traditional boundaries between organizations, sectors, and policy design and implementation" and their success depends on meaningful involvement from all stakeholder groups in a community (Page, 2010, p. 246).

In this context, public libraries are supporting both their communities and their local governments in several key ways. As a community good, public libraries have expanded their contributions to the community to provide technology access and training necessary for residents to participate in Internet-enabled local government. The same contributions have also facilitated the ability of local governments to use more Internet-enabled services as part of local government. The collaborative community services that have developed allow libraries and their partners to meet community needs that would not otherwise be addressed, while freeing the local government to focus on other, yet-to-be-addressed issues. These initiatives also encourage community involvement from a range of individuals and groups who are stakeholders in the community, promoting a more engaged community. And, as discussed above, community engagement is important in supporting innovative and responsive local government. As a community good and as a conduit for collaborative community services, the public library fosters healthy communities and strong local government.

DISRUPT AND REBUILD

If the impacts of neoliberal economic and neoconservative political ideologies that so heavily frame the national political discourse on public libraries are to be thoroughly disrupted, the process starts at the local level. National government has become too entrenched and partisan for an effective rethink of the policies and politics that impact public libraries. The more dynamic nature of government at the local level, combined with the tremendous contributions of public libraries to their local communities, enables public libraries to have the opportunity to significantly shape policies and politics at the local level. Rebuilding a political and policy-making environment that is supportive of public libraries begins at the local level and will hopefully convey over time to the national level.

If these efforts are to succeed, however, public libraries and their supporters will need to step away from the fallacy of neutrality and political disengagement. Instead, they need to embrace advocacy based on data-driven value demonstrations of their contributions to the community. The coordinated response of public libraries and their supporters in Los Angeles demonstrates how the right kind of engagement in local politics can even reverse very negative decisions—the voices of libraries and library patrons reversed drastic cuts imposed by city leaders. Such engagement, however, is also a necessary part of building support for decisions made by the library.

A series of controversies impacting public libraries in the summer of 2013 demonstrated the range of ways in which political and policy processes can affect libraries and also showed the clear need for public libraries and their supporters to be engaged in these processes:

- The Urbana Free Library in Illinois tossed out over 66,000 books in a week in 2013, deselecting all nonfiction titles that were more than ten years old. The community was not informed of this pending action, and librarians were not given the chance to check circulation statistics to see which older books were actually being used. Not surprisingly, the resulting controversy did not improve local perceptions of the library (Hart, 2013).
- The public library system of Miami-Dade lost nearly two hundred employees some two years ago and almost lost as many in 2013. Instead, Miami-Dade commissioners approved use of reserves to avoid cutting library workers and slashing library hours in the coming budget year. This action did not fix the long-term budget deficit, however, and the libraries will face a major overhaul in funding and service over the next year to try to cover the $20 million deficit (Mazzei & Rabin, 2013).
- Kentucky libraries were surprisingly stripped by state courts of their power to raise property taxes for support, an authority they have had under state law since 1979 (Morehart, 2013).
- The Fairfax County Public Library in Virginia adopted a modernization plan that deselected more than 250,000 print titles, eliminated the requirements for hiring trained librarians to staff or manage libraries, reduced hours, and cut time that children's librarians could spend with families in libraries (Jackman, 2013a). A reaction to a 23 percent budget reduction, this plan was greeted with much public resistance, and the library seemed to engage in no thought about how to gain support for it among supporters or local government (Dvorak, 2013; Jackman, 2013b). The trashing of 250,000 books—many of them new—in particular gained attention as the

library denied requests from the Friends of the Library group and
other local organizations to have the titles to donate or sell to raise
funds.

The Fairfax example includes the broadest impacts of political and policy
processes on public libraries. The library director engaged the library
board about the plan but failed to articulate the plan or the reasons for
the plan to the community. The community reacted negatively because it
was quite onerous in reductions of quality and quantity of service. After
cutting the library budget by 23 percent, the city council prevented the
library from making changes to accommodate the budget reduction following the community outcry. Imagine public reaction to the plan if the
library had released it earlier to the community as a sample of what
would happen if 23 percent of the library budget was cut. The community complaints would then have mostly been directed at the city council.

Engaging community members and local government officials offers
real hope in a bleak political climate, but this engagement by public libraries and their supporters must be active and coordinated. In the current political and economic climate, every gain will probably be hard
fought. But at this point, the only other option to fighting for support is
slowly fading away. Given their history, the fight to sustain libraries is
appropriately local and heavily weighted with symbolism about the state
of the American community. "One of the primary social functions of the
library remains symbolic: the staging of freedom in the local, often mundane struggle of individuals to craft a meaningful identity for themselves
amidst routine paths and standard choices for society" (Augst, 2007, p.
183).

As was detailed in earlier chapters of this book, public libraries have
become more engaged and organized in difficult times, defending the
principles of the ALA Bill of Rights in the face of censorship and using
the same principles to promote social integration. Public libraries have
helped the nation through world wars and the Great Depression, and
now the Great Recession. This same strength that public libraries have
collectively mustered in the face of enormous challenges in the past must
be drawn upon again. While the goal of changing political discourse and
policy-making processes is more obtuse than fighting segregation, it is
vitally important to the future of public libraries and of other community
goods.

To reiterate a key point from the first chapter, the main message of
this book is that there is a pressing need for public librarians and other
supporters of public libraries to be

1. aware of the political process and its implications for libraries;
2. attuned to the interrelationships between policy and politics; and
3. engaged in the policy process to articulate the need for policies that
   support public libraries and the community good.

The history, context, strategies, and goals offered in this book can serve as a blueprint for action and a starting point for larger discussions in the field.

Not everything presented here will work in every library, and some suggestions will probably fail utterly. As two statisticians once observed, "All models are wrong, but some models are useful" (Box & Draper, 1987, p. 424). The hope of this book is to present something useful in spurring discourse and action on an interrelated set of problems that threaten the nature and existence of public libraries and require engagement and action. Having debates on what to do and taking actions, even if not all of them work, are the necessary steps toward engaging and advocating so that public libraries have a chance to survive and thrive as a community good within current realities.

A few weeks before writer/activist/orator Frederick Douglass died in 1895, a young African American college student visited him. The student asked, in light of all that Douglass had accomplished in a long and distinguished life, what he should do as a man beginning his professional life. In response, "Douglass rose to his full height, looked at the young man and then up to the heavens, and in his rich baritone voice said 'Agitate! Agitate! Agitate!'" (Stauffer, 2008, p. 314).

Public libraries mean far too much to their patrons and their communities for libraries and their supporters to not throw everything they can at advocacy and engagement. Libraries in the United States have spent more than a century acting as agents of social change. Advocating for public libraries must now be part of that portfolio of advocating for social change. Many public librarians may feel uncomfortable in the role, but the profession and its supporters need to take the admonition of Frederick Douglass to heart completely and unabashedly.

References

Abbott-Hoduski, B. E. (2003). *Lobbying for libraries and the public's access to government information.* Lanham, MD: Scarecrow.

Ackermann, K. D. (2007). *Hoover, the Red Scare, and the assault on civil liberties.* New York: Carroll & Graf.

Adeyemon, E. (2009). Integrating digital literacies into outreach services for underserved youth populations. *Reference Librarian, 50,* 85–98.

Adler, M. (2012, June 12). Loud debate rages over N.Y. Library's quiet stacks. *NPR News.* Available from http://www.npr.org/2012/06/12/154786855/loud-debate-rages-over-n-y-librarys-quiet-stacks.

Aikin, J. (2013). "A search for better ways into the future": The Library of Congress and its users in the interwar period. In C. Pawley & L. S. Robbins (Eds.), *Libraries and the reading public in twentieth-century America* (pp. 78–93). Madison, WI: University of Wisconsin.

Alexander, O. D. (2008). Public library services to underrepresented groups: Poor and unemployed, emphasizing Danville, Virginia. *Public Library Quarterly, 27,* 111–133.

Alexander, O. D. (2013). Free public libraries charging for survival. *Public Library Quarterly, 32,* 138–149.

Alfino, M., & Pierce, L. (1997). *Information ethics for librarians.* Jefferson, NC: McFarland.

Allner, I. (2004). Copyright and the delivery of library services to distance learners. *Internet Reference Services Quarterly 9*(3), 179–192.

American Library Association. (2000). *12 ways libraries are good for the country.* Available from http://www.ala.org.

American Library Association. (2003). *Library advocate's handbook* (3rd ed.). Chicago: ALA Editions.

American Library Association. (2009). *Advocating in a tough economy toolkit.* Available from http://www.ala.org.

American Library Association. (2012a). *ALA policy manual.* Available from http://www.ala.org.

American Library Association. (2012b). *The 2012 State of America's Library Report.* Available from http://www.ala.org/news/mediapresscenter/americaslibraries/soal2012/social-networking.

Anderson, D. L. (2003). Selling a public good: The case of rechartering public libraries by referendum in New York State. *Public Library Quarterly, 22,* 5–23.

Ansell, C., & Gash, A. (2007). Collaborative governance in theory and practice. *Journal of Public Administration Research and Theory, 18,* 543–571.

Apesteguia, J., & Maier-Rigaud, F. P. (2006). The role of rivalry: Public goods versus common-pool resources. *Journal of Conflict Resolution, 50,* 646–663.

Audunson, R., Essmat, S., & Aabo, S. (2011). Public libraries: A meeting place for immigrant women? *Library & Information Science Research, 33,* 220–227.

Augst, T. (2001). Introduction: Libraries and agencies of culture. In T. Augst & W. Wiegand (Eds.), *Libraries as agencies of culture* (pp. 5–22). Madison: University of Wisconsin Press.

Augst, T. (2007). Faith in reading: Public libraries, liberalism, and the civil religion. In T. Augst & K. E. Carpenter (Eds.), *Institutions of readings: The social life of libraries in the United States* (pp. 148–183). Amherst: University of Massachusetts.

Auld, H. S. (2004, March/April). Patrons, customer, users, clients. *Public Libraries*, 81–87.

Axford, B., & Huggins, R. (2003). Towards a political sociology of the Internet and local governance. *Telematics and Informatics, 20*, 185–192.

Baker, N. (1996). The author vs. the library. *New Yorker, 72*(31), 51–62.

Baker, N. (2001). *Double fold: Libraries and the assault on paper*. New York: Random House.

Banfield, E. C., & Wilson, J. Q. (1963). *City politics*. Cambridge, MA: Harvard.

Barrett, J. R. (1992). Americanization from the bottom up: Immigration and the remaking of the working class in the United States. *Journal of American History, 79*, 996–1020.

Battistella, E. (2010). What a library closure taught me. *Library Journal*. Available from http://www.libraryjournal.com.

Baumgartner, F. R., Berry, J. M., Hojnacki, M., Leech, B. L., & Kimball, D. C. (2009). *Lobbying and policy change: Who wins, who loses, and why*. Chicago: University of Chicago.

Becker, S., Crandall, M. D., Fisher, K. E., Kinney, B., Landry, C., & Rocha, A. (2010). *Opportunity for all: How the American public benefits from Internet access at U.S. libraries*. Available from http://tascha.washington.edu/usimpact.

Beckerman, E. (1996). *Politics and the American public library: Creating political support for library goals*. Lanham, MD: Scarecrow.

Becvar, K. M., & Srinivasan, R. (2009). Indigenous knowledge and culturally-responsive methods in information research. *Library Quarterly, 79*, 421–441.

Bennett, S. (2001). The golden age of libraries. *Journal of Academic Librarianship, 27*, 256–259.

Berlin, I. (1953). *The hedgehog and the fox: An essay on Tolstoy's view of history*. New York: Simon & Schuster.

Berman, S. (1998). On my mind: Libraries, class, and the poor people's policy. *American Libraries, 29*(3), 38.

Berninghausen, D. K. (1948a). Current attacks on books. *American Library Association Bulletin, 42*(5), 58.

Berninghausen, D. K. (1948b). Book-banning and witch hunts. *American Library Association Bulletin, 42*(5), 204.

Berninghausen, D. K. (1953). The history of the ALA intellectual freedom committee. *Wilson Library Bulletin, 27*(10), 813–817.

Berninghausen, D. (1972). Antithesis in librarianship: Social responsibility vs. the Library Bill of Rights. *Library Journal, 97*(20), 3675–3681.

Berry, J. N., & Rawlinson, N. (1991). No time for neutrality. *Library Journal*. Available from http://www.libraryjournal.com.

Bertot, J. C. (2011). Public libraries and the Internet: A retrospective, challenges, and issues moving forward. In J. C. Bertot, P. T. Jaeger, & C. R. McClure (Eds.), *Public libraries and the Internet: Roles, perspectives, and implications* (pp. 15–35). Westport, CT: Libraries Unlimited.

Bertot, J. C., Gorham, U., Jaeger, P. T., & Taylor, N. G. (2012). Public libraries and the Internet 2012: Key findings, recent trends, and future challenges. *Public Library Quarterly, 31*(4), 303–325.

Bertot, J. C., & Jaeger, P. T. (2012). Implementing and managing public library networks, connectivity, and partnerships to promote e-government access and education. In S. Aikins (Ed.), *Managing e-government projects: Concepts, issues and best practices* (pp. 183–199). Hershey, PA: IGI Global.

Bertot, J. C., Jaeger, P. T., & Greene, N. N. (2013). Transformative e-government and public service: Public libraries in times of economic hardship. In V. Weerakkody & C. G. Reddick (Eds.), *Public sector transformation through e-government: Experiences from Europe and North America* (pp. 35–46). New York: Routledge.

Bertot, J. C., Jaeger, P. T., Langa, L. A., & McClure, C. R. (2006a). Drafted: I want you to deliver e-government. *Library Journal, 131*(13), 34–39.

Bertot, J. C., Jaeger, P. T., Langa, L. A., & McClure, C. R. (2006b). Public access computing and Internet access in public libraries: The role of public libraries in e-government and emergency situations. *First Monday, 11*(9). Available from http://www. firstmonday.org/issues/issue11_9/bertot/index.html.

Bertot, J. C., Jaeger, P. T., Munson, S., & Glaisyer, T. (2010). Engaging the public in open government: The policy and government application of social media technology for government transparency. *IEEE Computer, 43*(11), 53–59.

Bertot, J. C., Jaeger, P. T., & Sarin, L. C. (2012). Forbes folly: The lessons of being labeled the worst master's degree. *American Libraries, 43*(9/10), 30–33.

Bertot, J. C., Jaeger, P. T., Shuler, J. A., Simmons, S. N., & Grimes, J. M. (2009). Reconciling government documents and e-government: Government information in policy, librarianship, and education. *Government Information Quarterly, 26*, 433–436.

Bertot, J. C., McClure, C. R., & Jaeger, P. T. (2008). The impacts of free public Internet access on public library patrons and communities. *Library Quarterly, 78*, 285–301.

Bertot, J. C., McDermott, A., Lincoln, R., Real, B., & Peterson, K. (2012). *2011–2012 Public Library Funding and Technology Access Survey: Survey Findings and Results.* College Park, MD: Information Policy and Access Center.

Bethea, A. D. (2011). Has Charlotte survived? *Library Journal, 136*(9), 28–32.

Bier, V. (2006). Hurricane Katrina as bureaucratic nightmare. In R. J. Daniels, D. F. Kettl, & H. Kunreuther (Eds.), *On risk and disaster: Lessons from Hurricane Katrina* (pp. 243–254). Philadelphia: University of Pennsylvania Press.

Bishop, A. P., Bazzell, I., Mehra, B., & Smith, C. (2001). Afya: Social and digital technologies that reach across the digital divide. *First Monday, 6*(4). Available from http:// www.firstmonday.org/issues/issue6_4/bishop/index.html.

Bishop, B. W., & Veil, S. R. (2013). Public libraries as post-crisis information hubs. *Public Library Quarterly, 32*, 33–45.

Blanke, H. T. (1989, July). Librarianship & political values: Neutrality or commitment? *Library Journal*, 39–43.

Blumenstein, L. (2009, July 22). In Gainesville, FL, "The Library Partnership" merges branch, social services. *Library Journal.* Available from http://www.libraryjournal. com/article/CA6672422.html.

Boast, R., Bravo, M., & Srinivasan, R. (2007). Return to Babel: Emergent diversity, digital resources, and local knowledge. *Information Society, 23*, 395–403.

Borden, A. K. (1931). The sociological beginnings of the library movement. *Library Quarterly, 1*, 278–282.

Bossaller, J., & Raber, D. (2008). Reading and culture: The challenge of progressive era beliefs in the postmodern world. *Progressive Librarian, 31*, 17–28.

Bourke, C. (2005). Public libraries building social capital through networking. *Australasian Public Libraries and Information Services, 18*(2), 71–75.

Box, G. E., & Draper, N. R. (1987). *Empirical model-building and response surfaces.* New York: Wiley.

Braman, S. (2006). *Change of state: Information, policy, and power.* Cambridge, MA: MIT Press.

Brito, J., & Dooling, B. (2006, March). Who's your daddy? *Wall Street Journal*, A9.

Brophy, P. (2007). *The library in the twenty-first century* (2nd ed.). London: Facet.

Brown, J. L. (2001). Making a huge difference in so many little ways. *Public Libraries, 40*(1), 24.

Brown, J. S., & Duguid, P. (2002). *The social life of information.* Boston: Harvard Business School Press.

Brown, W. (2006). American nightmare: Neoliberalism, neoconservatism, and de-democraticization. *Political Theory, 34*, 690–714.

Budd, J. M. (1997, July). A critique of customer and commodity. *College & Research Libraries*, 309–320.

Budd, J. M. (2006). Politics and public library collections. *Progressive Librarian, 28*, 78–86.

154

References

Bureau of Labor Statistics. (2012). *Occupational outlook handbook: Librarians.* Available from http://www.bls.gov/ooh/education-training-and-library/librarians.htm.

Burger, R. H. (1993). *Information policies.* Norwood, NJ: Ablex.

Burke, S. K. (2008). Use of public libraries by immigrants. *Reference and User Services Quarterly, 48,* 164–174.

Burnett, G., Jaeger, P. T., & Thompson, K. M. (2008). The social aspects of information access: The viewpoint of normative theory of information behavior. *Library & Information Science Research, 30,* 56–66.

Burnham, W. D. (2010). *Democracy in peril: The American turnout problem and the path to plutocracy.* New York: Roosevelt Institute.

Burton, J. (2009). Theory and politics in public librarianship. *Progressive Librarian, 32,* 21–28.

Buschman, J. E. (2003). *Dismantling the public sphere: Situating and sustaining librarianship in the age of the new public philosophy.* Westport, CT: Libraries Unlimited.

Buschman, J. E. (2005). Libraries and the decline of public purposes. *Public Library Quarterly, 24*(1), 1–12.

Buschman, J. E. (2007a). Democratic theory in library and information science: Toward an emendation. *Journal of the American Society for Information Science and Technology, 58,* 1483–1496.

Buschman, J. E. (2007b). Transgression or stasis? Challenging Foucault in LIS theory. *Library Quarterly, 77,* 21–44.

Buschman, J. E. (2009). Information literacy, "new" literacies, and literacy. *Library Quarterly, 79,* 95–118.

Buschman, J. E. (2012). *Libraries, classrooms, and the interests of democracy: Marking the limits of neoliberalism.* Lanham, MD: Scarecrow.

Buschman, J. E., & Leckie, G. J. (Eds.). (2007). *The library as place: History, community, and culture.* Westport, CT: Libraries Unlimited.

Buschman, J. E., Rosenzweig, M., & Harger, E. (1994). The clear imperative for involvement: Librarians must address social issues. *American Libraries, 25*(6), 575–576.

Butler, R. P. (2003). Copyright law and organizing the Internet. *Library Trends, 52,* 307–317.

Byrne, A. (2003). Necromancy or life support? Libraries, democracy and the concerned intellectual. *Library Management, 24,* 116–125.

Caidi, N., & Allard, D. (2005). Social inclusion of newcomers to Canada: An information problem? *Library & Information Science Research, 27,* 302–324.

California ICT Digital Literacy Leadership Council. (2010, July). *Digital literacy pathways in California: ICT Leadership Council action plan report.* Available from http://www.cio.ca.gov.

Callahan, R. (2007). Governance: The collision of politics and cooperation. *Public Administration Review, 67,* 290–301.

Carlson, S. (2005). Whose work is it, anyway? *Chronicle of Higher Education, 51*(47), A33–A35.

Carlton, J. (2009, January 19). Folks are flocking to the library, a cozy place to look for a job: Books, computers and wi-fi are free, but staffs are stressed by crowds, cutbacks. *Washington Post,* A1.

Carnesi, M. S., & Fiol, M. A. (2000). Queens Library's New Americans Program: 23 years of services to immigrants. In Salvador Guerena (Ed.), *Library services to Latinos: An anthology* (pp. 133–142). Jefferson, NC: McFarland.

Carrico, J. C., & Smalldon, K. L. (2004). Licensed to ILL: A beginning guide to negotiating e-resources licenses to permit resource sharing. *Journal of Library Administration, 40*(1–2), 41–54.

Chatters, C. H. (1957). The outlook for support for public agencies with particular reference to libraries. *Library Quarterly, 27,* 249–254.

Chen, S. (2010). The new hungry: College-educated, middle-class cope with food insecurity. *CNN.com.* Available from http://www.cnn.com/2010/LIVING/12/13/food.insecurities.holidays.middle.class/index.html.

Chertoff, M. (2005, July 14). Statement before the Senate Committee on Homeland Security and Governmental Affairs, Department of Homeland Security: Second stage review.

Chu, C. M. (1999). Literacy practices of linguistic minorities: Sociolinguistic issues and implications for literacy services. *Library Quarterly, 69,* 339–359.

Cillizza, C. (2013a). Congress is really, really old. *Washington Post,* July 8. Available from http://www.washingtonpost.com.

Cillizza, C. (2013b, July 17). The least productive Congress ever. *Washington Post.* Available from http://www.washingtonpost.com.

Clark, L., & Visser, M. (2011). Digital literacy takes center stage. In *The transforming public library infrastructure.* Washington, DC: American Library Association, Office for Research and Statistics.

Clark, S. (2009). Marketing the library? Why librarians should focus on stewardship and advocacy. *Progressive Librarian, 33,* 93–100.

Clarke, J. (2004). Dissolving the public realm? The logics and limits of neo-liberalism. *Journal of Social Policy, 33,* 27–48.

CNN. (2009). Hard economic times: A boon for public libraries. *CNN.com.* Available from http://www.cnn.com/2009/US/02/28/recession.libraries/index.html.

Cocciolo, A. (2013). Public libraries and PBS partnering to enhance civic engagement: A study of a nationwide initiative. *Public Library Quarterly, 32,* 1–20.

Coffman, S., & Varek, B. (1998). What if you ran your library like a bookstore? *American Libraries, 29*(3), 40–42.

Cohen, L. (2003). *A consumer's republic: The politics of mass consumption in postwar America.* New York: Knopf.

Conant, R. W. (1965). *The public library and the city.* Cambridge, MA: MIT.

Congressional Research Service. (1984). Library Services and Construction Act. 97th Congress Reauthorization. Issue Brief 1B81064.

Constantino, R. (2005). Print environments between high and low socioeconomic status (SES) communities. *Teacher Librarian, 32*(3), 22–25.

Cook, B. (2012). Library heroes shelter evacuees from the summer of 2012. *American Libraries, 43*(9/10), 10–11.

Cornelius, I. (2004). Information and its philosophy. *Library Trends, 52,* 377–386.

Cornelius, I. (2010). *Information policies and strategies.* London: Facet.

Cossette, A. (1976/2009). *Humanism and libraries: An essay on the philosophy of librarianship.* Duluth, MN: Library Juice.

Cox, R. J. (2011). *The demise of the library school: Personal reflections on professional education in the modern corporate university.* Duluth, MN: Library Juice.

Cuban, L. (1995). Hedgehogs and foxes among educational researchers. *Journal of Educational Research, 89,* 6–12.

Cuban, S. (2007). *Serving new immigrant communities in the library.* Westport, CT: Greenwood.

Culnan, M. J. (1983). Environmental scanning: The effects of task complexity and source accessibility on information gathering behavior. *Decision Sciences, 14*(2), 194–206.

Culnan, M. J. (1984). The dimensions of accessibility to online information: Implications for implanting office information systems. *ACM Transactions on Office Information Systems, 2*(2), 141–150.

Culnan, M. J. (1985). The dimensions of perceived accessibility to information: Implications for the delivery of information systems and services. *Journal of the American Society for Information Science, 36*(5), 302–308.

Curley, A. (1974). Social responsibility and libraries. In M. J. Voight (Ed.), *Advances in Librarianship* (Vol. 4, pp. 77–90). New York: Academic.

Curley, A. (1990). Funding for public libraries in the 1990s. In E. J. Josey & K. D. Shearer (Eds.), *Politics and the support of libraries* (pp. 105–111). New York: Neal-Schuman.

D'Angelo, E. (2006). *Barbarians at the gates of the public library: How postmodern consumer capitalism threatens democracy, civil education and the public good.* Duluth, MN: Library Juice.

Daniel, H. (1961). *Public libraries for everyone: The growth and development of library services in the United States.* Garden City, NY: Doubleday.

Danton, J. P. (1934). Our libraries: The trend toward democracy. *Library Quarterly, 4,* 16–27.

Davies, D. W. (1974). *Public libraries as culture and social centers: The origin of the concept.* Metuchen, NJ: Scarecrow.

Davis, D. M. (2009). Challenges to sustaining library technology. *Public Libraries, 48*(4), 12–17.

Davis, D. M. (2011). Public library funding: An overview and discussion. In J. C. Bertot, P. T. Jaeger, & C. R. McClure (Eds.), *Public libraries and the Internet: Roles, perspectives, and implications* (pp. 193–214). Westport, CT: Libraries Unlimited.

Davlantes, A. (2010, June 28). Are libraries necessary, or a waste of tax money? *Fox News Chicago.*

Dean, J. (2013). Society doesn't exist. *First Monday, 18*(3–4).

Debono, B. (2002). Assessing the social impact of public libraries: What the literature is saying. *Australasian Public Libraries and Information Services, 15*(2), 80–95.

DellaVigna, S., & Kaplan, E. (2007, August). The Fox News effect: Media bias and voting. *Quarterly Journal of Economics,* 1187–1234.

Dempsey, B. (2009). Strategies from 2008 for an even tougher 2009. *Library Journal.* Available from http://www.libraryjournal.com.

Dempsey, B. (2010). Libraries win 84% of operating and 54% of building referenda in 2009. *Library Journal.* Available from http://www.libraryjournal.com.

DePillis, L. (2013, July 14). Barnes & Noble can succeed, but not by competing with Amazon. *Washington Post.* Available from http://www.washingtonpost.com.

DeProspo, E. R., Jr. (1977). Federal funds in the governance of local library institutions: A reappraisal. *Library Trends, 26,* 197–198.

Dervin, B. (1994). Information—democracy: An examination of underlying assumptions. *Journal of the American Society for Information Science, 45,* 369–385.

De Witte, K., & Geys, B. (2011). Evaluating efficient public good provision: Theory and evidence from a generalized conditional efficiency model for public libraries. *Journal of Urban Economics, 69,* 319–327.

De Witte, K., & Geys, B. (2013). Citizen coproduction and efficient public good provision: Theory and evidence from local public libraries. *European Journal of Operational Research, 224,* 592–602.

Diamond, S. (1998). *Not by politics alone: The enduring influence of the Christian right.* New York: Guilford.

Dilevko, J. (2009). *The politics of professionalism: A retro-progressive proposal for librarianship.* Duluth, MN: Library Juice Press.

Dionne, E. J., Jr. (2012). *Our divided political heart: The battle for the American idea in an age of discontent.* New York: Bloomsbury.

Ditzion, S. H. (1939). Social reform, education and the library. *Library Quarterly, 9,* 156–184.

Ditzion, S. H. (1947). *Arsenals of a democratic culture.* Chicago: American Library Association.

Dougherty, R. M. (2011). Library advocacy: One message, one voice. *American Libraries, 42*(5/6), 46–50.

Dowell, D. R. (2008). The "i" in libraries. *American Libraries, 39*(1/2), 42.

Doyle, T. (2001). A utilitarian case for intellectual freedom in libraries. *Library Quarterly, 71,* 44–71.

Dresang, E. T. (2006). Intellectual freedom and libraries: Complexity and change in the twenty-first century digital environment. *Library Quarterly, 76,* 169–192.

DuMont, R. R. (1977). *Reform and reaction: The big city public library in American life.* Westport, CT: Greenwood.

Durrance, J. C., & Fisher, K. E. (2002). *Online community information: Creating a nexus at your library.* Chicago: ALA Editions.

Durrance, J. C., & Fisher, K. E. (2005). *How libraries and librarians help: Assessing outcomes in your library.* Chicago: ALA Editions.

Durrani, S., & Smallwood, E. (2006). The professional is political: Redefining the social role of public libraries. *Progressive Librarian, 27,* 3–22.

Dvorak, P. (2013, September 13). Protest over tossed books couldn't be hushed. *Washington Post.* Available from http://www.washingtonpost.com.

Eberhart, G. (2013). The prescription for finding healthcare information. *American Libraries.* Available from http://www.americanlibrariesmagazine.org/blog/prescription-finding-healthcare-information.

El-Abbadi, M. (1990). *The life and fate of the ancient library of Alexandria.* Paris: UNESCO.

Eliot, T. H. (1959). Toward an understanding of public school politics. *American Political Science Review, 52,* 1032–1051.

Elliot, M. (2013). Impact of the public library district model on local funding of public libraries in New York State. *Public Library Quarterly, 32,* 124–137.

Ellis, P., Jacobs, D., & Stasch, J. (2012a, April 6). Beyond books: Why you should check out your public library. *Chicago Post-Tribune.* Available from http://posttrib.suntimes.com.

Ellis, P., Jacobs, D., & Stasch, J. (2012b, Winter). Investing in civic engagement and public libraries. *National Civic Review,* 5–10.

Ellsworth, R. E. (1948). Is intellectual freedom in libraries being challenged? *American Library Association Bulletin, 42*(2), 57–58.

Elmore, G. (2008, March 3). Pull the plug on the library. *Gainesville Sun.* Available from http://www.gainesvillesun.com.

Ennis, P. H., & Fryden, F. N. (1960). The library in the community use studies revisited. *Library Quarterly, 30,* 253–265.

Evans, P. B., & Wurster, T. S. (1997). Strategy and the new economics of information. *Harvard Business Review, 75*(5), 70–82.

Ezard, J. (2003, February 15). Buy lattes and get online at Britain's first Idea Store. *Guardian.* Available from http://www.theguardian.com.

Farrelly, M. G. (2009). Refuge in the library. *Public Libraries, 48*(4), 24–26.

Federal Communication Commission. (2010). *The national broadband plan: Connecting America.* Washington, DC: Author. Available from http://www.broadband.gov.

Ferullo, D. L. (2004). Major copyright issues in academic libraries: Legal implications of a digital environment. *Journal of Library Administration, 40*(1–2), 23–40.

Fisher, K. E., Durrance, J. C., & Hinton, M. B. (2004). Information grounds and the use of need-based services by immigrants in Queens, New York: A context-based, outcome evaluation approach. *Journal of the American Society of Information Science and Technology, 55,* 754–766.

Fiske, M. (1959). *Book selection and censorship: A study of school and public libraries in California.* Berkeley: University of California.

Floridi, L. (2002). On defining library and information science as applied philosophy of information. *Social Epistemology, 16,* 37–49.

Foerstel, H. N. (1991). *Surveillance in the stacks: The FBI's library awareness program.* Westport, CT: Greenwood.

Foerstel, H. N. (2004). *Refuge of a scoundrel: The Patriot Act in libraries.* Westport, CT: Libraries Unlimited.

Foskett, D. J. (1962). *The creed of the librarian: No politics, no religion, no morals.* London: Library Association.

Fourie, D. K., & Dowell, D. R. (2002). *Libraries in the information age: An introduction and career exploration.* Westport, CT: Libraries Unlimited.

Fuller, P. F. (1994). The politics of LSCA during the Reagan and Bush administrations: An analysis. *Library Quarterly, 64,* 294–318.

Gaffney, L. M. (2013). "Is your library family friendly?": Libraries as a site of conservative activism, 1992–2002. In C. Pawley & L. S. Robbins (Eds.), *Libraries and the read-*

ing public in twentieth-century America (pp. 185–199). Madison, WI: University of Wisconsin.

Gaines, E. J. (1980, September). Let's return to the traditional library service: Facing the failure of social experimentation. *Wilson Library Bulletin, 55,* 50–53.

Galbraith, J. K. (1998). *Created unequal: The crisis in American pay.* New York: Free Press.

Garceau, O. (1949). *The public library in the political process.* New York: Columbia University.

Garrison, D. (1993). *Apostles of culture: The public librarian and American society, 1876–1920.* Madison: University of Wisconsin.

Gasaway, L. N. (2000, Fall). Values conflict in the digital environment: Librarians versus copyright holders. *Columbia—VLA Journal of Law & the Arts,* 115–161.

Gathegi, J. N. (2005). The public library and the (de)evolution of a legal doctrine. *Library Quarterly, 75,* 1–19.

Gehner, J. (2010). Libraries, low-income people, and social exclusion. *Public Library Quarterly, 29*(1), 39–47.

Gellar, E. (1974). Intellectual freedom: Eternal principle or unanticipated consequence? *Library Journal, 99,* 1364–1367.

Gellar, E. (1984). *Forbidden books in American public libraries, 1876–1939: A study in cultural change.* Westport, CT: Greenwood.

Gerard, D. (1978). *Libraries in society: A reader.* London: Clive Bingley.

Gibbs, N. (2009, April 27). Thrift nation. *Time,* 24.

Gibson, A. N., Bertot, J. C., & McClure, C. R. (2009). Emerging roles of public libraries as e-government providers. *Proceedings of the 42nd Hawaii International Conference on Systems Sciences* (HICSS '09) (Waikoloa, Big Island, Hawaii, January 5–8, 2009). Washington, DC: IEEE Computer Society.

Given, L., & Leckie, G. L. (2003). "Sweeping" the library: Mapping the social activity space of the public library. *Library and Information Science Research, 25,* 365–385.

Goldberg, B. (2009). Board president denounces closing of Colton libraries. *American Libraries.* Available from http://www.americanlibrariesmagazine.org.

Goldstein, D. (2003). The spirit of an age: Iowa public libraries and professional librarians as solutions to society's problems, 1890–1940. *Libraries and Culture, 38,* 214–235.

Good, J. (2006–07). The hottest place in hell: The crisis of neutrality in contemporary librarianship. *Progressive Librarian, 28,* 25–29.

Gorham, U., Bertot, J. C., Jaeger, P. T., & Greene, N. N. (2013). E-government success in public libraries: Library and government agency partnerships delivering services to new immigrants. In J. Ramon Gil-Garcia (Ed.), *E-government success factors and measures: Concepts, theories, experiences, and practical recommendations* (pp. 41–59). Hershey, PA: IGI Global.

Gorham-Oscilowski, U., & Jaeger, P. T. (2008). National Security Letters, the USA PATRIOT Act, and the Constitution: The tensions between national security and civil rights. *Government Information Quarterly, 25,* 625–644.

Goulding, A. (2004). Libraries and social capital. *Journal of Librarianship and Information Science, 36*(1), 3–6.

Graham, J.-B. (2003). Now's not the time to be neutral? The myth and reality of the library as neutral entity. *Alabama Librarian, 53*(2), 9–11.

Graham, P. T. (2001). Public librarians and the civil rights movement. *Library Quarterly, 71,* 1–27.

Gray, C. M. (1993). The civic role of libraries. In J. E. Buschman (Ed.), *Critical approaches to information technology in librarianship: Foundations and applications.* Westport, CT: Greenwood.

Green, J. (2007). Subscription libraries and commercial circulating libraries in colonial Philadelphia and New York. In T. Augst & K. Carpenter (Eds.), *Institutions of reading: The social life of libraries in the United States* (pp. 24–52). Amherst, MA: University of Massachusetts.

Greenberg, K. J., & Dratel, J. L. (2005). *The torture papers: The road to Abu Ghraib.* New York: Cambridge.

Gubernick, L., & Conlin, M. (1997, February 10). The special education scandal. *Forbes*, 66–70.

Gutmann, A. (1995, April). Civic education and social diversity. *Ethics*, 557–579.

Gwinn, M. A. (2009, January 23). Library use jumps in Seattle area: Economy likely reason. *Seattle Times*. Available from http://www.seattletimes.com.

Hacker, J. S., Mettler, S., & Pinderhughes, D. (2005). Inequality and public policy. In R. L. Lawrence & T. Skocpol (Eds.), *Inequality and American democracy* (pp. 156–213). New York: Russell Sage.

Hafner, A. W. (1987). Public libraries and society in the information age. *Reference Librarian, 18*, 107–118.

Halsey, R. S. (2003). *Lobbying for public and school libraries: A history and political playbook*. Lanham, MD: Scarecrow.

Hanley, R. (1998, June 29). Jersey City librarians protest plan for private contractor. *New York Times*, B1, B6.

Hanley, R. P. (2004). Political science and political understanding: Isaiah Berlin on the nature of political inquiry. *American Political Science Review, 98*, 327–339.

Hansen, D., Koepfler, J., Jaeger, P. T., & Bertot, J. C. (in press). Action brokering for civic engagement: A case study of ACTion Alexandria, a web-based platform for local civic participation. In K. C. Desouza & E. W. Johnston (Eds.), *Policy informatics*. Cambridge, MA: MIT Press.

Hansen, D. L., Koepfler, J. A., Jaeger, P. T., Bertot, J. C., & Viselli, T. (2014). Civic action brokering platforms: Facilitating local engagement with ACTion Alexandria. *Proceedings of the 17th ACM Conference on Computer Supported Cooperative Work and Social Computing (CSCW 2014)*.

Harris, M. H. (1973). The purpose of the American public library: A revisionist interpretation of history. *Library Journal, 98*, 2509–2514.

Harris, M. H. (1976). Public libraries and the decline of the democratic dogma. *Library Journal, 101*, 2225–2230.

Harris, M. H. (1986). The dialectic of defeat: Antimonies in research in library and information science. *Library Trends, 34*, 515–531.

Harris, M. H., & Carrigan, D. P. (1990). The President and library policy. In E. J. Josey & K. D. Shearer (Eds.), *Politics and the support of libraries* (pp. 32–42). New York: Neal-Schuman.

Hart, R. S. (2013). Bookgate: When Urbana Free Library got rid of thousands of books. *Bookriot*. Available from http://bookriot.com/2013/06/21/bookgate-when-urbana-free-library-got-rid-of-thousands-of-books.

Hartman, T. (2007). The changing definition of U.S. libraries. *Libri, 57*, 1–8.

Hatch, J. (2004, October). Employment in the public sector: Two recessions' impact on jobs. *Monthly Labor Report*, 38–47.

Hauptman, R. (2002). *Ethics and librarianship*. Jefferson, NC: McFarland.

Heanue, A. (2001). In support of democracy: The library role in public access to government information. In N. Kranich (Ed.), *Libraries & democracy: The cornerstones of liberty* (pp. 121–128). Chicago, IL: American Library Association.

Heckart, R. J. (1991). The library as marketplace of ideas. *College and Research Libraries, 52*, 491–505.

Helling, J. (2012). *Public libraries and their national policies: International case studies*. Oxford: Chandos.

Herdman, M. M. (1943). The public library in the Depression. *Library Quarterly, 13*, 310–334.

Herndon, T., Ash, M., & Pollin, R. (2013). *Does high public debt consistently stifle economic growth? A critique of Reinhart and Rogoff*. Amherst, MA: Political Economic Research Institute.

Hernon, P., McClure, C. R., & Relyea, H. C. (Ed.). (1996). *Federal information policies in the 1990s: Views and perspectives*. Norwood, NJ: Ablex.

Hernon, P., Relyea, H. C., Dugan, R. E., & Cheverie, J. F. (2002). *United States government information: Policies and sources*. Westport, CT: Libraries Unlimited.

Hill, C. (2009a). Inside, outside, and online. *American Libraries, 40*(3), 39.

Hill, C. (2009b). *Inside, outside and online: Building your library community.* Chicago: ALA Editions.

Hill, N. M. (2009). Three views. *Public Libraries, 48*(4), 8–11.

Hillenbrand, C. (2005). Public libraries as developers of social capital. *Australasian Public Libraries and Information Services, 18*(1), 4–12.

Hinton, E. A. (1938). The public library under local government. *Public Administration, 16,* 453–465.

Hlebowitsh, P. (2010). Centripetal thinking in curriculum studies. *Critical Inquiries, 40,* 503–513.

Hoff, K., & Stiglitz, J. E. (2010). Equilibrium fictions: A cognitive approach to societal rigidity. *American Economic Review, 100,* 141–146.

Hoffert, B. (2009). It's the economy. *Library Journal, 134*(3), 34–36.

Hoffman, J., Bertot, J. C., & Davis, D. M. (2012). *Libraries connect communities: Public Library Funding and Technology Access Study 2011–2012.* Digital supplement of American Libraries magazine, June 2012. Available from http://viewer.zmags.com/publication/4673a369.

Holland, S., & Verploeg, A. (2009). No easy targets: Six libraries in the economy's dark days. *Public Libraries, 48*(4), 27–38.

Holt, G. E. (2005). Asking the right but hard questions. *Public Library Quarterly, 24*(2), 77–82.

Holt, G. E. (2009). Future economic realities of libraries: A lesson in current events. *Public Library Quarterly, 28,* 249–268.

Holt, G. E. (2013). A future-oriented budget narrative for the King County Library System: A presentation and an analysis. *Public Library Quarterly, 32,* 68–86.

Holt, L. E., & Holt, G. E. (2010). *Public library services for the poor: Doing all we can.* Chicago: ALA Editions.

Hummel, P. (2012). Library advocacy in hard times. *Oregon Library Association Quarterly, 18*(2), 4–5.

Hussey, L. K., & Velasquez, D. L. (2011). Forced advocacy: How communities respond to library budget cuts. *Advances in Librarianship, 34,* 59–93.

Imhoff, K. R. T. (2006). Creating advocates for public libraries. *Public Library Quarterly, 25*(1/2), 155–170.

Institute of Museum and Library Services. (2006). *Library statistics: Public libraries.* Available from http://harvester.census.gov/imls/publib.asp.

Institute of Museum and Library Services. (2011a). *Building digitally inclusive communities.* Available from http://www.imls.gov/resources/resources.shtm.

Institute of Museum and Library Services. (2011b). *Library statistics: Public libraries.* Available from http://harvester.census.gov/imls/publib.asp.

Institute of Museum and Library Services. (2013). *FY2011 public library (public use) data file.* Washington, DC. Available from http://www.imls.gov/research/pls_data_files.aspx.

Jackman, T. (2013a, September 10). In Fairfax libraries' bid for renewal, books are trashed. *Washington Post.* Available from http://www.washingtonpost.com.

Jackman, T. (2013b, September 13). Library plan put on hold in Fairfax. *Washington Post.* Available from http://www.washingtonpost.com.

Jackson, D. Z. (2009). The library-a recession sanctuary. *Boston Globe,* January 3. Available from http://www.bostonglobe.com.

Jackson, S. L. (1974). *Libraries and librarianship in the West: A brief history.* New York: McGraw-Hill.

Jaeger, P. T. (2009). Public libraries and local e-government. In C. G. Reddick (Ed.), *Handbook on research on strategies for local e-government adoption and implementation: Comparative studies.* Hershey, PA: IGI Global.

Jaeger, P. T., & Bertot, J. C. (2009). E-government education in public libraries: New service roles and expanding social responsibilities. *Journal of Education for Library and Information Science, 50,* 40–50.

Jaeger, P. T., & Bertot, J. C. (2010). Public libraries and e-government. In J. C. Bertot, P. T. Jaeger, & C. R. McClure (Eds.), *Public libraries and the Internet: Roles, perspectives, and implications* (pp. 39–57). Westport, CT: Libraries Unlimited.

Jaeger, P. T., & Bertot, J. C. (2011). Responsibility rolls down: Public libraries and the social and policy obligations of ensuring access to e-government and government information. *Public Library Quarterly, 30,* 91–116.

Jaeger, P. T., Bertot, J. C., & Gorham, U. (2013). Wake up the nation: Public libraries, policy-making, and political discourse. *Library Quarterly, 83,* 61–72.

Jaeger, P. T., Bertot, J. C., Kodama, C. M., Katz, S. M., & DeCoster, E. J. (2011). Describing and measuring the value of public libraries: The growth of the Internet and the evolution of library value. *First Monday, 11*(7). Available from http://www.uic.edu/htbin/cgiwrap/bin/ojs/index.php/fm/article/viewArticle/3765/3074.

Jaeger, P. T., Bertot, J. C., & McClure, C. R. (2003). The impact of the USA Patriot Act on collection and analysis of personal information under the Foreign Intelligence Surveillance Act. *Government Information Quarterly, 20*(3), 295–314.

Jaeger, P. T., Bertot, J. C., & McClure, C. R. (2004). The effects of the Children's Internet Protection Act (CIPA) in public libraries and its implications for research: A statistical, policy, and legal analysis. *Journal of the American Society for Information Science and Technology, 55*(13), 1131–1139.

Jaeger, P. T., Bertot, J. C., McClure, C. R., & Rodriguez, M. (2007). Public libraries and Internet access across the United States: A comparison by state from 2004 to 2006. *Information Technology and Libraries, 26*(2), 4–14.

Jaeger, P. T., Bertot, J. C., & Shuler, J. A. (2010). The Federal Depository Library Program (FDLP), academic libraries, and access to government information. *Journal of Academic Librarianship, 36,* 469–478.

Jaeger, P. T., Bertot, J. C., Shuler, J. A., & McGilvray, J. (2012). A new frontier for LIS programs: E-government education, library/government partnerships, and the preparation of future information professionals. *Education for Information, 29,* 39–52.

Jaeger, P. T., Bertot, J. C., Thompson, K. M., Katz, S. M., & DeCoster, E. J. (2012). The intersection of public policy and public access: Digital divides, digital literacy, digital inclusion, and public libraries. *Public Library Quarterly, 31*(1), 1–20.

Jaeger, P. T., & Bowman, C. A. (2005). *Understanding disability: Inclusion, access, diversity, and civil rights.* Westport, CT: Praeger.

Jaeger, P. T., & Burnett, G. (2005). Information access and exchange among small worlds in a democratic society: The role of policy in redefining information behavior in the post-9/11 United States. *Library Quarterly, 75*(4), 464–495.

Jaeger, P. T., & Burnett, G. (2010). *Information worlds: Social context, technology, & information behavior in the age of the Internet.* London: Routledge.

Jaeger, P. T., & Fleischmann, K. R. (2007). Public libraries, values, trust, and e-government. *Information Technology and Libraries, 26*(4), 35–43.

Jaeger, P. T., Fleischmann, K. R., Preece, J., Shneiderman, B., Wu, F. P., & Qu, Y. (2007). Community response grids: Facilitating community response to biosecurity and bioterror emergencies through information and communication technologies. *Biosecurity and Bioterrorism, 5*(4), 335–346.

Jaeger, P. T., Gorham, U., Sarin, L. C., & Bertot, J. C. (2013). Libraries, policy, and politics in a democracy: The four historical epochs. *Library Quarterly, 83,* 166–181.

Jaeger, P. T., Gorham, U., Sarin, L. C., & Bertot, J. C. (in press). Democracy, neutrality, and value demonstration in the age of austerity. *Library Quarterly.*

Jaeger, P. T., Langa, L. A., McClure, C. R., & Bertot, J. C. (2006). The 2004 and 2005 Gulf Coast hurricanes: Evolving roles and lessons learned for public libraries in disaster preparedness and community services. *Public Library Quarterly, 25*(3/4), 199–214.

Jaeger, P. T., & McClure, C. R. (2004). Potential legal challenges to the application of the Children's Internet Protection Act (CIPA) in public libraries: Strategies and issues. *First Monday, 9*(2). Available from http://www.firstmonday.org/issues/issue9_2/jaeger/index.html.

Jaeger, P. T., McClure, C. R., & Bertot, J. C. (2005). The E-rate program and libraries and library consortia, 2000–2004: Trends and issues. *Information Technology and Libraries, 24*(2), 57–67.

Jaeger, P. T., McClure, C. R., Bertot, J. C., & Langa, L. A. (2005). CIPA: Decisions, implementation, and impacts. *Public Libraries, 44*(2), 105–109.

Jaeger, P. T., McClure, C. R., Bertot, J. C., & Snead, J. T. (2004). The USA PATRIOT Act, the Foreign Intelligence Surveillance Act, and information policy research in libraries: Issues, impacts, and questions for library researchers. *Library Quarterly, 74*(2), 99–121.

Jaeger, P. T., Paquette, S., & Simmons, S. N. (2010). Information policy in national political campaigns: A comparison of the 2008 campaigns for President of the United States and Prime Minister of Canada. *Journal of Information Technology & Politics, 7*, 1–16.

Jaeger, P. T., Shneiderman, B., Fleischmann, K. R., Preece, J., Qu, Y., & Wu, F. P. (2007). Community response grids: E-government, social networks, and effective emergency response. *Telecommunications Policy, 31*, 592–604.

Jaeger, P. T., Subramaniam, M., Jones, C. B., & Bertot, J. C. (2011). Diversity and LIS education: Inclusion and the age of information. *Journal of Education for Library and Information Science, 52*, 166–183.

Jaeger, P. T., Taylor, N. G., Bertot, J. C., Perkins, N., & Wahl, E. E. (2012). The Co-evolution of e-government and public libraries: Technologies, access, education, and partnerships. *Library & Information Science Research, 34*, 271–281.

Jaeger, P. T., & Thompson, K. M. (2003). E-government around the world: Lessons, challenges, and new directions. *Government Information Quarterly, 20*(4), 389–394.

Jaeger, P. T., & Thompson, K. M. (2004). Social information behavior and the democratic process: Information poverty, normative behavior, and electronic government in the United States. *Library & Information Science Research, 26*(1), 94–107.

Jaeger, P. T., Thompson, K. M., & Lazar, J. L. (2012). The Internet and the evolution of library research: The perspective of one longitudinal study. *Library Quarterly, 82*, 75–86.

Jaeger, P. T., & Yan, Z. (2009). One law with two outcomes: Comparing the implementation of the Children's Internet Protection Act in public libraries and public schools. *Information Technology and Libraries, 28*(1), 8–16.

James, S. E. (1985). The relationship between local economic conditions and the use of public libraries. *Library Quarterly, 55*, 255–272.

James, S. E. (1986). Economic hard times and public library use: A close look at the Librarian's Axiom. *Public Library Quarterly, 7*(3–4), 61–70.

Jayakar, K., & Park, E.-A. (2012). Funding public computing centers: Balancing broadband availability and expected demand. *Government Information Quarterly, 29*, 50–59.

Jenkins, C. (1990). The political processes and library policy. In E. J. Josey & K. D. Shearer (Eds.), *Politics and the support of libraries* (pp. 45–51). New York: Neal-Schuman.

Jerrard, J., Bolt, N., & Strege, K. (2012). *Privatizing libraries*. Chicago: American Library Association.

Joeckel, C. B. (1935). *The government of the American public library*. Chicago: University of Chicago Press.

Johnson, C. A. (2010). Do public libraries contribute to social capital? A preliminary investigation into the relationship. *Library & Information Science Research, 32*, 147–155.

Jones, P. A., Jr. (1993). From censorship to intellectual freedom to empowerment: The evolution of the social responsibility of the American public library. *North Carolina Libraries, 52*, 135–137.

Jones, P. A., Jr. (1999). *Libraries, immigrants, and the American experience*. Westport, CT: Greenwood.

Josey, E. J. (Ed.). (1980). *Libraries in the political process*. Phoenix: Oryx.

Josey, E. J., & Shearer, K. D. (1990). *Politics and the support of libraries.* New York: Neal-Schuman.

Kajberg, L. (2011). Revisiting the concept of the political library in the world of Web 2.0 technologies. *Progressive Librarian, 36/37,* 30–41.

Kearney, R. C., Feldman, B. M., & Scavo, C. P. F. (2000). Reinventing government: City manager attitudes and actions. *Public Administration Review, 60,* 535–548.

Kelley, M. (2011). Los Angeles Public Library wins big with votes, Measure L passes. *Library Journal.* Available from http://www.libraryjournal.com.

Kelley, M. (2012). The new normal. *Library Journal.* Available from http://www.libraryjournal.com.

Kent, S. G. (1996). American public libraries: A long transformation. *Daedalus, 125*(4), 207–220.

Kermeny, J. G. (1962). A library for 2000 A.D. In M. Greenberger (Ed.), *Computers and the world of the future.* Cambridge, MA: MIT.

Kerslake, E., & Kinnell, M. (1998). Public libraries, public interest and the information society: Theoretical issues in the social impact of public libraries. *Journal of Librarianship and Information Science, 30*(3), 159–167.

Kim, E. K. (2013, March 28). More than just books: Arizona libraries add public health nurses. *NBC News.* Available from http://www.today.com.

Kingma, B. R. (2001). *The economics of information: A guide to economic and cost benefit analysis for information.* Littleton, CO: Libraries Unlimited.

Kinney, B. (2010). The Internet, public libraries, and the digital divide. *Public Library Quarterly, 29*(2), 104–161.

Kintz, L. (1997). *Between Jesus and the market: The emotions that matter to right-wing America.* Durham, NC: Duke University Press.

Kliff, S. (2012, July 6). The incredible shrinking public health workforce. *Washington Post.* Available from http://www.washingtonpost.com.

Knack, S. (2002). Social capital and the quality of government: Evidence from the states. *American Journal of Political Science, 46,* 772–785.

Kniffel, L. (1996). Criticism follows hoopla at new San Francisco library. *American Libraries, 27*(7), 12–13.

Kniffel, L. (2002). Who wants to be the first to go to jail? *American Libraries, 33*(7), 46.

Knox, E. (2013). The challengers of West Bend: The library as a community institution. In C. Pawley & L. S. Robbins (Eds.), *Libraries and the reading public in twentieth-century America* (pp. 200–213). Madison, WI: University of Wisconsin.

Kramp, R. S. (1975/2010). *The great depression: Its impact on forty-six large American public libraries.* Duluth, MN: Library Juice.

Kranich, N. (2001a). Libraries, the Internet, and democracy. In N. Kranich (Ed.), *Libraries and democracy: The cornerstones of liberty* (pp. 383–395). Chicago: American Library Association.

Kranich, N. (Ed.). (2001b). *Libraries and democracy: The cornerstones of liberty.* Chicago: American Library Association.

Kranich, N. (2010). Promoting adult learning through civil discourse in the public library. *New Directions for Adult and Continuing Education, 127*(4), 15–24.

Krummel, D. W. (1999). *Fiat lux, fiat latebra: A celebration of historical library functions.* Campaign, IL: University of Illinois Press.

Labaree, D. F. (1997). Public goods, private goods: The American struggle over educational goals. *American Educational Research Journal, 34*(1), 39–81.

Lancaster, F. W. (Ed.) (1993). *Libraries and the future: Essays on the library in the twenty-first century.* New York: Haworth.

Landoy, A., & Zetterlund, A. (2013). Similarities and dissimilarities among Scandinavian library leaders and managers. In P. Hernon & N. O. Pors (Eds.), *Library leadership in the United States and Europe: A comparative study of academic and public libraries* (pp. 93–108). Santa Barbara, CA: Libraries Unlimited.

Lankes, R. D., Silverstein, J., & Nicholson, S. (2007). Participatory networks: The library as conversation. *Information Technology and Libraries, 26*(4), 17–33.

LaRose, R., Strover, S., Gregg, J. L., & Straubhaar, J. (2011). The impact of rural broadband development: Lessons from a natural field experiment. *Government Information Quarterly, 28,* 91–100.

Larson, K. C. (2001). The Saturday Evening Girls: A progressive era library club and the intellectual life of working class and immigrant girls in turn-of-the century Boston. *Library Quarterly, 71,* 195–230.

LaRue, J. (2009). Tough times and eight ways to deal with them. *American Libraries.* Available from http://www.americanlibrariesmagazine.org.

LaRue, J. (2011). Keeping our message simple. *American Libraries.* Available from http://www.americanlibrariesmagazine.org.

Lasswell, H. D. (1958). *Politics: Who gets what, when, how.* New York: Meridian.

Learned, W. (1924). *The American public library and the diffusion of knowledge.* New York: Harcourt Brace.

Learned, W. (1926). *Libraries and adult education.* Chicago: American Library Association.

Leckie, G. J. (2004). Three perspectives on libraries as public space. *Feliciter, 50*(6), 233–236.

Leckie, G. J., & Hopkins, J. (2002). The public place of central libraries: Findings from Toronto and Vancouver. *Library Quarterly, 72,* 326–372.

Lee, R. E. (1966). *Continuing education for adults through the American public library.* Chicago: American Library Association.

Leibovich, M. (2013). *This town: Two parties and a funeral—and plenty of valet parking!—in America's gilded capital.* New York: Penguin.

Leigh, R. D. (1957). Changing concepts of the public library's role. *Library Quarterly, 27,* 223–234.

Lerner, F. (2009). *The story of libraries: From the invention of writing to the computer age.* New York: Continuum.

Licklider, J. C. R. (1965). *Libraries of the future.* Cambridge, MA: MIT.

Lievrouw, L. A. (1994). Information resources and democracy: Understanding the paradox. *Journal of the American Society for Information Science, 45,* 350–377.

Lin, G. T.-R., & Lin, J. (2006). Ethical customer value creation: Drivers and barriers. *Journal of Business Ethics, 67,* 93–105.

Line, M. B. (2003). Democracy and information: Transmitters and receivers. *Library Management, 24,* 386–392.

Lukenbill, W. B. (2006). Helping youth at risk: An overview of reformist movements in public libraries to youth. *New Review of Children's Literature and Librarianship, 12,* 197–213.

Lukensmeyer, C. J. (2012, Winter). Public libraries and the future of democracy. *National Civic Review,* 13–14.

Luyt, B. (2001). Regulating readers: The social origins of the readers' advisor in the United States. *Library Quarterly, 71,* 443–466.

Lynch, M. J. (2002). Economic hard times and public library use revisited. *American Libraries, 33*(7), 62–63.

Lyons, C. (2007). The library: A distinct local voice? *First Monday, 12*(3). Available from http://www.uic.edu/htbin/cgiwrap/bin/ojs/index.php/fm/article/view/1629/1544.

Lyons, R. (2009). Critiquing advocacy research findings: An illustration from the OCLC report. *Public Library Quarterly, 28,* 212–226.

Lyons, R. (2013). Rainy day statistics: U.S. public libraries and the Great Recession. *Public Library Quarterly, 32,* 97–118.

Manchester, W. (1993). *A world lit only by fire: The medieval mind and the Renaissance; portrait of an age.* New York: Little, Brown.

Mann, T. E., & Ornstein, N. J. (2012). *It's even worse than it looks: How the American constitutional system collided with the new politics of extremism.* New York: Basic.

Manoff, M. (2001). The symbolic meaning of libraries in a digital age. *Portal: Libraries and the Academy, 1,* 371–381.

Martell, C. (2009). Hanging tough at our neighborhood libraries. *Public Library Quarterly, 28,* 336–343.

Matthews, J. R. (2007). *The evaluation and measurement of library services.* Westport, CT: Libraries Unlimited.

Matz, C. (2008). Libraries and the USA Patriot Act. *Journal of Library Administration, 47* (3/4): 69–87.

Mazzei, P., & Rabin, C. (2013, September 11). Miami-Dade will raid reserves to avoid library layoffs, maintain hours. *Miami Herald.* Available from http://miamiherald. com.

McChesney, K. (1984). History of libraries, librarianship, and library education. In A. R. Rogers & K. McChesney (Eds.), *The library in society* (pp. 33–60). Littleton, CO: Libraries Unlimited.

McClelland, E. (2013). *Nothin' but blue skies: The heyday, hard times, and hopes of America's industrial heartland.* New York: Bloomsbury.

McClure, C. R., Feldman, S., & Ryan, J. (2006). Politics and advocacy: The role of networking in selling the library to your community. *Public Library Quarterly, 25*(1/ 2), 137–154.

McClure, C. R., & Jaeger, P. T. (2008). Government information policy research: Importance, approaches, and realities. *Library & Information Science Research, 30,* 257–264.

McCook, K. d.l.P. (2011). *Introduction to public librarianship* (2nd ed.). New York: Neal-Schuman.

McCook, K. d.l.P., & Barber, P. (2002). Public policy as a factor influencing adult lifelong learning, adult literacy and public libraries. *Reference & User Services Quarterly, 42*(1), 66–75.

McCook, K. d.l.P., & Brand, K. (2001). Community indicators, genuine progress, and the golden billion. *Reference and User Services Quarterly, 40,* 337–340.

McCreadie, M., & Rice, R. E. (1999). Trends in analyzing access to information, part I: Cross-disciplinary conceptions of access. *Information Processing and Management, 35,* 45–76.

McCrossen, A. (2006). "One more cathedral" or "mere lounging places for bummers?" The cultural politics of leisure and the public library in Gilded Age America. *Libraries and the Cultural Record, 41,* 169–188.

McDowell, K. (2010). Which truth, what fiction? Librarians' book recommendations for children, 1877–1890. In A. R. Nelson & J. L. Rudolph (Eds.), *Education and the culture of print in modern America* (pp. 15–35). Madison, WI: University of Wisconsin.

McDowell, K. (2011). Children's voices in librarians' words, 1890–1930. *Libraries & the Cultural Record, 46,* 73–100.

McMenemy, D. (2007). Librarians and ethical neutrality: Revisiting *The Creed of a Librarian. Library Review, 56,* 177–181.

McMullen, H. (2000). *American libraries before 1876.* Westport, CT: Greenwood.

Meade, R. (2013, May 14). A librarian's response to "what's a library?" *Huffington Post.* Available from http://www.huffingtonpost.com.

Mehra, B., & Srinivasan, R. (2007). The library-community convergence framework for community action. *Libri, 57*(3), 123–139.

Mergel, I. (2010). Government 2.0 revisited: Social media strategies in the public sector. *American Society for Public Administration, 33*(3), 7, 10.

Michel, D. (2009). Foxes, hedgehogs, and greenhouse governance: Knowledge, uncertainty, and international policy-making in a warming world. *Applied Energy, 86,* 258–264.

Milam, D. P. (2001). Access for all: Public library contributions to civic connectivity. *National Civic Review, 90*(3), 213–220.

Milbank, D. (2013, July 18). On Obamacare, testing the definition of insanity. *Washington Post.* Available from http://www.washingtonpost.com.

Miranda-Murillo, D. (2006). New immigrants centers at the Austin public library. *Texas Library Journal, 82*(4), 144–147.

Molz, K. (1976). *Federal policy and library support.* Cambridge, MA: MIT.

Moon, M. J. (2002). The evolution of e-government among municipalities: Rhetoric or reality? *Public Administration Review, 62*, 424–433.

Moon, M. J., & Norris, D. F. (2005). Does managerial orientation matter? The adoption of reinventing government and e-government at the municipal level. *Information Systems Journal, 15*, 43–60.

Morehart, P. (2013). Lawsuits impact Kentucky libraries. *American Libraries*. Available from http://www.americanlibrariesmagazine.org/blog/lawsuits-impact-kentucky-libraries.

Morehead, J. (1998). *Introduction to United States government information sources* (6th ed.). Westport, CT: Libraries Unlimited.

Morrongiello, G. (2013, July 3). White House vetoes public seeing Obama's thanks to librarians. *Washington Examiner*. Available from http://washingtonexaminer.com.

Moyn, S. (2012, May 12). Human rights, not so pure anymore. *New York Times*. Available from http://www.nytimes.com.

Musman, K. (1993). *Technological innovations in libraries, 1860–1960*. Westport, CT: Greenwood.

Naficy, H. (2009). Centering essential immigrant help on the library Web site: The American Place (TAP) at Hartford Public Library. *Public Library Quarterly, 28*(2), 162–175.

Nalbandian, J. (1999). Facilitating community, enabling democracy: New roles for local government managers. *Public Administration Review, 59*, 187–197.

National Center for Education Statistics. (2009). *Financial accounting for local and state school systems*. Available from http://www.nces.ed.gov.

National Telecommunications and Information Administration. (2013). *Exploring the digital nation: America's emerging online experience*. Available from http://www.fcc.gov.

Nelson, J. A. (2006). Marketing and advocacy: Collaboration in principle and practice. *Public Library Quarterly, 25*(1/2), 117–135.

Newman, J. (2007). Re-mapping the public: Public libraries and the public sphere. *Cultural Studies, 21*, 887–909.

Newsom, G., & Dickey, L. (2013). *Citizenville: How to take the town square digital and reinvent government*. New York: Penguin.

Nieves, E. (2010, March 7). California library reaches out to homeless patrons. *Boston Globe*. Available from http://www.boston.com/news/nation/articles/2010/03/07/san_francisco_hires_social_worker_for_homeless_library_patrons.

Novotny, E. (2010). Hard choices in hard times: Lessons from the Great Depression. *Reference & User Services Quarterly, 49*, 222–224.

Nyquist, E. B. (1968). Poverty, prejudice, and the public library. *Library Quarterly, 38*, 78–89.

O'Leary, R., Gerard, C., & Bingham, L. B. (2006). Introduction to the symposium on collaborative public management. *Public Administration Review, 66*(s1), 6–9.

O'Neil, S. L., & Hansen, J. W. (2001). Productivity. In B. S. Kaliski (Ed.), *Encyclopedia of Business and Finance* (Vol. 2, pp. 708–710). New York: Macmillan.

Online Computer Library Center. (2007). *Sharing, privacy and trust in our networked world*. Dublin, OH: Author.

Osborne, D. (1993). Reinventing government. *Public Productivity and Management Review, 16*, 349–356.

Oxford English Dictionary. (2013a). Value. Available from http://www.oed.com/view/Entry/221253.

Oxford English Dictionary. (2013b). Value, n. Available from http://www.oed.com/view/Entry/221253.

Page, S. (2010). Integrative leadership for collaborative governance: Civic engagement in Seattle. *Leadership Quarterly, 21*, 246–263.

Park, J. C. (1980). Preachers, politics, and public education: A review of right-wing pressures against public schooling in America. *Phi Delta Kappan, 61*(9), 608–612.

Parker, R., Kaufman-Scarborough, C., & Parker, J. C. (2007). Libraries in transition to a marketing orientation: Are librarians' attitudes a barrier? *International Journal of Nonprofit and Voluntary Sector Marketing, 12*, 320–337.

Pawley, C. (2001). *Reading on the middle border: The culture of print in late-nineteenth-century Osage, Iowa.* Amherst: University of Massachusetts.

Pawley, C. (2009). Seeking significance: Actual readers, specific reading communities. *Book History, 5*, 143–160.

Pearlstein, S. (2012, April 12). Turned off by politics? That's exactly what politicians want. *Washington Post.* Available from http://www.washingtonpost.com.

Pensa, P. (2009, December 4). Chicago Public Library starts a new, lean chapter. *Chicago Tribune.* Available from http://www.chicagotribune.com.

Pera, M. (2013). Libraries and the Affordable Care Act. *American Libraries.* Available from http://www.americanlibrariesmagazine.org.

Perlstein, R. (2008). *Nixonland: The rise of a president and the fracturing of America.* New York: Scribner.

Pirolli, P., Preece, J., & Shneiderman, B. (2010). Cyberinfrastructure for social action on national priorities. *Computer, 43*(11), 20–21.

Pittman, R. (2001). Sex, democracy, and videotape. In N. Kranich (Ed.), *Libraries and democracy: The cornerstones of liberty* (pp. 113–118). Chicago: American Library Association.

Porter, M., & King, D. L. (2009). Save money-use the web. *Public Libraries, 48*(4), 18–20.

Preer, J. L. (2006). "Louder please": Using historical research to foster professional identity in LIS students. *Libraries and the Cultural Record, 41*, 487–496.

Preer, J. (2008). Promoting citizenship: How librarians helped get out the vote in the 1952 presidential election. *Libraries & the Cultural Record, 43*, 1–28.

Provizer, N. W. (2008). On hedgehogs, foxes and leadership: Uncovering the Other Tolstoy. *Leadership Quarterly, 19*, 453–458.

Public Agenda. (2006). *Long overdue: A fresh look at public and leadership attitudes about libraries in the 21st century.* New York: Author. Available from http://publicagenda.org.

Pungitore, V. L. (1995). *Innovation and the library: The adoption of new ideas in public libraries.* Westport, CT: Greenwood.

Raber, D. (1995). Ideological opposition to federal library legislation: The case of the Library Services Act of 1956. *Public Libraries, 34*, 162–169.

Raber, D. (2007). ACONDA and ANACONDA: Social change, social responsibility, and librarianship. *Library Trends, 55*, 675–697.

Rabin, M., & Schrag, J. L. (1999, February). First impressions matter: A model of confirmatory bias. *Quarterly Journal of Economics*, 37–82.

Rainie, L. (2010). *Internet, broadband, and cell phone statistics.* Pew Internet and American Life Project. Available from http://www.pewinternet.org/Reports/2010/Internet-broadband-and-cell-phone-statistics.aspx.

Ramey, J. B. (2013). For the public good: Urban youth advocacy and the fight for public education. *Children and Youth Services Review, 35*, 1260–1267.

Randall, J. (2013, July 10). Comcast profits off poverty. *Salon.* Available from http://www.salon.com/2013/07/10/comcasts_new_partner.

Raven, J. (2007). Social libraries and library societies in eighteenth century North America. In T. Augst & K. Carpenter (Eds.), *Institutions of reading: The social life of libraries in the United States* (pp. 1–23). Amherst, MA: University of Massachusetts.

Raymond, B. (1979). ACONDA and ANACONDA revisited: A retrospective glance at the sounds of fury of the sixties. *Journal of Library History, 14*, 349–362.

Rayward, W. B., & Jenkins, C. (2007). Libraries in times of war, revolution, and social change. *Library Trends, 55*(3), 361–369.

Reddick, C. G., & Aikins, S. K. (2012). Web 2.0 technologies and democratic governance. In C. G. Reddick & S. K. Aikins (Eds.), *Web 2.0 technologies and democratic governance: Political, policy and management implications* (pp. 1–7). New York: Springer.

Reith, D. (1984). The library as social agency. In A. R. Rogers & K. McChesney (Eds.), *The library in society* (pp. 5–16). Littleton, CO: Libraries Unlimited.

Repo, A. J. (1989). The value of information: Approaches in economics, accounting, and management science. *Journal of the American Society for Information Science, 40,* 68–85.

Resmovits, J. (2011, May 31). Librarian positions cut in schools across the country. *Huffpost Education.* Available from http://www.huffingtonpost.com/2011/05/31/librarian-positions-cutschools_n_869458.html.

Rettig, J. (2009). Once in a lifetime. *American Libraries.* Available from http://americanlibrariesmagazine.org/junejuly-2009/once-lifetime.

Reuters. (2010). Nearly half of elderly in U.S. will face poverty. *MSNBC.com.* Available from http://www.msnbc.com.

Richards, N. M. (2013). The perils of social reading. *Georgetown Law Journal, 101,* 689–724.

Richards, P. S. (2001). Cold War librarianship: Soviet and American activities in support of national foreign policy, 1946–1991. *Libraries & the Cultural Record, 36,* 183–203.

Robbins, L. S. (1996). *Censorship and the American library: The American Library Association's response to threats to intellectual freedom.* Westport, CT: Greenwood.

Robbins, L. S. (2000). *The dismissal of Miss Ruth Brown: Civil rights, censorship, and the American library.* Norman: University of Oklahoma Press.

Robbins, L. S. (2007). Responses to the resurrection of Miss Ruth Brown: An essay on the reception of a historical case study. *Libraries & the Cultural Record, 42,* 422–437.

Rogers, R. A. (1984). An introduction to philosophies of librarianship. In A. R. Rogers & K. McChesney (Eds.), *The library in society* (pp. 17–32). Littleton, CO: Libraries Unlimited.

Rosenblum, M. (2013, May 8). What's a library? *Huffington Post.* Available from http://www.huffingtonpost.com.

Rothbauer, P. (2007). Locating the library as place among lesbian, gay, bisexual, and queer patrons. In J. Buschman & G. J. Leckie (Eds.), *The library as place: History, community, and culture.* Westport, CT: Libraries Unlimited.

Rothstein, R., & Jacobsen, R. (2006). The goals of education. *Phi Delta Kappan, 88*(4). Available from http://www.epi.org.

Samek, T. (2001). *Intellectual freedom and social responsibility in American librarianship, 1967–1974.* Jefferson, NC: McFarland.

Sandel, M. (1996). *Democracy's discontent: America in search of a public philosophy.* Cambridge, MA: Belknap.

Sargent, G. (2013, July 9). Sabotage governing. *Washington Post.* Available from http://www.washingtonpost.com.

Schattschneider, E. E. (1935). *Politics, pressures and the tariff: A study of free private enterprise in pressure politics, as shown in the 1929–1930 revision of the tariff.* New York: Prentice Hall.

Schneck-Hamlin, D., Han, S.-H., & Schneck-Hamlin, B. (in press). Library-led forums on broadband: An inquiry into public deliberation. *Library Quarterly.*

Schwartz, M. (2013, January). The budget balancing act. *Library Journal,* 38–41.

Scott, P., Richards, E., & Martin, B. (1990). Captives of controversy: The myth of the neutral social researcher in contemporary scientific controversies. *Science, Technology, and Human Values, 15,* 474–494.

Scott, R. (2011). The role of public libraries in community building. *Public Library Quarterly, 30*(3), 191–227.

Seattle Foundation. (2009). *A healthy community: What you need to know to give strategically.* Seattle, WA: Author. Available from http://www.seattlefoundation.org/aboutus/Documents/10029170_HCReport_web.pdf.

Sennett, R. (1974). *The fall of public man.* New York: Norton.

Senville, W. (2009). Libraries at the heart of our communities. *Planning Commissioners Journal, 75*(3), 12–18.

Seymour, W. N., Jr. (1980). *The changing roles of public libraries.* Metuchen, NJ: Scarecrow.

Shavit, D. (1985). *Federal aid and state library agencies: Federal policy implementation.* Westport, CT: Greenwood.

Shavit, D. (1986). *The politics of public librarianship.* Westport, CT: Greenwood.

Shera, J. H. (1933). Recent social trends and future library policy. *Library Quarterly, 3,* 339–353.

Shera, J. H. (1949). *Foundations of the public library: Origins of public library movement in New England, 1629–1855.* Chicago: University of Chicago.

Shera, J. H. (1952). On the value of library history. *Library Quarterly, 22,* 240–251.

Shera, J. H. (1963). Toward a new dimension for library education. *ALA Bulletin, 57,* 313–317.

Shera, J. H. (1964, July). Automation and the reference librarian. *Reference Quarterly, 3,* 3–7.

Shera, J. H. (1970). *The sociological foundations of librarianship.* New York: Asia Publishing House.

Shields, G. R. (1980). Federal legislation and libraries. In E. J. Josey (Ed.), *Libraries in the political process* (pp. 3–14). Phoenix: Oryx.

Shneiderman, B. (2008, March 7). Science 2.0. *Science, 319,* 1349–1350.

Shuler, J. A. (2002). Freedom of public information versus the right to public information: The future possibilities of library advocacy. *Journal of Academic Librarianship, 28*(3), 157–159.

Shuler, J. A., Jaeger, P. T., & Bertot, J. C. (2010). Implications of harmonizing e-government principles and the Federal Depository Library Program (FDLP). *Government Information Quarterly, 27,* 9–16.

Shuman, B. A. (2001). *Issues for libraries and information science in the Internet age.* Englewood, CO: Libraries Unlimited.

Sigler, K. I., Jaeger, P. T., Bertot, J. C., McDermott, A. J., DeCoster, E. J., & Langa, L. A. (2011). The role of public libraries, the Internet, and economic uncertainty. In A. Woodsworth (Ed.), *Advances in librarianship: Vol. 34. Librarianship in times of crisis* (pp. 19–35). London: Emerald.

Silver, N. (2012a). *The signal and the noise: Why so many predictions fail but some don't.* New York: Penguin.

Silver, N. (2012b). As swing districts dwindle, can a divided house stand? *FiveThirtyEight.* Available from http://www.fivethirtyeightblog.com.

Sin, S.-C. J. (2011). Neighborhood disparities in access to information resources: Measuring and mapping U.S. public libraries' funding and service landscapes. *Library & Information Science Research, 33,* 41–53.

Sin, S.-C. J. (2012). Modeling the impact of individuals' characteristics and library service levels on high school students' public library usage: A national analysis. *Library & Information Science Research, 34,* 228–237.

Smith, A. (2011). *Why Americans use social media.* Pew Internet & American Life Project. Available from http://www.pewinternet.org.

Smith, J. (2012, June 8). The best and worst master's degrees for jobs. *Forbes.* Available from http://www.forbes.com/sites/jacquelynsmith/2012/06/08/the-best-and-worst-masters-degrees-for-jobs-2/2.

Smith, J. (2013, June 7). The best and worst master's degrees for jobs right now. *Forbes.* Available from http://www.forbes.com/sites/jacquelynsmith/2013/06/07/the-best-and-worst-masters-degrees-for-jobs-rightnow.

Somashekhar, S. (2013, August 28). States find new ways to resist health law. *Washington Post.* Available from http://www.washingtonpost.com.

Srinivasan, R. (2006a). Where information society and community voice intersect. *Information Society, 22,* 355–365.

Srinivasan, R. (2006b). Indigenous, ethnic and cultural articulations of new media. *International Journal of Cultural Studies, 9,* 497–518.

Srinivasan, R. (2007). Ethnomethodological architectures: Information systems driven by cultural and community visions. *Journal of the American Society for Information Science and Technology, 58*, 723–733.

Stauffer, J. (2008). *Giants: The parallel lives of Fredrick Douglass and Abraham Lincoln.* New York: Twelve.

Stauffer, S. M. (2005). Polygamy and the public library: The establishment of public libraries in Utah before 1910. *Library Quarterly, 75*, 346–370.

Stauffer, S. M. (2006). Introduction. In R. Litwin (Ed.), *Library daylight: Tracing of modern librarianship, 1874–1922* (pp. 1–11). Duluth, MN: Library Juice.

Stephens, M. (2007). Web 2.0 and libraries, part 2: Trends and technologies. *Library Technology Reports, 43*(5), 10–14.

Stielow, F. (2001). Reconsidering "arsenals of a democratic culture": Balancing symbol and practice. In N. Kranich (Ed.), *Libraries and democracy: The cornerstones of liberty* (pp. 3–14). Chicago: American Library Association.

Stiglitz, J. E. (2012). *The price of inequality: How today's divided society endangers our future.* New York: Norton.

Stoffle, C. J., & Tarin, P. A. (1994, July). No place for neutrality: The case for multiculturalism. *Library Journal*, 46–49.

Strover, S., Chapman, G., & Waters, J. (2004). Beyond community networking and CTCs: Access, development, and public policy. *Telecommunications Policy, 28*, 465–485.

Sullivan, M. (2012, July 9). The worst master's degree? *Washington Post.* Available from http://www.washingtonpost.com/blogs/answer-sheet/post/the-worst-masters-degree/2012/07/08/gJQAfm6BXW_blog.html.

Svendsen, G. L. H. (2013). Public libraries as breeding grounds for bonding, bridging and institutional social capital. *Sociologia Ruralis, 53*, 52–73.

Svenonius, E. (2000). *The intellectual foundation of information organization.* Cambridge, MA: MIT.

Swan, D. W., Grimes, J., Owens, T., Vese, R. D., Jr., Miller, K., Arroyo, J., Craig, T., Dorinski, S., Freeman, M., Isaac, N., O'Shea, P., Schilling, P. Scotto, J. (2013). *Public libraries survey: Fiscal year 2010 (IMLS-2013-PLS-01).* Washington DC: Institute of Museum and Library Services.

Swanson, D. R. (1979). Libraries and the growth of knowledge. *Library Quarterly, 49*, 3–25.

Swigger, B. K. (2012). *The MLS project: An assessment after sixty years.* Lanham, MD: Scarecrow.

Sykes, J. (2003). Value as calculation and value as contribution to the organization. *Information Outlook, 7*(3), 10–13.

Taylor, J. B. (2013). Locating the library in the non-library censorship of the 1950s: Ideological negotiations in the professional record. In C. Pawley & L. S. Robbins (Eds.), *Libraries and the reading public in twentieth-century America* (pp. 168–184). Madison, WI: University of Wisconsin.

Taylor, N. G., Gorham, U., Jaeger, P. T., & Bertot, J. C. (in press). IT and collaborative community services: The roles of the public library, local government, and nonprofit entity partnerships. *International Journal of Public Administration in the Digital Age.*

Taylor, N. G., Jaeger, P. T., McDermott, A. J., Kodama, C. M., & Bertot, J. C. (2012). Public libraries in the new economy: 21st Century skills, the Internet, and community needs. *Public Library Quarterly, 31*, 191–219.

Tetlock, P. E. (2006). *Expert political judgment.* Princeton, NJ: Princeton University.

Thatcher, M. (1987). Transcript archived at the Margaret Thatcher Foundation. Available from http://www.margaretthatcher.org/document/106689.

Tisdale, S. (1997, March). Silence, please: The public library as entertainment center. *Harper's*, 65–73.

Travis, H. (2006). Building universal digital libraries: An agenda for copyright reform. *Pepperdine Law Review, 33*, 761–833.

Turner, A. M. (1997). *Getting political: An action guide for librarians and library supporters.* New York: Neal-Schuman.

Urban Libraries Council. (2010). *Partners for the future: Public libraries and local governments creating sustainable communities.* Chicago, IL: Author.

U.S. Centers for Medicare and Medicaid Services. (n.d.). Table 145. Medicaid—Summary by State: 2000 and 2006. *Medicaid, Program Statistics, Medicaid Statistical Information System.* Available from http://www.census.gov/compendia/statab/2010/tables/10s0145.pdf.

U.S. House Committee on the Judiciary, Subcommittee on Civil and Constitutional Right. (1988, June 20, July 13). *FBI counterintelligence visits to libraries.* 100th Cong., 2nd sess.

U.S. Office of Retirement and Disability Policy. (n.d.). Table 2. Supplemental Security Income. *Social Security Administration, Supplemental Security Record.* Available from http://www.ssa.gov/policy/docs/factsheets/cong_stats/2009/al.html.

U.S. Senate Committee on Labor and Public Welfare, Subcommittee on Education. (1956, May 23). *Library Services.* 84th Cong., 2nd Sess.

U.S. Supplemental Nutrition Assistance Program. (n.d.). Table of Participation and Benefits as of October 28, 2010. Available from http://www.fns.usda.gov/pd/34SNAPmonthly.htm.

U.S. Women, Infants and Children Program. (n.d.). Table of WIC Program: Total Participation. Available from http://www.fns.usda.gov/pd/26wifypart.htm.

Van Moorsel, G. (2005). Client value models provide a framework for rational library planning (or, phrasing the answer in the form of a question). *Medical Reference Services Quarterly, 24*(2), 25–40.

Van Sant, W. (2009, June 8). Librarians now add social work to their resumes. *St. Petersburg Times.* Available from http://www.tampabay.com.

Van Slyck, A. A. (1995). *Free to all: Carnegie libraries and American culture, 1890–1920.* Chicago: University of Chicago Press.

Varheim, A. (2010). Gracious space: Library programming strategies towards immigrants as tools in the creation of social capital. *Library & Information Science Research, 33,* 12–18.

Ver Eecke, W. (1998). The concept of a "merit good": The ethical dimensions. *Journal of Socio-Economics, 27*(1), 133–153.

Ver Eecke, W. (1999). Public goods: An ideal concept. *Journal of Socio-Economics, 28*(2), 139–156.

Vollmer, T. (2010, June). *There's an app for that! Libraries and mobile technology: An introduction to public policy considerations.* ALA Office for Information Technology Policy. Policy Brief No. 3. Available from http://www.ala.org/offices/sites/ala.org.offices/files/content/oitp/publications/policybriefs/mobiledevices.pdf.

Wakeman, J. (1962). The context of librarianship. *Wilson Library Bulletin, 37*(12), 348.

Wall, T. B. (1990). Federal library policy-making: An overview. In E. J. Josey & K. D. Shearer (Eds.), *Politics and the support of libraries* (pp. 9–22). New York: Neal-Schuman.

Waller, V. (2009). The relationship between public libraries and Google: Too much information. *First Monday, 14*(9). Available from http://www.uic.edu/htbin/cgwrap/bin/ojs/index.php/fm/article/viewArticle/2477/2279.

Waples, D., Carnovsky, L., & Randall, W. M. (1932). The public library in the Depression. *Library Quarterly, 2,* 321–343.

Watson, L. (2010). The future of the library as a place of learning: A personal perspective. *New Review of Academic Libraries, 16*(1), 45–56.

Watson, P. D. (1994). Founding mothers: The contribution of women's organizations to public library development in the United States. *Library Quarterly, 64,* 233–269.

Webster, F. (1995). *Theories of the information society.* London: Routledge.

Webster, F. (2002). *Theories of the information society* (2nd ed.). London: Routledge.

Webster, F. (2005). The end of the public library? *Science as Culture, 14,* 283–287.

Wellisch, J. B., Patrick, R. J., Black, D. V., & Cuardra, C. A. (1974). *The public library and federal policy.* Westport, CT: Greenwood.

Wheeler, W. (2011). Economics of information: A brief introduction. *Progressive Librarian, 36/37,* 42–50.

White, H. S. (1990, January). My truths are more moral than your biases. *Library Journal,* 72–73.

White House. (2006). *The federal response to Hurricane Katrina: Lessons learned.* Washington: Author.

Wiegand, W. A. (1976). *The politics of an emerging profession: The American Library Association, 1876–1917.* New York: Greenwood.

Wiegand, W. A. (1989). *An active instrument for propaganda: The American public library during World War I.* Westport, CT: Greenwood.

Wiegand, W. A. (1996). *Irrepressible reformer: A biography of Melvil Dewey.* Chicago: American Library Association.

Wiegand, W. A. (2011). *Main Street Public Library: Community Places and Reading Spaces in the Rural Heartland, 1876–1956.* Iowa City: University of Iowa.

Wilcox, C. (2011). *Onward Christian soldiers? The religious right in American politics.* Boulder, CO: Westview.

Williamson, K., & Roberts, J. (2010). Developing and sustaining a sense of place: The role of social information. *Library & Information Science Research, 32,* 281–287.

Williamson, M. (2000). Social exclusion and the public library: A Habermasian insight. *Journal of Librarianship and Information Science, 32*(4), 178–186.

Winkel, J. (2007). Lessons on evaluating programs and collections for immigrant communities at the Queens Borough Public Library. *Colorado Libraries, 33*(1), 43–46.

Wohlstetter, R. (1962). *Pearl Harbor: Warning and decision.* Stanford, CA: Stanford University Press.

Wolff, K. (2009). *Culture club: The curious history of the Boston Athenaeum.* Boston: University of Massachusetts.

Wolfinger, R. E., & Field, J. O. (1966). Political ethos and the structure of city government. *American Political Science Association Review, 60,* 306–326.

Wolin, S. S. (1981). The new public philosophy. *Democracy, 1*(4), 23–36.

Wolin, S. S. (1993). Democracy, difference, and re-cognition. *Political Theory, 21,* 464–483.

Wooden, R. A. (2006). The future of public libraries in an Internet age. *National Civic Review, 95*(4), 3–7.

Yaniv, O. (2005, October 19). Immigrants warned on green card cons. *New York Daily News.* Available from http://articles.nydailynews.com/2005-10-19/local/18313877_1_immigrants-application-eligible-countries.

Young, I. M. (2006). Social responsibility and global justice: A social connection model. *Social Philosophy and Policy, 23,* 102–130.

Zabriskie, C. (2013, April 30). Libraries in New York City: Why we give a damn and why you should too. *Huffington Post.* Available from http://www.huffingtonpost.com.

Zickuhr, K. (2013). Who's not online and why. Pew Internet and American Life Project. Available from http://www.pewinternet.org.

Zickuhr, K., Rainie, L., & Purcell, K. (2013). *Library services in the digital age.* Pew Internet and the American Life Project. Available from http://www.pewinternet.org.

Zickuhr, K., & Smith, A. (2012). *Digital differences.* Pew Internet and American Life Project. Available from http://www.pewinternet.org.

Zweizig, D. (1973). *Predicting amount of library use: An empirical study of the public library in the life of the adult public.* Unpublished PhD dissertation, Syracuse University.

Zweizig, D., & Rodger, E. J. (1982). *Output measures for public libraries: A manual of standardized procedures.* Chicago, IL: American Library Association.

Index

About the Authors

Paul T. Jaeger, PhD, JD, is associate professor and diversity officer of the College of Information Studies and co-director of the Information Policy and Access Center at the University of Maryland. Dr. Jaeger's research focuses on the ways in which law and public policy shape information behavior, particularly for underserved populations. He is the author of more than 130 journal articles and book chapters. This is his eighth book. His other recent books are *Information Worlds: Social Context, Technology, and Information Behavior in the Age of the Internet* (2010) with Gary Burnett; *Public Libraries and the Internet: Roles, Perspectives, and Implications* (2011) with John Carlo Bertot and Charles R. McClure; and *Disability and the Internet: Confronting a Digital Divide* (2012). His research has been funded by the Institute of Museum and Library Services, the National Science Foundation, the American Library Association, the Smithsonian Institution, and the Bill and Melinda Gates Foundation, among others. Dr. Jaeger is co-editor of *Library Quarterly*, co-editor of the Information Policy Book Series from MIT Press, and associate editor of *Government Information Quarterly*.

Ursula Gorham, JD, is a doctoral candidate in the College of Information Studies at the University of Maryland and a graduate research associate at the Information Policy and Access Center (iPAC). She holds a law degree, as well as graduate degrees in library science and public policy, from the University of Maryland. She is admitted to practice law in Maryland and, prior to pursuing her doctoral degree, served as a law clerk in Maryland appellate and federal bankruptcy courts. Ursula's work at iPAC has focused on e-government partnerships in public libraries, and she has co-authored a number of papers on this topic. Her research interests also include the accessibility of legal information and court documents, with an emphasis on self-represented litigants.

John Carlo Bertot, PhD, is professor and co-director of the Information Policy and Access Center in the College of Information Studies at the University of Maryland. His research spans library and government agency technology planning and evaluation, information and telecommunications policy, and e-government. He is president of the Digital Government Society of North America and serves as chair of the International Standards Organization's Library Performance Indicator (ISO

11620) working group and is past chair of the American Library Association's Library Research Round Table. John is editor of *Government Information Quarterly* and co-editor of *Library Quarterly*. Over the years, John
has received funding for his research from the National Science Foundation, the Bill and Melinda Gates Foundation, the Government Account-
ability Office, the American Library Association, and the Institute of Museum and Library Services.

Lindsay C. Sarin is MLS program coordinator and a research fellow at
the Information Policy and Access Center in the College of Information
Studies at the University of Maryland. Lindsay previously worked in a
number of diverse academic library settings, where she provided information literacy instruction and outreach services. She is active in both
state and national library associations; she also works with new librarians
and LIS students in order to help them become active and engaged in the
profession. Her research interests include the relationship between information policy and library advocacy, outreach, information services to
diverse populations, and information literacy pedagogy and methodology.

For more information about the authors' work and related research,
please visit the Information Policy and Access Center: http://ipac.umd.
edu.